CLARENDON LIBRARY OF LOGIC AND PHILOSOPHY
General Editor: L. Jonathan Cohen

RELATIVE IDENTITY

RELATIVE
IDENTITY

——

NICHOLAS GRIFFIN

OXFORD
AT THE CLARENDON PRESS
1977

Oxford University Press, Walton Street, Oxford OX2 6DP

OXFORD LONDON GLASGOW NEW YORK
TORONTO MELBOURNE WELLINGTON CAPE TOWN
IBADAN NAIROBI DAR ES SALAAM LUSAKA ADDIS ABABA
KUALA LUMPUR SINGAPORE JAKARTA HONG KONG TOKYO
DELHI BOMBAY CALCUTTA MADRAS KARACHI

ISBN 0 19 824409 6

© *Oxford University Press 1977*

*Printed in Great Britain
at the University Press, Oxford
by Vivian Ridler
Printer to the University*

Salvador Allende

in memoriam

Preface

As philosophical theories go, the classical theory of identity, which stems from Leibniz's Law, has had a long innings. Recently, however, attention has been attracted by non-standard identity theories in which the classical two-place identity operator is replaced, or supplemented, by a range of three-place identity operators, the third place in each being occupied by a general noun which expresses the respect in which identity is intended. One such theory is defended here. The theory is approached somewhat obliquely in Chapters 2 to 5, where different types of general noun are distinguished and their relevance to questions of identity and distinctness considered. Chapters 6 and 7 reject the frequently made claim that classical identity statements are incomplete or senseless. A feature of the theory proposed here is that it incorporates the classical theory. In Chapters 8 to 10 the thesis that items identical with respect to one general noun may be distinct with respect to another is defended, and formal principles for a relative identity theory are set out.

The book was written during three years' research at the Australian National University, and I am grateful to A.N.U. not merely for the opportunity to work there but for all manner of assistance which made the work very much less burdensome. Among more personal debts the greatest is to Richard Routley. I have benefited immensely from discussions with him over the last three years, and his detailed criticisms of earlier drafts have saved me from more mistakes than I care to remember. Peter Sheehan, who first aroused my interest in the topic, deserves my special gratitude for his unfailing kindness and encouragement during the difficult initial stages. I am also grateful to numerous colleagues at A.N.U. for their comments: in particular to Robert Brown, Peter Herbst, Malcolm Rennie, and Stephen Voss.

Outside A.N.U. my debts are also numerous: Professor P. T. Geach (University of Leeds) sent me detailed comments on an earlier draft which helped me to understand his own position. Professors M. J. Cresswell (Victoria University of Wellington); C. L. Hamblin (University of New South Wales); Hugh Montgomery (University of Auckland); and R. Ziedens (University of Waikato) all read the draft and provided me with comments, both particular and general, which were immensely helpful. Several authors were kind enough to send me unpublished work and I am happy to thank them here: Dr. Tyler Burge (University of California); Dr. Carl Calvert (University of Washington); Professor Jack Nelson (Temple University); Dr. Ross Poole (Macquarie University); Dr. Leslie Stevenson (University of St. Andrews); Professor Gerald Vision (Temple University); Professor David Wiggins (University of London); and Dr. John Woods (University of Victoria, Canada).

Finally, Helen Fleming typed my baroque manuscript with amazing efficiency; and Cheryl Griffin gave sympathy and encouragement during a busy period of her life, and help with the index during a busy period of mine. Last but not least, I am greatly indebted to the Printer's Reader who saved me from innumerable inconsistencies both philosophic and typographic.

NICHOLAS GRIFFIN

11 September 1975

Contents

Note

As this book goes to press, Professor David Wiggins has been kind enough to send me details of revisions he intends to make in a second edition of his *Identity and Spatio-Temporal Continuity*. Were I starting to write this book now, there would be a number of points of detail which I should express differently in view of his alterations. There are one or two substantial points, however, which I need to note here.

First: It is now clear that the (D)-thesis I attack in Chapter 7 is not one which Wiggins defends. Wiggins's new statement of his position makes it appear much closer to the position I outline in § 7.5. The main differences between us as to the import of (D) are now due to Wiggins's rejection and my acceptance of (R). Wiggins holds both the Leibniz's Law account and what I've called the $(\exists f)$-account of '$a = b$'. In consequence, given '$a =_{\mathscr{F}} b$' he can immediately infer '$(\forall \phi)(\phi(a) \equiv \phi(b))$'. Such an inference would be invalid on my own theory, which includes (R). None the less it is gratifying to learn that what I suggested in § 7.5 was Wiggins's true and important insight into the relation between sortals and identity is, in fact, closer to his stated position than his earlier formulations of (D) suggested.

Second: Wiggins has replaced the argument I attack at great length in Chapter 5. However, he still adheres to the conclusion of the original argument, namely that if an item falls under two distinct sortals in the course of its history there must be exactly one ultimate sortal which both sortals restrict. His new argument is much briefer and clearer than the original but is still, I think, invalid since, like the old one, it ignores the possibility that the two sortals in question merely intersect.

Hamlet. But come, for England! Farewell, dear mother.

King. Thy loving father, Hamlet.

Hamlet. My mother—father and mother is man and wife, man and wife is one flesh, and so, my mother. Come, for England!

(*Hamlet* IV. iii)

I
Absolute and Relative Identity

1.1 The Theory of Absolute Identity

The theory of identity which appears in most (if not all) of our logic books is the theory of absolute identity. The theory can be set up in a variety of ways, by adding either one or two axioms on to ordinary quantification logic. Historically the first formulation was essentially that given by Frege in the *Begriffsschrift* (1879) using two axiom schemata. Following Church,[1] we may express these:

$$x = x \qquad \text{(reflexivity)}$$

and
$$x = y \ \& \ \phi(x) \supset. \ \phi(y)$$
$$\text{(indiscernibility of identicals)}$$

where (for present purposes only) 'x' and 'y' are syntactical individual variables and '$\phi(\zeta)$' a syntactical predicate variable. The completeness of these axiom schemata, in the sense that every valid schema of identity theory is provable within the system, follows from the completeness of quantification theory and was first shown by Gödel in 1930.

A second version is due to Hao Wang and is based on the single axiom schema, Wang's Law:

$$\phi(y) \equiv (\exists x)(x = y \ \& \ \phi(x)).$$

Both reflexivity and the indiscernibility of identicals can be proved from Wang's Law.[2] It follows that Wang's formulation and Frege's are equivalent.

In second-order predicate calculus we can avoid the use of '$=$' as a primitive. Working from Leibniz's Law:

(LL) $\qquad (\forall x)(\forall y)[x = y \equiv (\forall \phi)(\phi(x) \equiv \phi(y))]$

[1] *Introduction to Mathematical Logic* (Princeton: Princeton University Press, 1956), p. 281.
[2] See W. V. O. Quine, *Set Theory and its Logic* (Cambridge, Mass.: Harvard University Press, 1963), p. 13.

we can derive very simply[3] all the valid propositions of identity theory, of which the following are the most important for what follows: the indiscernibility of identicals:

(In. Id.) $(\forall x)(\forall y)[x = y \supset (\forall \phi)(\phi(x) \equiv \phi(y))]$;

the identity of indiscernibles:[4]

(Id. In.) $(\forall x)(\forall y)[(\forall \phi)(\phi(x) \equiv \phi(y)) \supset x = y]$;

the reflexivity, symmetry, and transitivity of identity, respectively:

(Refl.) $(\forall x)(x = x)$

(Symm.) $(\forall x)(\forall y)(x = y \supset y = x)$

(Trans.) $(\forall x)(\forall y)(\forall z)(x = y \ \& \ y = z \supset. \ x = z)$.

It is this theory that I shall henceforth call the theory of absolute identity.

1.2 Difficulties with Absolute Identity

It is clear that absolute identity theory is a well-established branch of logic. Not only that, but its principles seem to be employed in almost all our everyday or philosophical reasoning in which questions of identity arise. It is with good reason that both Geach and Perry, who take opposite sides on the issue of relative identity, call the absolute theory 'the classical theory of identity'.[5] The power and simplicity of this theory is such that, as Geach says, it seems 'an enterprise worthy of a circle-squarer to challenge [it]'.[6] None the less, the theory is open to objections to which I shall briefly advert: some are well known enough not to require detailed treatment, and my comments are not intended to be conclusive.

---

[3] Where they are not obvious appropriate proofs can be adapted from Church, op. cit., § 52, for example.

[4] Although the identity of indiscernibles is a theorem of absolute identity theory, its pre-theoretical validity is controversial. See, for example, G. E. Moore, *Philosophical Studies* (London: Routledge and Kegan Paul, 1922), p. 307, who thinks it obviously false; and C. S. Peirce, *Collected Papers* (Cambridge, Mass.: Harvard University Press, 1933), 4.311, who thinks it 'all nonsense'. (Id. In.), by contrast, is trivial: substitute '$\zeta = y$' for '$\phi(\zeta)$'. (Authors differ on exactly which formulae to label 'Leibniz's Law', 'identity of indiscernibles', and 'indiscernibility of identicals'. In what follows (LL), (Id. In.), and (In. Id.) will be intended.)

[5] John R. Perry, 'Identity' (Unpublished doctoral dissertation, Cornell University, 1968), p. 4; P. T. Geach, 'Identity', in his *Logic Matters* (Oxford: Blackwell, 1972), p. 239.   [6] 'Identity', p. 239.

The best known of the problems is the failure of Leibniz's Law when non-extensional predicates are substituted for '$\phi(\zeta)$'.[7] To take the most hackneyed example:

(1.1)   The number of the planets = 9.

is true, and so is:

(1.2)   Necessarily 9 is greater than 7.

From these, together with Leibniz's Law, we can derive the false conclusion:

(1.3)   Necessarily the number of planets is greater than 7.

There is also a proof to show that, given (LL) and the necessity of reflexivity,[8] there are no contingent true identity statements.[9] The proof runs as follows:[10]

[1] $a = b \supset (\forall\phi)(\phi(a) \equiv \phi(b))$ ((In. Id.), U.I., a/x, b/y)

[2] $a = b$ (premiss)

[3] $\Box(a = a) \supset \Box(a = b)$ ([1][2]M.P., U.I., $\Box(a = \zeta)/\phi(\zeta)$)

[4] $\Box(a = a)$ ((Refl.), Nec.)

[5] $\Box(a = b)$ ([3][4] M.P.)

[6] $a = b \supset \Box(a = b)$ ([2]–[5] C.P.)

[7] See, inter alia, W. V. O. Quine, 'Reference and Modality', in his From a Logical Point of View (New York: Harper and Row; 2nd edn., 1961), pp. 139–59.

[8] Which follows from (Refl.) by necessitation (Nec.) in even such weak modal logics as Feys's system, T. (Cf. G. E. Hughes and M. J. Cresswell, An Introduction to Modal Logic [London: Methuen; 2nd edn., 1972], p. 31.)

[9] The result was first proved by Ruth Barcan in 'The Identity of Individuals in a Strict Functional Calculus of Second Order', Journal of Symbolic Logic, 12 (1947), 15, prop. 2.31; but the present version of the proof was first given by Prior in his Formal Logic (Oxford: The Clarendon Press; 2nd edn., 1962), pp. 205–6. The proof given here is adapted from Wiggins, 'Identity-Statements', in R. J. Butler (ed.), Analytical Philosophy (Oxford: Blackwell, 1965), 2nd series, pp. 40–1. Wiggins, however, is no longer troubled by the proof. Cf. his Identity and Spatio-Temporal Continuity (Oxford: Blackwell, 1967), fn. 26 (p. 68); also 'Sentence-Sense, Word-Sense, and Difference of Word-Sense', in D. D. Steinberg and L. A. Jakobovits (eds.), Semantics: An Interdisciplinary Reader in Philosophy, Linguistics and Psychology (Cambridge: Cambridge University Press, 1971), note (b), p. 16.

[10] In this and subsequent proofs the natural deduction system used is essentially that of Quine's Methods of Logic. The 'explanation' of the derivation of each line appears between parentheses to the right of that line. The abbreviations used there are taken from Copi's Symbolic Logic; use of the classical propositional calculus or standard quantification theory is marked by the letters 'C.P.C.' and 'Q.T.', respectively. Letters and numerals appearing in brackets within the 'explanation' are references to earlier lines in the proof or text used in the derivation.

Attempts to avoid the first modal problem have been made[11] by reinterpreting (1.3) as:

(1.4)   Necessarily the number which numbers the planets is greater than 7.

which is less obviously false. The argument is that 'the number which numbers the planets' is just another way of referring to the number 9 and (1.4) therefore amounts to no more than (1.2). The same manœuvre also deals with the Barcan–Wiggins proof because if '$a = b$' is true 'a' and 'b' are simply different names for the same thing and that thing is necessarily identical with itself; and thus, if we have '$a = b$', we ought not to baulk at '$\Box(a = b)$'. However, both arguments will go through if the necessity operator is replaced by an epistemic operator such as 'it was believed by Julius Caesar that'. It is scarcely plausible to maintain that if $a = b$, it was believed by Julius Caesar to be so (where 'a' and 'b' are singular terms—not rigid designators), although Kripke, Montague, Prior, and Scott, for example, seem prepared to accept this conclusion.

Quine introduced the term 'referential opacity' for those contexts in which (LL) leads from truth to falsity:[12] and it is generally held that restrictions must be placed on the range of the predicate variable '$\phi(\zeta)$' in (LL) in order to exclude referentially opaque contexts, for example by allowing '$\phi(\zeta)$' to range only over traits or 'real' properties. It is, of course, one thing to recognize the need for such exclusions but quite another to decide how to draw the line. Despite much discussion it is still not clear what restricted version of (LL) would be valid.

Quite apart from the modal paradoxes (LL) suffers other disadvantages. It makes no allowance for change through which one self-same object gains or loses properties. As we have stated the law a man who is athletic in youth and sedentary in middle age will constitute a counter-example to the principle of the indiscernibility of identicals. If we reject Hume's solution that there is no identity through change,[13] there are at least two

[11] For example by Bede Rundle, 'Modality and Quantification', in R. J. Butler (ed.), *Analytical Philosophy*, p. 31. See also Prior, op. cit., p. 206.

[12] W. V. O. Quine, 'Reference and Modality', op. cit., p. 142. Quine took the term as 'roughly the opposite' of Russell's use of 'transparent' in Appendix C, 'Truth-Functions and Others', of *Principia Mathematica* (Cambridge: Cambridge University Press; 2nd edn., 1927), vol. i, pp. 659–66.

[13] Cf. the *Treatise*, Bk. I, Part IV, § 6 (pp. 301–6 of the Penguin edition).

possible remedies within the absolute theory: either we can restrict the range of the second-order quantifier to dated predicates so that both the youth and the man have the properties of being-athletic-when-young and also being-sedentary-when-middle-aged. Dating, of course, needn't be precise, but only sufficient to distinguish periods when certain predicates apply from periods when they don't. On the other hand, we can rewrite (LL) thus:

$$(LL_t) \qquad a = b \equiv (\forall \phi)(\forall t)[R_t(\phi(a)) \equiv R_t(\phi(b))]$$

where 'R' is Rescher and Urquhart's primitive realization operator and '$R_t(p)$' reads 'it is realized at time t that p'.[14] Either way it becomes possible for an object to change without thereby becoming a different object.[15]

The trouble now is that we appear to have licensed too much: an object may now change in any way we please, however radical, without ceasing to be that self-same object. Suppose our man changes into a balloon; or, to put the matter more neutrally, suppose the man disappears and a balloon somewhat later occupies his place. There is nothing (except our common sense, nothing at least in our account of identity) to stop us saying that the man and the balloon are the same so long as the existence of the balloon doesn't overlap with that of the man. So long as the balloon appears after the man has disappeared then, for any dated balloonish predicate, 'ϕ-at-$t'(\zeta)$', which applied to the balloon, there is nothing to stop us saying that it also applied to the man, and any dated mannish predicate, 'ψ-at-$t(\zeta)$', could also have applied to the balloon (where $t < t'$ and the balloon appeared and the man disappeared somewhere in between). Similarly there is nothing to stop the man and the balloon switching between any number of different roles, becoming first a car, then a book, and then a distant star, so long as no two roles overlap.[16]

Of course, common sense requires us to say that 'ζ was

[14] See their *Temporal Logic* (New York: Springer Verlag, 1971), p. 31.

[15] I shall refer to both (LL$_t$) and the version with second-order quantification restricted to dated predicates as 'tensed Leibniz's Law'.

[16] This is argued by Peter Herbst in 'Names and Identities and Beginnings and Ends' (Unpublished, 1972), *passim*, but especially pp. 30–40 where he successfully argues that, on the classical view of identity, he is identical with Alexander the Great. At least there is no way in which we can refute the hypothesis by means of the classical theory alone.

popped at t'' applies to the balloon and not to the man, and hence (the absolutist urges) the two are distinct by tensed Leibniz's Law. But to argue this way we have first to be sure that the two are distinct and hence that our common sense premiss is correct, for unless we exclude the possibility that the two are identical we cannot be sure that 'ζ was popped at t''' applies only to the balloon and not also to the man. Herbst's argument is to the conclusion that tensed Leibniz's Law gives us no help in the matter. Of course, we can't prove that the man is identical with the balloon but we can't disprove it either. By the very nature of the case we are debarred from having evidence one way or the other.

We could add to our account of identity a requirement of spatio-temporal continuity and this would exclude the case where there was a gap between the disappearance of the man and the appearance of the balloon, but it does not solve the problem completely. Firstly, we can easily construct a case in which the balloon is spatio-temporally continuous with the man. Secondly, spatio-temporal continuity would be a purely *ad hoc* addition to the theory of absolute identity which would destroy its great formal appeal (without necessarily improving its standing as an analysis of the notion of identity we normally use). Thirdly, the most important distinction between the absolute and the relative theories of identity (as we shall see) is that the relative theory employs several distinct identity relations, each related to a general noun (i.e. each acting as the identity relation for a given category of items). On the other hand, in the absolute theory, though it may contain more than one identity relation (e.g. contingent, necessary, intensional, extensional identities etc.[17]), each identity relation is absolute in that it is not restricted to expressing identity within a particular category of items. If the absolutist is going to characterize identity by tensed Leibniz's Law plus some condition of spatio-temporal continuity then this identity relation will be appropriate only for certain categories of items—those for which spatio-temporal

---

[17] For an example of the way in which an absolutist may be prepared to split up his notion of identity see D. Gabbay and J. M. Moravcsik, 'Sameness and Individuation', *Journal of Philosophy*, 70 (1973), 514 n.; although the authors seem to think that only one of their four types of identity can be called 'absolute identity'. At any rate it is clear that all their identity relations are absolute in the sense in which we use the term to distinguish absolute from relative identity.

continuity is an appropriate identity requirement (i.e., presumably, material bodies). Already, therefore, the absolutist's position would be giving way if he were to admit spatio-temporal continuity. I suspect that all three difficulties would recur if we sought to supplement tensed Leibniz's Law with any other principle instead of spatio-temporal continuity.[18]

We can, moreover, make Herbst's argument more general.[19] If we are to use Leibniz's Law to decide whether items are identical or distinct we need to see whether they share all their predicates. But we can only do this when we can decide whether two predicates apply to the same item and this presupposes exactly the sort of judgement which we were hoping Leibniz's Law would enable us to make. Of course, this problem applies to synchronic as well as to diachronic identity statements. Suppose there are two cages, A and B, with a tiger, a and b respectively, in each. Let the predicate '$\phi(\zeta)$' be 'ζ is in A at t' and let the predicate '$\psi(\zeta)$' be 'ζ is in B at t'. Assume that $A \neq B$. If we had $\phi(a)$ & $\sim \phi(b)$ and $\sim \psi(a)$ & $\psi(b)$ we could use (LL) to establish that $a \neq b$. But how can we be sure we don't have $\phi(a)$ & $\phi(b)$ and $\psi(a)$ & $\psi(b)$? Obviously by appeal to the fact that no tiger can be in two places at once. But this fact does not follow from (LL). It appears that even if (LL) is adequate as a purely formal account of identity it still needs to be supplemented with some other account if it is to generate the valid principles we normally use in assessing identity claims. Moreover, there will be certain predicates for which it will be difficult, if not impossible, to decide whether they apply to the bearers of both names in an identity relation, without first knowing that both names are borne by the same item. How, for instance, could we decide whether 'ζ is visible before sunrise' is applicable to the Evening Star without knowing whether the Evening Star is identical with the Morning Star?[20]

---

[18] Attempts to develop the absolute theory in this way are open to objections raised by Baruch Brody: If C is a necessary and sufficient condition for identity, and C^* a necessary and sufficient condition for identity in a certain category of items, then C can only be satisfied by items of that category when C^* is, but this is open to empirical counter-examples. Cf. Brody, 'Locke on the Identity of Persons', *American Philosophical Quarterly*, 9 (1972), 331–2.

[19] Cf. Herbst, op. cit., p. 4.

[20] Cf. Michael Dummett, *Frege: Philosophy of Language* (London: Duckworth, 1973), pp. 544–5. See also David Wiggins, 'Individuation of Things and Places', *Proceedings of the Aristotelian Society*, Supplementary Volume 37 (1963), 195–6.

Clearly Leibniz's Law, unless supplemented, provides no criterion against which we can judge identity claims; to achieve this the absolutist must go outside his formal treatment of identity. There is, of course, no reason why the provision of necessary and sufficient conditions for a concept should enable us to judge individual cases of the applicability of that concept, though it might be regarded as desirable where possible. At any rate, the absolutist owes us some such account if his theory is to be useful.

We have already seen that the principle of the identity of indiscernibles has been called in question by philosophers. Their opposition stems from the fact that even if we could check all the properties of two items, and found that they were common to both, we would still have no guarantee that they were one and the same item: the universe might, after all, repeat itself in various ways. Because we can imagine such a case we cannot treat (LL) as an account of what we mean by 'identity'. Attempts (e.g. by Dummett) to overcome this problem make essential (but usually disguised) use of the verification principle. Dummett takes Leibniz's Law to provide a definition of identity. In arguing against the objections to the identity of indiscernibles he writes: 'If it is really the case that we can find[21] no predicate . . . which is true of a but not of b, then nothing can possibly form an obstacle to our regarding a as identical with b.'[22] But if he is really to support his conclusion that Leibniz's Law provides a *definition* of identity then he needs the full verificationist claim that if there is no discernible difference between a and b then that means the same as the claim that a and b are identical, rather than the disguised verificationist claim that 'nothing can possibly form an obstacle' to our regarding them as identical. The fact that we can envisage circumstances in which indiscernibility does not imply identity shows that indiscernibility does not mean the same as identity. So it appears that Leibniz's Law not only fails to give us a criterion by which to judge identity claims, but also to give a correct account of what identity claims mean.

With all this against it, it may seem puzzling that the absolute

---

[21] I'm sure this weak antecedent is unintended. What Dummett surely means is 'if it is really the case that there *is* no predicate . . .'

[22] Dummett, *Frege*, pp. 543–4.

theory ever commanded any respect at all, let alone the all but universal assent that has, in fact, been accorded it. I think the reason the theory has proved so popular is that (LL) achieved its first successes in mathematics. If we take (LL) to define the identity relation between mathematical items the problems we've just been considering most often don't arise. The success of (LL) in mathematics has been convincing and has made it seem worth-while to exercise a lot of ingenuity to equip the principle for use elsewhere. It is not my concern to argue here that absolute identity is indefensible but rather to argue that an alternative account is defensible and, in many ways, is advantageous. To this I shall now turn.

1.3 Some Advantages of Relative Identity

We need, first of all, to have at least a vague idea of what the theory of relative identity is. It is not too easy to state the theory precisely and, in fact, there are several distinct theories not all of which have been explicitly differentiated in the literature. For the purposes of this section I shall content myself with three quotations from Geach which give a general idea of the theory and follow these with some comments on why this type of theory is attractive. In the next section I shall make some necessary distinctions between the different theories of relative identity.

First, then, Geach's statement of his own point of view:

(I)   When one says 'x is identical with y', this, I hold, is an incomplete expression; it is short for 'x is the same A as y', where 'A' represents some count noun understood from the context of utterance—or else, it is just a vague expression of a half-formed thought.[23]

(II) 'Being the same water' cannot be analysed as 'being the same (something-or-other) and being water'.[24]

(III) On my own view of identity I could not object in principle to different As being one and the same B . . .[25]

From this alone it appears that there are three relativist theses, all interrelated, but by no means all equivalent.

The motivation for (I) and (II) is rather different from that

[23] Geach, 'Identity', p. 238.
[24] Geach, *Reference and Generality* (Ithaca: Cornell University Press; 2nd edn., 1968), p. 151.   [25] Ibid., p. 157.

for (III). The most obvious motive for (I) and (II), but one which has not, to my knowledge, been avowed, is that in ordinary language we use the relation 'ζ is the same such-and-such as η' very frequently (if anything, more frequently than we use 'ζ is identical with η'). Moreover, we do use it in ways which are not adequately captured by 'ζ is identical with η' let alone by '$\zeta = \eta$', its counterpart in absolute identity theory. As even an absolutist like Perry is forced to admit, the connection between the concept of absolute identity in second-order predicate calculus and the concept of identity employed in natural language 'is not clear, and may even seem quite puzzling'.[26] If we are interested in the analysis of ordinary language and seek to use the techniques of formal logic in that analysis, we should not assume that the absolute theory copes with everything we would want to call an identity statement and that everything that it doesn't cope with can conveniently be assigned to some other category.

The motivation which Geach avows is one derived from Frege. Clearly the notions of unity and identity are closely related. Frege held that to say 'x is one' was either an incomplete way of saying 'x is one F' or else lacked clear sense.[27] However, while Frege accepted this thesis about 'ζ is one' he did not extend the thesis to identity: 'Identity is a relation given to us in such a specific form that it is inconceivable that various forms of it should occur.'[28] This puzzles Geach because the connection between unity and identity which comes out in English as 'one and the same' comes out similarly in German as '*ein und dasselbe*'. (In fact, this isn't quite so strange as Geach thinks it for, according to Frege, identity applies to objects while number applies to concepts, so we can't expect all the traits of number to pass over to identity.[29]) At any rate Geach regards his own doctrine of relativized identity as an extension of Frege's views about 'ζ is one'.

However, this sort of philosophical motivation is both older and more general than Geach's references to Frege make clear. It involves what G. E. L. Owen has engagingly called 'polygam-

26 Perry, 'Identity', p. 1.
27 Frege, *The Foundations of Arithmetic*, transl. by J. L. Austin (Oxford: Blackwell, 1950), p. 40.
28 Frege, *Grundgesetze der Arithmetik* (Jena: Verlag Hermann Pohle, 1903), vol. ii, p. 254.   29 Frege, *Foundations of Arithmetic*, p. 61.

ous predicates', that is, predicates which require the addition of a general term in order to complete their sense and which may therefore be regarded as having different forms depending on the general term which is added.[30] A stock example is 'ζ is better than η': to say that a is better than b is incomplete in sense until the respect in which a is held to be better is specified. This doctrine can be traced back to Aristotle. There is evidence that Aristotle held that 'good',[31] 'being' and 'existent',[32] and 'one'[33] were polygamous. Other philosophers have added to the list: 'resemblance' is often suggested as a candidate,[34] and Russell, at one stage at least, proposed 'truth' and 'falsity'.[35] Geach's theory of identity can be interpreted, at least in part, as the claim that identity is a polygamous concept. And this is not implausible, for while we know what it is to be the same dog or the same number (just as we know what it is for a dog or a number to exist) the question of what it is to be the same *simpliciter* is rather odd (just as the question of what it is to exist *simpliciter* is rather odd).

What of the motivation for (III)? Again, ordinary language provides the best justification. We might well say, e.g., that two cars were the same type of car, two word tokens are the same word type, two toys are the same colour, and so on. If this is all (III) commits us to it is hard to see why it has been so controversial. The examples given don't challenge (LL) so long as the absolutist can maintain a distinction between numerical and qualitative identity. The absolutist can fairly easily find an

---

[30] G. E. L. Owen, 'Aristotle on the Snares of Ontology', in R. Bambrough (ed.), *New Essays on Plato and Aristotle* (London: Routledge and Kegan Paul, 1965), p. 72. Geach has acknowledged this source and called such predicates 'transcendental' because of the way they 'jump across any conceptual barriers between different kinds of discourse'. Geach, 'Ontological Relativity and Relative Identity', in M. K. Munitz (ed.), *Logic and Ontology* (New York: New York University Press, 1973), p. 287. For every polygamous (or transcendental) predicate there is a corresponding polygamous concept or general term—viz., the general term from which the predicate in question was formed (e.g. 'existent' from 'ζ exists').

[31] *Topics* A (107a 4–17).

[32] *Sophistici Elenchi* (182b 13–27); *Posterior Analytics* (92b 14); *De Anima* B (415b 13); *Metaphysics* H (998b 22–7; 1042b 15–1043a 7).

[33] *Sophistici Elenchi* (182b 13–27); *Physics* H (248b 19–21); *Metaphysics* I (1053b 25–1054a 19).

[34] Butchvarov, *Resemblance and Identity* (Bloomington, Ind.: Indiana University Press, 1966), pp. 111–24. Also D. J. O'Connor, 'On Resemblance', *Proceedings of the Aristotelian Society*, 46 (1945/6), 47–76.

[35] *Principia Mathematica*, vol. i, p. 42.

analysis of them by accepting that, while the distinctness involved in each case is numerical distinctness (and is thus captured by (LL)), the sameness in each case is not numerical sameness (and thus requires some other analysis than that provided by (LL)). Of course this looks somewhat self-serving as the only means we have so far of distinguishing the two is whether or not they meet the requirements of (LL); but this need not, perhaps, be so. However, there are cases where the distinction between numerical identity and qualitative identity is not very obvious. There is at least a *prima facie* case for having a theory of identity (or, if you like, of 'sameness') which treats the two even-handedly.

There is another group of examples which are inclined to be more puzzling and on occasion to lead to irresolvable wrangles about whether two things are 'really' the same. For example, people who agree on all the facts might still argue about whether two people who spoke different dialects really spoke the same language. A not unreasonable conclusion to such a discussion might be that they spoke the same language but not the same dialect. Quite how the absolutist might handle such a conclusion is difficult to see. He could scarcely claim that while 'ζ is the same dialect as η' expresses numerical identity 'ζ is the same language as η' does not. At any rate it is clear that ordinary language has a use for such sentences, that sometimes they make true statements, and in at least some cases the absolutist account of them is not clear cut.

1.4 Some Theories of Relative Identity

Identity statements in natural language come in two syntactic varieties. Some are of the form '*a* is the same as *b*' or '*a* is identical with *b*'. These are absolute identity statements. Others have the form '*a* is the same so-and-so as *b*'. These are relative identity statements. In seeking a logical analysis of natural language identity statements a number of policies are open. The most draconian is that proposed by the early Wittgenstein which would eliminate identity statements altogether in favour of special constraints upon the singular terms of the language.[36] As we shall see, much can be done

---

[36] *Tractatus Logico-Philosophicus*, transl. D. F. Pears and B. F. McGuinness (London: Routledge and Kegan Paul, 1961), 5.53–5.534.

with identity relations so long as we are prepared to impose the requisite conditions on the singular terms which might flank the relations; in this case the condition that no item has more than one name in the canonical language. There are two alternative reductionist policies which are less sweeping than Wittgenstein's. The first is the classical theory which reduces all natural language identity statements to absolute identity statements; the second is a relativist reduction theory which reduces them all to relative identity statements. Finally there is a non-reductionist policy, defended here, which admits both absolute and relative identity statements into the canonical language. Of these four policies I shall be concerned here almost entirely with the last two. The absolutist reduction policy will be used mainly as a foil for these two, and Wittgenstein's policy will be entirely ignored.

What, then, of the two types of theory with which I am concerned, the theories which permit relative identity statements in their canonical language? Consider again Geach's claim (II) which rejects the principle that, e.g., 'being the same water' can be analysed as 'being the same (something-or-other) and being water'. It is clear some such principle is basic to the absolutist reduction policy since it converts a relative identity statement into an absolute identity statement. For example, 'a is the same man as b' in Quine's canonical notation becomes:

$$(1.5) \qquad \mathrm{man}(a) \ \& \ \mathrm{man}(b) \ \& \ a = b$$

and if one happens to like Quine's canonical notation there seems very little harm in this: the canonical paraphrase isn't obviously inadequate to the English original. However, if one accepts the point that Geach makes in (I), then (1.5) is not adequate because either the third conjunct requires completion by a general noun understood from the context (a completion which ought to be explicit in canonical notation) or it is 'just a vague expression of a half-formed thought', i.e. (presumably) deficient in sense. Thus if Geach is right in (I), he is right in (II).[37]

[37] As they stand there is a tension between the first quotation and the second, because the first requires completion by a count noun, while the second uses an example involving completion by 'water' which is a mass term. The difficulty is more apparent than real, since Geach has admitted that his restriction of completions to count nouns was 'a slip of the pen' and that he allows mass terms as

Hence, we turn to (I). Geach is here making a claim, central to the relativist reductionist policy, which, following Wiggins,[38] I shall call '(D)'. Stated very generally, it might run:[39]

(D) Absolute identity statements require completion to give a statement of the form '*a* is the same $\mathscr{A}$ as *b*'.

Although '$\mathscr{A}$', '$\mathscr{B}$', and '$\mathscr{C}$' are general nouns and not predicates, let the expression '$\mathscr{A}(\zeta)$' be the associated (general noun) predicate 'ζ is (an) $\mathscr{A}$'. Following Wiggins[40] rather loosely in terminology I shall say that a general term which follows 'same' in sentences of the form '*a* is the same $\mathscr{A}$ as *b*' is in *covering concept position*. Such a term '$\mathscr{A}$' will be said to express (or, briefly: to be) a *covering concept* for that statement when it is such that '$\mathscr{A}(a)$' and '$\mathscr{A}(b)$' are both true. Thus in 'W. S. Porter is the same number as O. Henry', 'number' is in covering concept position but is not a covering concept.

(D) leads to two questions: Why do absolute identity statements require completion? and What sort of completion do they require? At least the options for answering the second question are easier to be clear about, and a satisfactory answer to the first can be given only in the course of analysing the theory (or theories) of relative identity. It is clear that the completing term must be a general term and that this general term must be either a noun or a noun phrase: nothing else would do grammatically. But general nouns come in several varieties and this gives us our first variants of the simple but vague (D). The first variant (D_1) construes the possible completions very widely: any general noun will serve as a completion. A much more restrictive version (D_2) requires that the completion be by a sortal general noun. And a third variant (D_3) might lie somewhere between the two, admitting other completions than just those by sortals but not admitting every general noun. Such a

---

well. Cf. Geach, 'Identity—A Reply', *Logic Matters*, p. 247; and 'Ontological Relativity and Relative Identity', p. 289.

[38] *Identity and Spatio-Temporal Continuity*, p. 1.

[39] In what follows the upper case letters '$\mathscr{A}$', '$\mathscr{B}$', '$\mathscr{C}$' are constants standing for general nouns, the corresponding lower case letters are variables taking general nouns as values. The special type-face will be reserved for general noun constants and variables. The notation for general nouns will be developed further in Chapter 2. In future I shall take the liberty of altering quotations to make them conform with this notation.

[40] *Identity and Spatio-Temporal Continuity*, p. 2.

version might be Geach's admission of both sortals and mass terms. (The distinction between sortals and mass terms will be treated at length in Chapters 2 and 3.)

But other things said by relativists suggest that a relativist policy might be none of (D_1)–(D_3). For example: 'I maintain that it makes no sense to judge whether x and y are "the same", or whether x remains "the same", unless we add or understand some general term—"the same $\mathscr{A}$". That in accordance with which we thus judge as to the identity, I call a *criterion* of identity . . .'[41] What is meant by a 'criterion of identity' is not yet clear (it will become so, I hope, in Chapter 4) and it is not obvious that if we confine completions to general nouns which provide criteria of identity we shall have a (D)-thesis coextensive with any of (D_1), (D_2), or (D_3). Thus there is scope for (D_4) which limits completions to general nouns conveying criteria of identity. As a final option I shall include (D_5) which limits completions to ultimate sortals. The motivation for this will become clearer when sortals are discussed. A general noun which acts as an adequate completion for identity statements on a given theory of relative identity will be said to be a *completing concept* on that theory. Thus while all completing concepts are covering concepts, the converse is not true.

Quotation (III) introduces a thesis which has become known as (R):

(R) a may be the same $\mathscr{A}$ as b and not the same $\mathscr{B}$.

As it stands the truth of (R) is rather uninteresting. We have already noted cases in which statements of this form may be true, e.g.

(1.6)   This car is the same type of car as that car, but they are not the same car.

(1.7)   'Dog' is the same type word as 'Dog' but they are not the same token word.

(1.8)   This toy is the same colour as that toy but they are not the same toy.

There is a second group of statements, clearly distinct from those of the first group, which also have the form (R) and

41 Geach, *Reference and Generality*, p. 39. Cf. also G. E. M. Anscombe, 'The Principle of Individuation', *Proceedings of the Aristotelian Society*, Supplementary Volume 27 (1953), 91.

which are also clearly true, at least within a two-valued logic. These are cases in which the general noun in covering concept position is not, in fact, a covering concept. Examples are:

(1.9)   W. S. Porter is the same man as O. Henry but they are not the same number.

(1.10)   W. S. Porter is the same man as O. Henry but they were not the same boy (because Porter did not assume the name 'O. Henry' when he was a boy).

In a two-valued logic both conjuncts would be true. In a three-valued logic with conjunction defined by the matrix:

&	T	N	F
T	T	N	F
N	N	N	F
F	F	F	F

we would assign the value 'N' ('nonsense') to (1.9) if we assigned the value 'N' to its second conjunct. Whether we would be happy assigning the same value to the second conjunct of (1.10) is more debatable.[42]

So far the relativist's case looks good and will remain so for a while as we shall reserve the absolutist reply for later. There are, of course, at least as many variants of (R) as there are of (D), for each variant of (D) will give a different method of completing 'a is the same . . . as b' and hence give a different variant of (R). Of the two theses, (D) and (R), the latter has not received as much support as the former. Many philosophers, with what might roughly be termed Aristotelian motivations, have accepted (D) and rejected (R).[43] Some have embraced them both,[44] while some, following the non-reduction-

---

[42] R. H. Thomason, 'A Semantic Theory of Sortal Incorrectness', *Journal of Philosophical Logic*, 1 (1972), 226, suggests that the relativist is forced to assign the value 'N' to statements such as the second conjunct of (1.9). I see no reason (and Thomason doesn't provide one) for saying that the relativist is *forced* to do this, although I can see that he might wish to and might find such a position congenial.

[43] Chief among them is, of course, Wiggins: cf. his *Identity and Spatio-Temporal Continuity*, Parts I and II. But others include Leslie Stevenson, 'Relative Identity and Leibniz's Law', *Philosophical Quarterly*, 22 (1972), 155–8; Michael Durrant, 'Numerical Identity', *Mind*, 82 (1973), 95–103; J. W. Cook, 'Wittgenstein on Privacy', in George Pitcher (ed.), *Wittgenstein: The 'Philosophical Investigations'* (London: Macmillan, 1968), pp. 311–18.

[44] P. T. Geach, *Reference and Generality* and 'Identity'; Peter Sheehan, 'The

ist policy, have accepted (R) but not (D).[45] The latter Odegard calls 'Lockean-relativists'.[46]

Odegard does not quote Locke, but a passage which apparently supports his attribution comes in Book II, Chapter 27, of the *Essay*. Talking of the way in which an oak grows from a plant into a great tree or a colt grows into a horse by the incorporation of new matter and the loss of old, Locke says: '. . . so that truly they are not either of them the same masses of matter, though they be truly one of them the same oak, and the other the same horse'.[47] But then Locke goes on to say: 'The reason whereof is, that in these two cases, a mass of matter, and a living body, identity is not applied to the same thing.'[48] Without pursuing exegetic details this passage does raise problems for Odegard's attribution, because Locke seems to be saying not:

(1.11)   The plant is the same oak as the great tree but they are not the same mass of matter.

but, where '*a*' and '*b*' are two names of an oak, and '*c*' and '*d*' names of masses of matter:

(1.12)   *a* is the same oak as *b* & *c* is not the same mass of matter as *d* & *a* is not the same thing as *c* & *b* is not the same thing as *d*.

The text supports this interpretation for Locke says that 'identity is not applied to the same thing' in saying that the plant and the tree are the same oak but not the same mass of matter, which suggests that in each conjunct the terms of the identity relation are different. And it is clear from other things Locke says[49] that he regards the oak and the parcel of matter which composes it as distinct absolutely. Moreover, 'identity *is* applied' suggests that there is only one identity relation and not two involved.

Relativity of Identity' (Unpublished, 1972); E. M. Zemach, 'In Defence of Relative Identity', *Philosophical Studies*, 26 (1974), 207–18; George Pitcher, 'About the Same', in A. Ambrose and M. Lazerowitz (eds.), *Ludwig Wittgenstein: Philosophy and Language* (London: Allen and Unwin, 1972), pp. 120–39.

[45] Douglas Odegard, 'Identity Through Time', *American Philosophical Quarterly*, 9 (1972), 29–38.
[46] Ibid., p. 29 and Appendix, p. 38.
[47] Locke, *Essay*, Bk. II, Ch. 27, § 4 (vol. i, p. 442 of Fraser's edition).
[48] Ibid.   [49] Cf. ibid., §§ 2, 5 (Fraser, vol. i, pp. 441, 443).

But there are other passages concerned with person-identity which show that Locke, if he did not actually believe (R), came creditably close to doing so. He says for example: '[I]f the same consciousness . . . can be transferred from one thinking substance to another, it will be possible that two thinking substances may make but one person.'[50] It is not clear that all such passages can be dealt with in the same way that we dealt with the oak tree example. Sometimes, he does seem to suggest such a treatment, for example, when he imagines that the 'soul of a prince . . . enter[s] . . . the body of a cobbler' he asks rhetorically: '. . . everyone sees he would be the same *person* with the prince . . .: but who would say it was the same *man*?'[51] But then he seems to retreat: 'I know that, in the ordinary way of speaking, the same person, and the same man, stand for one and the same thing',[52] which plainly suggests that Locke thinks that the man and the person are distinct absolutely. But when he considers whether they do stand for the same thing, the only evidence he offers for saying that they do not is that 'person' and 'man' convey different criteria of identity—which was what was needed to generate a case of (R) in the first place. And, in an elaboration of this, where he gets closest to discussing our problem, he says:

It is not therefore unity of substance that comprehends all sorts of identity, or will determine it in every case; but to conceive and judge of it aright, we must consider what idea the word it applies to stands for: it being one thing to be the same *substance*, another the same *man*, and a third the same *person*, if *person*, *man* and *substance*, are three names for three different ideas;—for such as is the idea belonging to that name, such must be the identity; . . .[53]

But this leaves it unclear whether he believes (R), a version of (D), or something else altogether. Not surprisingly Locke was confused on the topic and seems to have stumbled upon, rather than adopted, the non-reductionist policy: thinking that while it was important to know whether you were talking about man-identity or person-identity or substance-identity you could

---

[50] Locke, *Essay*, Bk. II, Ch. 27, § 13 (Fraser, vol. i, p. 454). Cf. also the tortuous passage (too long to quote) on the identity of Socrates in which he admits that 'it is hard to conceive that Socrates, the same individual man, should be two persons' (§ 21; Fraser, vol. i, pp. 461–2).

[51] Ibid., § 15 (Fraser, vol. i, p. 457).

[52] Ibid.   [53] Ibid., § 8 (Fraser, vol. i, p. 445).

still inquire whether they were the same or different absolutely. This tangled discussion of Locke is of more than merely historical interest, for the difficulties into which Locke, as a proto-relativist, got himself have been raised more recently by Perry and Calvert in objection to Geach, and we shall consider them more carefully in due course.

1.5 *The Relation Between Absolute and Relative Identity*

Geach seems to think that only the interpretation and not the syntax of absolute identity theory need be challenged by relative identity. He writes: 'Absolute identity seems at first sight to be presupposed in the branch of formal logic called identity theory',[54] which clearly implies that he thinks that relative identity could as well be expressed in classical identity theory. This might well be so for (D)-relativism, but for (R)-relativism things are not so simple.

Wiggins has a proof which, he claims,[55] shows that (R) is incompatible with the formal requirements of classical identity theory. However, the proof requires him to extend the classical theory in a way which the person who wishes to combine the relativist and absolutist positions is not compelled to accept. Some preliminary formalization of the relativist theories is required here. Following Wiggins,[56] I shall take '$a =_{\mathscr{A}} b$' to read 'a is the same $\mathscr{A}$ as b'. On account of (D), the antecedent of (LL) is incomplete; but Wiggins gives a version of (In. Id.) which meets this objection:[57]

(DLL) $(\forall x)(\forall y)[(\exists a)(x =_a y) \supset (\forall \phi)(\phi(x) \equiv \phi(y))]$.

Given the following example of (R):

(1.13) $a =_{\mathscr{A}} b \; \& \sim (a =_{\mathscr{B}} b)$

where

(1.14) $\mathscr{A}(a) \; \& \; \mathscr{A}(b) \; \& \; \mathscr{B}(a)$

and the following, surely unexceptionable, premiss:

(1.15) $\mathscr{B}(a) \supset a =_{\mathscr{B}} a$

---

[54] 'Identity', p. 238.
[55] *Identity and Spatio-Temporal Continuity*, p. 3.   [56] Ibid., p. 2.
[57] Ibid., p. 3. In fact (DLL) differs slightly, in ways not relevant here, from the formula Wiggins gives.

Wiggins can derive a contradiction from (DLL).[58] The argument, reconstructed, runs as follows:

[1] $(\forall x)(\forall y)(\forall a)(x =_a y \supset (\forall \phi)(\phi(x) \equiv \phi(y))$ ((DLL) Q.T.)

[2] $a =_{\mathscr{A}} b \supset (\forall \phi)(\phi(a) \equiv \phi(b))$ ([1] U.I., a/x, b/y, $\mathscr{A}/a$)

[3] $(\forall \phi)(\phi(a) \equiv \phi(b))$ ((1.13) Simp., [2] M.P.)

[4] $a =_{\mathscr{B}} a \supset a =_{\mathscr{B}} b$ ([3] U.I., $a =_{\mathscr{B}} \zeta/\phi(\zeta)$)

[5] $a =_{\mathscr{B}} a$ ((1.14) Simp., (1.15) M.P.)

[6] $a =_{\mathscr{B}} b$ ([4], [5] M.P.)

[7] $a =_{\mathscr{B}} b \;\&\; \sim (a =_{\mathscr{B}} b)$ ((1.13) Simp., [6] Conj.)

Thus, if we permit a relative identity claim to carry a commitment to unrestricted indiscernibility, we cannot simultaneously accept (R). That (DLL) is an unreasonable formula to adopt irrespective of (R), is seen by instantiating 'colour' for 'a', 'Mars' for 'x', and 'the Soviet flag' for 'y'. None the less, a consistent theory based on (DLL) is possible, and the theory can even be made plausible if we add appropriate constraints on what can serve as a completing concept and on the relation between the completing concept and the singular terms of the identity statement.[59]

Alternatively, we can preserve (R) in a consistent theory provided that we drop (DLL) in favour of a more limited substitutivity principle, such that if a and b are the same $\mathscr{A}$ then it follows that for every predicate $\phi(\zeta)$ within a certain restricted range of predicates $\phi(a)$ iff $\phi(b)$.[60] Such a theory will be a theory for (D) as well as (R) when the string '$a = b$' is not a wff of the theory. However, we can produce a consistent Lockean theory from the (R)-relativist theory by adding Leibniz's Law as a definition for absolute identity.[61] It turns out that the relations

---

[58] *Identity and Spatio-Temporal Continuity*, pp. 3–4.

[59] See Leslie Stevenson, 'A Formal Theory of Sortal Quantification', *Notre Dame Journal of Formal Logic*, 16 (1975), 185–207, where such a theory is formulated and its consistency proved. See also his 'Relative Identity and Leibniz's Law', p. 157, where he states the constraints required on the completing concept and its relation to the singular terms. This second issue is discussed below in § 10.2.

[60] See Richard Routley and Nicholas Griffin, 'Towards a Logic of Relative Identity' (unpublished) where such a logic is set up within classical second-order logic. See below, § 8.2 for further discussion of these restricted substitutivity principles.

[61] See Routley and Griffin, op. cit., for details.

between the absolute and the relative theories of identity are more complex than either Wiggins or Geach seem to have thought, for we can construct consistent absolute, (D)-relative, (R)-relative, and Lockean identity theories if we take sufficient care in selecting basic principles.

In what follows I shall argue against (D). It seems to me that the arguments in its favour are very weak and often rely on unacceptable postulates, such as the verification principle. Moreover, it seems too restrictive a principle for comfort—ruling out as defective or even nonsensical a good deal which it seems wise to retain. On the other hand, I think the (D)-relativists have discovered, or perhaps rediscovered, an important truth, but one which it is misleading to express by means of (D). This is the claim that the notion of an individual is incoherent without individuation, and the individuative resources required for individuals are provided by (certain types of) general nouns in natural language.

This doctrine is compatible with both (R) and the theory of absolute identity. However, taking it together with (R), as I do, requires some changes in the semantics of absolute identity. What these changes might be I shall try and suggest in § 8.5, though their formal treatment is still a long way off. Chapters 8, 9, and 10 present my defence of (R). The next four chapters, however, deal with different types of general noun and their functions in relative identity theory.

2

General Terms

2.1 Singular and General Terms

So far as I can tell my use of 'general term' and 'singular term' is co-extensive with Quine's,[1] despite the fact that Quine's method of making the distinction is not entirely satisfactory. According to Quine 'a singular term names or purports to name just one object, though as complex or diffuse an object as you please, while a general term is true of each, severally, of any number of objects',[2] which leaves it open to the sort of objections raised by Strawson.[3] However, I do not intend to provide a more satisfactory criterion partly because I think the distinction is well understood and partly because one has to start somewhere. Thus 'Al Capone', 'the Napoleon of Notting Hill', 'Pegasus', 'the round square', and 'that river' are singular terms; while 'river', 'queen', 'round', 'square', and 'unicorn' are general terms. In what follows I shall be almost entirely concerned with those general terms which are nouns or noun phrases, and which I call general nouns.

In theories of relative identity general nouns play a far more important role than they do in Quine's predicate calculus. Quine is quite content to make the singular term/general term distinction vaguely because in his canonical notation a general term counts for little more than a constituent syllable of a predicate. On at least one occasion he does imply that a predicate simply is a general term,[4] but either way, general terms in their own right are given little standing. However, in order to

---

[1] See, e.g., *Word and Object* (Cambridge, Mass.: The M.I.T. Press, 1960), pp. 90–5; 'Identity, Ostension, and Hypostasis', in *From a Logical Point of View*, p. 75; *Methods of Logic* (New York: Holt, 1950), pp. 203–8.

[2] *Word and Object*, pp. 90–1.

[3] *Individuals* (London: Methuen, 1959), p. 155.

[4] 'The Scope and Language of Science', in *The Ways of Paradox* (New York: Random House, 1966), p. 224.

formulate a theory of relative identity it is necessary to be able to mark general nouns as distinct from the predicates in which they occur. It is also necessary to be able to distinguish sortal general nouns (e.g. 'dog', 'car', 'unicorn', 'cup') from mass terms (e.g. 'water', 'sugar', 'bread', 'phlogiston').

2.2 +Count and −Count General Terms

The first great division among general terms is the division between +count and −count general terms. The distinction between them is very easy to draw:

(2.1) A general term 'T' is +count if 'There are n Ts . . .' makes sense, where 'n' is a variable taking numerals as values; otherwise 'T' is −count.[5]

The +count/−count distinction among general terms partially cuts across the distinction between general nouns and other types of general term, for while all +count general terms are general nouns some −count general terms are also general nouns (e.g. 'gold', 'chastity'). Criteria for +count and −count general nouns can easily be derived from (2.1) by replacing the requirement that 'T' be a general term by the requirement that it be a general noun.

2.3 Notation for General Nouns

In §§ 1.4 and 1.5 it was necessary to introduce some notation for general nouns in order to be able to formalize the theory of relative identity. Here it will be necessary to extend that notation somewhat. The script type-face introduced in § 1.4 will continue to be reserved for general nouns with the exception of their use in forming general noun predicates—e.g. '$\mathscr{A}(\zeta)$'. As in § 1.5 the upper-case letters '$\mathscr{A}$', '$\mathscr{B}$', '$\mathscr{C}$' will be general noun constants, and the corresponding lower-case letters variables taking general nouns as values. To ensure sufficient supplies of such constants and variables priming and subscripted numerals may be added.

Within the class of general nouns we will chiefly be concerned

---

[5] Fred Feldman ('Sortal Predicates', *Nous*, 7 (1973), 270) considers a rather similar criterion as a criterion for sortals. It seems to me that the distinction between +count nouns and sortals is worth preserving. A further objection to Feldman's criterion is that it admits proper names; since it does not require the term in question to be a general term.

with two subgroups: sortals within the group of +count general nouns; and mass terms within the group of −count general nouns.[6] (In what follows sortals will feature very much more than mass terms.) The term 'sortal' derives from Locke's happy use of the word 'sort'—he coins 'sortal' from 'sort' on analogy with 'general' from 'genus'.[7] The expression 'mass term' stems originally from Jespersen's use of 'mass word'.[8] The letters '$\mathscr{F}$', '$\mathscr{G}$', '$\mathscr{H}$' will henceforth be sortal constants, and 'f', 'g', 'h' sortal variables. Likewise '$\mathscr{M}$' and '$\mathscr{N}$' will be mass term constants and 'm' and 'n' mass term variables. Priming and subscript numerals will also be allowed, though there will not be much call for them with mass terms. Sortal and mass term predicates will be constructible in the same way as general noun predicates. I shall alter quotations to conform to this notation.

The task of the remainder of this chapter and of the whole of the next is to provide adequate criteria for mass terms and sortals, respectively. Although the issue for mass terms is, it seems to me, very much more complicated than for sortals the comparative unimportance of mass terms for present purposes explains my cursory treatment of their complexities.

[6] A third group of some importance are non-sortal +count nouns or dummy sortals, e.g. 'thing', 'entity', 'individual', 'set', 'collection of plants', etc.

[7] Cf. *Essay*, Bk. III, Ch. 3, § 15 (Fraser, vol. ii, p. 27). The Lockean term is chosen in preference to a variety of contenders. Strawson used to use 'individuative' which begs at least one of the questions of this work (cf. 'Particular and General', *Proceedings of the Aristotelian Society*, 54 (1954), 254 n.) and, taking his cue from Aristotle, 'substance-name' (ibid., p. 239), but later changed to 'sortal' (*Individuals*, p. 168). Geach uses 'count noun' ('Ontological Relativity and Relative Identity', p. 289) and thereby obscures a distinction I want to make. Woodger, to whom Wiggins is much indebted, uses 'shared name' (*Biology and Language* [Cambridge: Cambridge University Press, 1952], p. 17). Quine talks of 'divided reference' (*Word and Object*, p. 90) thereby suggesting a mereological criterion I wish to reject.

[8] Cf. *The Philosophy of Grammar* (London: Allen and Unwin, 1924), p. 198. As with 'sortal' there are many alternatives: Strawson uses 'material name' ('Particular and General', p. 238) which conveys the unfortunate impression that all mass terms are names of materials. Terence Parsons tries to correct this impression by suggesting that we construe terms such as 'music' and 'hunger' as naming 'abstract substances' ('Analysis of Mass and Amount Terms', *Foundations of Language*, 6 (1970), 369). Goodman uses 'collective predicate' (*The Structure of Appearance* [New York: Bobbs-Merrill; 2nd edn., 1966], p. 54) which unfortunately suggests 'flock' or 'shoal'. Quine considers 'partitive term' (*Word and Object*, p. 91 n.) which is also used by Strawson (op. cit., p. 238) but this suggests a mereological criterion which I reject. The terminology I have chosen has been sanctioned rather by tradition than by principle.

2.4 Mass Terms

Intuitively ⁻count nouns seem to fall into at least three distinct groups. The first consists of what might be called the names of materials: e.g. 'gold', 'water', 'iron', 'wrought iron', 'frozen water', etc. To this list should be added, also, terms which behave in exactly the same way but which we would be less inclined to call the names of materials, e.g. 'groceries', 'meat', 'wheat', 'garbage', 'housing', and 'footwear'. The second group contains terms which behave similarly but are abstract, e.g. 'music', 'cricket', 'mathematics', 'information', and 'entertainment'. Colour words such as 'red', when glossed as 'redness', also belong to the second list. Terms on these two lists are what seem to be paradigm examples of mass terms, and it will not be necessary for our purposes to distinguish very carefully between the two lists. The third group is much more miscellaneous and includes such terms as 'intelligence', 'chastity', 'indigence', 'quality', 'viscosity', and 'efficiency'—typically abstract names of qualities. In many uses these terms are singular rather than general, as in 'Chastity is its own punishment' (example due to Stephen Voss). But in this they do not apparently differ from such uses of mass terms as 'Snow is white'. They do, however, have general uses (e.g. 'John has intelligence') and in these uses it is tempting to distinguish nouns of this third group by the fact that they are so closely related to adjectives ('intelligence' to 'intelligent', 'virtue' to 'virtuous', etc.). This has led some linguists to suggest that all abstract nouns can be derived from adjectives.[9] While this does not seem to be the case with what I called 'abstract mass terms' it certainly has plausibility with the third group, which I shall call (following Strawson)[10] 'characterizing terms'. As this expression is generally understood[11] it includes adjectives, adverbs, and verbs in addition to certain nouns. In view of the account I shall give of mass terms it seems likely that characterizing nouns are a type of mass term. It also seems fairly clear that,

[9] For example, F. Bowers, 'The Deep Structure of Abstract Nouns', *Foundations of Language*, 5 (1969), 520–33. See also Strawson, 'Particular and General', p. 239; and Dummett, *Frege*, pp. 77–8. (Dummett claims that there could not be a language in which the noun form appeared but not the adjective.)

[10] *Individuals*, p. 168.

[11] For example, by Strawson, ibid.; and John Lyons, *Introduction to Theoretical Linguistics* (Cambridge: Cambridge University Press, 1968), p. 338.

as far as relative identity is concerned, the two groups behave in the same way. The issues involved in the analysis of characterizing terms are very obscure and it would take us too far out of our way to reach a satisfactory resolution of them.

Certain uses of mass terms can be construed on analogy with sortals. For example, if we say '*a* is $\mathscr{M}$' we are saying what sort of material *a* is, in very much the same way as when we say '*a* is an $\mathscr{F}$' we are saying what sort of a thing *a* is. However, subject uses of mass terms are quite different. In 'Snow is falling', 'snow' looks as if it might refer to one, particular, sprawling object, so that 'snow' in this sense is not a general term at all;[12] or to the universal *snow*, in which case we seem to be asserting that the universal is falling—from Plato's heaven presumably.[13] These are difficult problems but there's no need to solve them now, all we need to do now is to say what mass terms are. My purpose in adverting to problems of wider philosophic interest is simply to show that the semantics of mass terms is in a peculiar state of indecision and that a really satisfactory semantic characterization of mass terms may be fairly hard to come by unless we are prepared to resolve these issues.

Despite the fact that the literature on mass terms is already quite large, very few authors have attempted to define what they are. Instead the literature abounds with various interesting suggestions, few of which we are invited to take as supplying necessary and sufficient conditions. Grammatical criteria are, of course, fairly popular, but also fairly prone to counter-examples. Chappell provides a convenient summary:

Mass nouns are distinguished grammatically from count nouns by not having plural forms and by not taking either the indefinite article or numerical adjectives; on the other hand they do, and count nouns do not, admit quantitative adjectives. Thus, though any common noun, including the plural forms of count nouns, can be preceded by 'the' and 'the same', and by 'any', 'no', and 'some', only singular count nouns can occur after 'one', or after 'a', 'each',

---

[12] The nearest analogue with sortals to certain cases like this is the use of the generic 'the' preceding a sortal. Cf. John Bacon, 'Do Generic Descriptions Denote?', *Mind*, 82 (1973), 331–47; also 'The Semantics of Generic THE', *Journal of Philosophical Logic*, 2 (1973), 323–39. For this view of mass terms in subject position see Quine, *Word and Object*, p. 98.

[13] The second alternative is the one adopted by Strawson.

and 'every'; and only plural count nouns can follow 'two', 'three', etc. and 'many' and 'few'. On the other hand, only mass nouns are preceded by 'much', 'little', and 'less' (note that 'more' has a numerical as well as a quantitative use, being opposed in the former to 'fewer' rather than to 'less').[14]

The two major features here, failure of pluralization and admission of quantitative adjectives, are both open to counter-examples. 'Oats', 'groceries', 'spaghetti', certain uses of 'beans' and 'potatoes', are all mass terms which take the plural ending —though not numerical adjectives. In much more common-place mass terms there are counter-examples: 'water' sometimes admits the plural ending, as in 'Spa waters'. What seals the fate of grammatical criteria, however, is that many words double both as sortals and mass terms. There are quite a number of such terms: e.g. 'lamb', which is ambiguous between a type of meat and a juvenile sheep; others are 'rope', 'apple', 'sugar', 'beer', 'coffee', 'paper', 'cake', etc. The existence of this class of words effectively frustrates any attempt to distinguish between sortals and mass terms by purely grammatical criteria.[15]

Strawson[16] attempts to distinguish between sortals, mass terms, and characterizing terms by treating them all as names of universals and then considering the different latitudes permitted in what is to count as an instance of the universal. With sortals the situation is quite simple: only a cat can be an instance of *cat*. With characterizing terms, by contrast, the latitude is very great: a person, an action, or a plan are among the things which can be instances of *intelligence*. Mass terms, it seems, fall somewhere between the two: a lump of gold, a piece of gold, and a ring of gold may all be instances of *gold*. But despite their differences lumps, pieces, and rings of gold all have something more in common than their goldenness: they are all material objects.

Geach has objected to this, that we cannot treat persons, actions, or plans as instances of *intelligence* since 'we cannot say of persons, actions or plans that they are intelli*gence*'.[17] If Geach

---

[14] Chappell, 'Stuff and Things', *Proceedings of the Aristotelian Society*, 71 (1970/1), 61–2.

[15] Cf. Jespersen's *Philosophy of Grammar*, pp. 199–200.

[16] 'Particular and General', pp. 239–40. See also, Chappell, 'Stuff and Things', pp. 72–3.   [17] Personal communication, 6 January 1975.

is right here then we cannot use Strawson's point to distinguish
characterizing terms from other general terms. If persons,
actions, and plans are not themselves instances of *intelligence*
then it is presumably the case that they all may have properties or features which are such instances. But if this is so
then Strawson's point fails since only properties (of various
types of things) can be instances of *intelligence*. Let us, however,
assume that Geach is not right. Can Strawson's point be made
to do the work we want it to do? One of the troubles with
Strawson's account is that it is scarcely, as it stands, sharp
enough to do what we want. We can, however, sharpen it
somewhat in the following way. An instance of $\mathscr{F}$ is always a
member of one sort, namely $\mathscr{F}$. By contrast an instance of $\mathscr{M}$
can fall under many sortals, but all instances of $\mathscr{M}$ must fall
under the same dummy sortal, namely that appropriate to $\mathscr{M}$.
Finally, instances of a characterizing noun need not even fall
under the same dummy sortal but may be of radically different
types. Of these three statements only the first seems to be un-
impeachable. The third, while it doubtless works well for
'intelligence' and 'courage', fails with 'brittleness' and 'viscosity' for only a material object can be an instance of *brittleness*
and only a fluid of *viscosity*. The objection to the second statement, which is the one we are chiefly interested in, is more
fundamental. We can seriously doubt whether a piece of gold
is an instance of *gold* at all. For surely a piece of gold is an
instance of the universal named by the sortal 'piece of gold'.[18]
Of course, this leaves us open to the possibly embarrassing
question: What *is* an instance of *gold*? But we don't have to
answer this in order to attack Strawson's criterion. We can also
find counter-examples to the second statement: for example,
'red' (in its mass term sense) has instances of such diverse forms
as pillar-boxes, sunsets, and after-images—and so fails Strawson's criterion for mass terms. (Strawson, however, includes
'red' among characterizing nouns—a classification which rather
runs against my intuitions.) Strawson's criterion does not seem
to me to be a promising line for further investigation.

   D. S. Clarke claims that: 'Unlike ordinary substantives [mass
terms] do not express attributes of shape and boundary by

---

[18] Laycock makes this objection, 'Some Questions of Ontology', *Philosophical
Review*, 81 (1972), 13.

which we identify an object as the same on different occasions and distinguish it from other objects of the same general kind.'[19] He calls this the 'fundamental feature' of mass terms. Clarke is concerned simply to distinguish sortals from mass terms, but even for this task his 'fundamental feature' fails. 'Colony of ants', 'lump of coal', and 'number' are all sortals yet do not in any obvious sense express 'attributes of shape and boundary'. If we take these attributes very broadly so that 'number' expresses attributes of boundary which, for example, distinguish numbers from other mathematical entities, then it seems to me that a mass term such as 'gold' will express attributes of boundary which, for example, distinguish gold from other chemical elements. Moreover, dummy sortals such as 'thing' pass this criterion for mass terms.

Although Clarke does not provide us with a criterion he does, I think, provide us with a clue. The clue is that, within broad limits, mass terms refer to relatively undifferentiated bodies of stuff and that a mereological criterion might be the most useful way of distinguishing them. There are a variety of such criteria to choose from, some of which we can dispose of very briefly. The following criterion might be suggested:

(2.2) A term '$\mathscr{A}$' is a mass term iff if you divide something which is $\mathscr{A}$ into two parts then each part is $\mathscr{A}$.

But on this criterion 'water' will fail as a mass term for if the method of division is electrolysis then the result of dividing water will not be water. And similarly for every chemical substance, there is some method of division which does not preserve the sort of substance we started with. So let us rephrase the criterion in such a way as to avoid this reliance on the actual process of fission:

(2.3) A term '$\mathscr{A}$' is a mass term iff all parts of a thing which is $\mathscr{A}$ are $\mathscr{A}$.[20]

But this is no better: on the atomic theory of matter any chemical substance will have parts which are not of that same type of substance. Chappell draws attention to a related feature,

---

[19] 'Mass Terms as Subjects', *Philosophical Studies*, 21 (1970), 25.
[20] Cf. Chappell, 'Stuff and Things', p. 72. Terms satisfying this condition are called 'dissective' by Goodman, *The Structure of Appearance*, p. 53.

which he calls the homogeneity of stuffs.[21] Anything which is gold is gold uniformly, unlike something which is a cat (and which is not therefore a cat uniformly). This amounts to the criterion we've just considered and rejected. It is open to all the same objections and we may note some more: a cheese may have holes in it, gold rings are not always gold uniformly but often comprise gems as well.

If fission and parts fail to provide the criterion perhaps fusion and wholes will do better:

(2.4)   A term '$\mathscr{A}$' is a mass term iff the fusion of any two parts which are $\mathscr{A}$ is $\mathscr{A}$.

This works much better as it captures the cumulative reference feature of mass terms which Quine has pointed out.[22] It lets through all the terms in our first group, which is all to the good. It is still, however, open to counter-examples: for one thing it admits characterizing adjectives. For example, the fusion of any two parts which are heavy will be heavy. Thus 'heavy' is a mass term on (2.4). We could avoid this result by imposing the additional restriction that '$\mathscr{A}$' is a noun, to exclude adjectival characterizing terms. However, the criterion would still include 'thing' and other dummy sortals as mass terms for the sum of any two parts which are things is also a thing. However, we could effect the appropriate exclusions in the following way:

(2.5)   A term '$\mathscr{A}$' is a mass term iff '$\mathscr{A}$' is a ⁻count noun and the fusion of any two disjoint parts which are $\mathscr{A}$ is $\mathscr{A}$.

In the criterion 'fusion' is to be taken with the sense it is given in the calculus of individuals: The fusion of two individuals is defined as that individual which overlaps all and only those individuals which overlap at least one of the two.[23] 'Disjoint' is also used in Goodman's sense, namely, two individuals are dis-

---

[21] Chappell, ibid. The most detailed statement of the homogeneity condition I know of appears in an unpublished paper by Barry Taylor, 'Tense, Energia and Kinesis'.

[22] *Word and Object*, pp. 91, 97.

[23] More formally,

$$a+b =_{df} (\imath x)[(\forall y)(y \circ x \equiv . \ y \circ a \vee y \circ b)]$$

where 'o' is Goodman's primitive, two-place overlapping operator. Cf. *The Structure of Appearance*, pp. 50–1.

joint iff there is no individual which overlaps them both. It is useful to give a more formal version of (2.5) because substituting English nouns for '$\mathscr{A}$' in the last part of the criterion doesn't always give an easy English reading. Using the calculus of individuals and our notion of a general term predicate gives us:

(2.6)   A term '$\mathscr{A}$' is a mass term iff '$\mathscr{A}$' is a ⁻count noun and
$$(\forall x)(\forall y)(\mathscr{A}(x) \,\&\, \mathscr{A}(y) \,\&\, x \dagger y \supset. \mathscr{A}(x+y))$$

where '$x \dagger y$' reads 'x and y are disjoint' and is defined as above.

The reason for adding the disjointness condition is that without it singular terms might get included as mass terms. For example, 'Napoleon Bonaparte' would be a mass term, for the fusion of any two parts each of which is Napoleon will be Napoleon: it being the case that any two parts which are each Napoleon Bonaparte must be identical and will thus be identical with their fusion.[24] It might be thought that the most natural way to exclude singular terms would be to impose on the first clause of the criterion the requirement that only ⁻count *general* nouns could be mass terms. But this I am reluctant to do for Quine's sake. According to Quine mass terms in subject position are singular terms referring to one sprawling object. This view has some plausibility and ought not, I think, be ruled out as a matter of definition.

Criterion (2.5) seems to me to be adequate in that it lets through all the terms in the first and second lists. The problem now is whether (2.5) lets through characterizing nouns. It seems that it does: if we can talk of fusing parts which are cricket to get more cricket then we can surely talk of fusing parts which are intelligence to get more intelligence. Perhaps we don't so often do it with 'intelligence' as we do with 'cricket' but that is beside the point. So we have a criterion which lets in all mass terms and whose only defect is that it lets in characterizing terms as well. What remedy is there? It seems to be doubtful whether we need a remedy. Characterizing terms are

<hr>

[24] Richard Routley has suggested amending (2.1) to let in proper names as ⁺count nouns. This would enable us to drop the disjointness condition in (2.5)— 'Napoleon' would then be excluded as not being ⁻count. This approach would produce a parallel amongst ⁺count nouns to the singular uses of ⁻count nouns. For a sub-classification of nouns which cuts across the singular term/general term distinction see D. Gabbay and J. M. Moravcsik, 'Sameness and Individuation', pp. 520–4.

a little understood group of terms and a lot more work on their analysis is needed. It goes far beyond the scope of this project to do any of that work here, but in lieu of it we might hazard the following guess. If, as I suspect, characterizing nouns in surface structure are derived from adjectival forms in deep structure, it would not be counter-intuitive that the nouns so derived turn out to be mass terms. The fact that some characterizing nouns seem to fit the criterion so oddly (e.g. 'the fusion of any two parts which are viscosity is viscosity') might be explained by means of the adjectival origin of the nouns (from 'viscous'). This would explain the grammatical similarities between mass terms and characterizing nouns, which we noted in discussing Chappell's grammatical criteria. This is so far only a speculation, but our ignorance of characterizing nouns is so great that I see no reason to amend (2.5) to exclude them at present.[25] Of course, it may turn out, when they are investigated, that they should not be lumped together with mass terms but that is a bridge we should cross when we are forced to it.

A final point needs to be made concerning the criterion: it admits plural sortals. Consider the plural sortal 'cows', it passes the first clause of the criterion for 'There are n cowses in r' does not make sense, so 'cows' is a ⁻count noun. Moreover, it passes the second clause of the criterion for the fusion of any two parts which are separately cows results in more cows. The grammar of plural sortals and mass terms is almost identical: we have 'the cows' but not *'a cows', *'each cows', *'every cows'. Numerical adjectives need a little more care. What we have in 'two cows' is not a sortal, but the pluralization of a sortal, admitting a numerical adjective. So we have the schema:

(2.7)   two pl(. . .)

rather than the schema:

(2.8)   two . . .

where the blanks are filled by sortals and 'pl(. . .)' is a function from general nouns to pluralizations of them. Now neither plural sortals nor mass terms satisfy schema (2.7)—there being no pluralization of a plural sortal nor of a mass term—while

[25] Jespersen, for example, includes them. Cf. *Philosophy of Grammar*, p. 198.

plural sortals (and not mass terms) satisfy the erroneous (2.8). The main grammatical difference between plural sortals and mass terms is in quantitative adjectives. Plural sortals do not take 'much', or 'little', and only colloquially 'less'. But since the grammatical criteria do not provide a hard and fast rule on what terms are to be mass terms, some exceptions are tolerable. The admission of plural sortals as mass terms is not as disastrous as might at first be thought. Indeed it is the sort of move which a number of people have urged quite independently of our criterion for mass terms.[26] So far as I can see it constitutes no ground for rejecting the criterion.

[26] e.g. Henry Laycock, 'Some Questions of Ontology', op. cit. In Pidgin exactly the same construction may be used for mass terms as is used for pluralizing sortals. (Thanks to Peter Mühlhäusler for information on this point.)

3

Sortals

3.1 Intuitive and Grammatical Criteria for Sortals

The distinction between sortals and other general terms is one that is obvious to pre-philosophic common sense. To say of something that it is a book is very different from saying that it is a thing, or that it is red or large. In saying that it is a book we may be said to be classifying it; in saying that it is red or large, to be characterizing it; while in saying that it is a thing we don't seem to be saying much at all. But the use of these two terms, 'classifying' and 'characterizing', certainly does not provide the required demarcation line, for clearly we may, in calling something large, be said to be classifying it; and there is no clear sense in which, in calling something a book, we can be said not to be characterizing it. Clearly, we need something better than this rough and ready intuition to make the required distinction.[1]

The first philosophical discussion of the distinction seems to have been given by Aristotle in the *Categories* but what he says is so obscure that it is more likely to confuse than to clarify. Aristotle distinguishes as 'secondary substances' those substances the terms for which tell us what a thing is.[2] Although this way of talking has been adopted by Wiggins[3] it does not seem to me to provide anything like a viable and precise distinction between sortal and non-sortal terms—at least, unless we can give some characterization of what it is to say what something is. The distinction is sometimes made between substantival and adjectival terms (e.g. by Aquinas),[4] but grammar

---

[1] For heroic efforts to make do with this intuition see Stuart Hampshire, 'Identification and Existence', in H. D. Lewis (ed.), *Contemporary British Philosophy* (London: Allen and Unwin, 1956), Third Series, pp. 199–208.

[2] See *Categories*, Chapter Five, especially 2a 11; 2b 29; 3b 10.

[3] *Identity and Spatio-Temporal Continuity*, e.g. p. 27; fn. 2 (p. 65).

[4] *Summa Theologica*, Ia q. 39, art 3 c; ad 1um, art 5 ad 5um. This distinction is echoed by John Lyons, *An Introduction to Theoretical Linguistics*, p. 338.

can be misleading here for some substantival terms (e.g. 'gold'
and 'water') are not sortals but mass terms. On the other hand,
if the discussion is pursued as a distinction between substance
and properties it leads to metaphysical deep waters which we
might well wish to avoid. Thus, while it is easy to appreciate
the intuitive distinction between sortals and non-sortals, it
proves very difficult to draw a precise boundary between the
two which doesn't do violence to our intuitions.

While 'large scale' grammatical distinctions, such as that
between substantival and adjectival, do not provide us with
the required criterion, there are a number of grammatical
features which, we might hope, would pick out sortals. John
Wallace summarizes these features: 'Sortal predicates are grammatically substantival. They admit the definite article, the
plural ending, the pronouns "same", "other", and "another",
and quantity words: "all", "every", "some", "a", "many",
"few", "one", "two", "three", . . . They admit the demon-
stratives "this", "that", ' these", and "those". They do not
admit "much".'[5] However, these features do not provide a
means of distinguishing sortals from other types of term. There
are three main objections. In the first place there are a large
number of quirky exceptions. For example, both mass terms
and some characterizing terms admit 'same'. We can talk of
'Spa waters' though 'water' is a mass term. 'Will' (in the sense
of volition rather than that of a legal document) has many
peculiarities for we can talk of 'the will' and also of 'a will'
(as in 'He has a will of his own'). On the other hand, we can
make no sense of *'wills', *'all wills', *'every will', and *'much
will' (though 'much effort of will' is all right). But quirks are
the least of the three problems. More important is that the
grammatical criterion lets in all dummy sortals; often +count
nouns of extremely wide applicability (e.g. 'thing', 'entity',
'item', 'object', 'individual', etc.) but not invariably since
'possession', 'element', 'part', and 'set' are all dummy sortals.
However, Wallace hopes that dummy sortals may be excluded
by further restrictions, so this need not concern us unduly at

---

[5] 'Philosophical Grammar' (Unpublished Doctoral Dissertation, Stanford
University, 1964), p. 70. It has become common in the literature to refer to sortal
terms as 'sortal predicates'. I want to keep the two expressions distinct but I shall
not amend quotations.

this stage. To my mind the most conclusive argument against
the grammatical criterion is that it fails to distinguish the sortal
and mass term roles of those words, noted in § 2.4, which can
be both sortals and mass terms. It seems to me that a purely
grammatical criterion for sortals, even if sufficiently sophisti-
cated to exclude the odd exceptions, and even if supplemented
by a restriction against dummy sortals, would be inadequate
to mark out the class of terms intuitively accepted as sortals.

Another reason supports this view. Our intuitive notions of
what a sortal is are semantically based. Even were we able to
formulate a set of purely grammatical criteria co-extensive
with sortalhood, we would still have missed the main point of
making the distinction, which lies in the different ways in
which the different types of term refer. Moreover, the grammatical features which Wallace suggests are mostly peculiar to
English (e.g. admitting 'another', 'few', etc., although taking
the definite article and the plural ending are more general).
Although categorization of terms varies very much from language to language[6] we might hope to provide a criterion which
would tell us whether a term in a given language was a sortal
in that language or not. The distinction must, therefore, be
sought semantically instead of grammatically.

An initial criterion we can rule out quickly is that a sortal is
that which covers an identity[7] statement. Now it is true that
any sortal can act as covering concept in some identity statement, indeed as Wiggins says it is 'one of the clear facts'[8] about
them. Yet a simple definition of a sortal as that which covers
an identity statement is unsatisfactory in several respects.
Firstly, such a characterization fits our intuitions very badly.
'Clay' in 'This clay is the same clay as that on the potter's
wheel last week' is certainly a covering concept for what has
every appearance of being an identity statement and yet is
paradigmatically a mass term. Of course, we might add the
requirement that '$\mathscr{A}$' be a completing concept for the identity
statement and then hope to be able to show that all non-sortals

---

[6] For example, the English 'grape' is a sortal whereas the German '*Traube*'
and the Russian '*vinograd*' are mass terms, like the English 'fruit'. On the other hand,
the French '*fruit*' and the Russian '*frukt*' are sortals.

[7] Sometimes, as now, I shall use 'identity statement' to include what are strictly
distinctness statements. This almost universal practice should not cause any
confusion.   [8] *Identity and Spatio-Temporal Continuity*, p. 29.

somehow failed as completing concepts. But completing concepts are relative to a theory of (D)-relative identity and the only version of (D) which would be sure of excluding non-sortals would be (D₂), which precisely limits completing concepts to sortals, and that would make the whole thing circular. Secondly, the concept of an identity statement is not perhaps the best understood notion to take as a primitive in the definiens. Authors—particularly those who disagree about absolute and relative identity—disagree on whether a given statement is an identity statement in at least some cases. Thirdly, we are hoping to throw some light on the notion of an identity statement by investigating sortals; not vice versa. Finally, it becomes clear that if we simply equate sortals with covering concepts we will not be able to draw up a list of sortals irrespective of the sentences in which they occur. For example, Wiggins would have to claim that in

(3.1)   This book is the same colour as that book.

'colour' is not a covering concept for an identity statement because he holds that (3.1) is not an identity statement. On the other hand, he would presumably claim that

(3.2)   The colour of this book is the same colour as the colour of that book.

was an identity statement and 'colour' a covering concept. Thus 'colour' would be a sortal in (3.2) but not in (3.1). Sheehan[9] holds that we can classify only uses of terms as sortal or non-sortal uses. This seems to me to be mistaken since the sortal/non-sortal distinction is commonly taken to be a distinction between terms rather than between their uses, and, as the whole of language is sortal ridden, to attempt a criterion for every context in which a term might have a sortal use is going to be virtually impossible. For the moment, at any rate, I want to leave the question of the relation between sortals and identity statements open.

3.2 Mereological Criteria

Since a mereological criterion worked well for mass terms, and since sortals are often directly contrasted with mass terms, it

---

[9] 'The Relativity of Identity', p. 14.

seems reasonable to begin our search for a semantic criterion
for sortals by looking at mereological criteria. One feature
noted by Frege[10] and Quine[11] is that sortals divide their reference in a certain way. Wallace provides a criterion, or at least,
a necessary condition, thus:

> 'If "$\mathscr{A}$" is a sortal predicate then you cannot divide an $\mathscr{A}$ in
> two parts and get two $\mathscr{A}$s.'[12]

This, as he says, rules out 'thing', 'red thing', and 'physical
object'. However, 'cloud', 'garden hose', 'perfect diamond',
'amoeba', 'cell', and 'protozoon' all fail this criterion, though all
are sortals. Thus the criterion is not a necessary condition for
sortalhood. Moreover, we cannot use it as a sufficient condition either, since 'indivisible thing' would pass, as Wallace
points out in a later article.[13] To deal with some of these objections Wallace proposes taking 'divide' metaphorically in the
sense of 'divide conceptually'. This is not at all clear, but
Wallace then restates his criterion as:

> 'If "$\mathscr{A}$" is a sortal predicate, then no $\mathscr{A}$ has two parts that
> are $\mathscr{A}$s.'[14]

I'm not sure that this new criterion will do the work Wallace
expects it to. A garden hose which consists of two garden hoses
taped together has parts which are garden hoses. What has to
do the work here is the gloss we put on 'part', but it is not
obvious that 'part' will do any more work than 'divide' in the
old criterion, at least unless we give it a new gloss. Perhaps we
could gloss it (rather vaguely) as 'natural division' with the

---

[10] *Foundations of Arithmetic*, p. 66.

[11] *Word and Object*, § 19, pp. 90–5.

[12] 'Philosophical Grammar', p. 72; also R. Ackermann, 'Sortal Predicates
and Confirmation', *Philosophical Studies*, 20 (1969), 2.

[13] 'Sortal Predicates and Quantification', *Journal of Philosophy*, 62 (1965), 10.

[14] 'Philosophical Grammar', p. 73. Both versions of the criterion are stated
simultaneously in his article, op. cit., pp. 9–10. In the article Wallace seems to
have given up the hope that any or all of his criteria provide necessary and sufficient conditions for sortalhood. He says, for example, 'it is impossible to extract . . .
any short, clear, true formula for distinguishing sortal predicates from others'
(p. 9) and he seems to accept (p. 10) that the notion of a sortal is unanalysable and
obscure. He hopes that his theory of sortal-restricted quantification may clarify
the concept (p. 11). However, since in that theory sortals are merely loaded into
pockets in the quantifiers it does not seem that much clarification results—we
still do not know precisely which terms may be thus loaded.

paradigm in mind of (say) a car's being 'naturally divided' into such parts as a chassis, a body, and an engine. But, surely, our garden hose is thus naturally divided. And, of course, a work of art may divide naturally into parts, each of which is itself a work of art. Wagner's *Ring Cycle* and Lawrence Durrell's *Alexandrian Quartet* do so.

An alternative mereological criterion is the following:

> If '$\mathscr{A}$' is a sortal then no $\mathscr{A}$ results from the fusion of two (or more) $\mathscr{A}$s.[15]

But this suffers from some of the same problems as the earlier criteria. 'Garden hose', 'pile of stones', 'table', and 'garden' all fail this criterion. We can reject all three mereological criteria.

3.3 Countability Criteria

Strawson presents a brief and simple—too simple—criterion thus:

> A sortal universal supplies a principle for distinguishing and counting individual particulars which it collects. It presupposes no antecedent principle, or method, of individuating the particulars it collects. Characterizing universals, on the other hand, whilst they supply principles of grouping, even of counting, particulars, supply such principles only for particulars already distinguished, or distinguishable, in accordance with some antecedent principle or method.[16]

Wallace makes Strawson's criterion a little more precise:

> If '$\mathscr{A}$' is a sortal predicate, you can find how many $\mathscr{A}$s there are in such and such a space by counting $\mathscr{A}$s. And, if '$\mathscr{A}$' is a sortal predicate, it makes perfectly good sense to ask someone how many $\mathscr{A}$s there are in such and such a space.[17]

In his subsequent paper Wallace develops this a bit more:

> (a) A sortal predicate '$\mathscr{A}$' provides a criterion for counting things that are $\mathscr{A}$. (b) If '$\mathscr{A}$' is a sortal predicate, you can find out how many $\mathscr{A}$s there are in such and such a space by counting. (c) If

---

[15] Cf. Feldman, 'Sortal Predicates', p. 275; Daniel Bennett, 'Essential Properties', *Journal of Philosophy*, 66 (1969), 496–8.

[16] P. F. Strawson, *Individuals*, p. 168.

[17] Wallace, 'Philosophical Grammar', pp. 70–1.

'$\mathscr{A}$' is a sortal predicate, it makes sense to ask someone how many $\mathscr{A}$s there are in such and such a space.[18]

The counting criterion seems to be essential in some way or another to sortals. But we find that it is very difficult to formulate the criterion in such a way as to include all and only sortals. In Wallace's (b) and (c) we must construe 'space' very widely for 'number' is a sortal but numbers are not spatial items in any literal sense. Wallace takes care of numbers by noting that we can say 'how many natural numbers there are less than seven'. Moreover, we may not permit the space in which we are counting $\mathscr{A}$s to be infinite because again it would (in general) be impossible to say how many $\mathscr{A}$s there were in such a space. Some of these problems can be solved by rephrasing Wallace's (b) as follows:

> If '$\mathscr{A}$' is a sortal term then we can, in principle, find out by counting how many $\mathscr{A}$s there are in a certain, finite space appropriate to $\mathscr{A}$s.

But this refined version doesn't help us with sortals such as 'fraction', for we cannot, even in principle, find out by *counting* how many fractions there are between certain limits, though we can, of course, say there are $\aleph_0$ of them.[19] Yet 'fraction' is a perfectly good sortal. It may be possible to include 'fraction' if we treat the space appropriate to fractions as the space occupied by one fraction. But this looks like a gerrymander.

The counting criteria considered so far are such that even with obvious sortals there can be problems. For example, 'car' is as good an example of a sortal as we could wish and yet on entering a car-breaker's yard we may not be able to say how many cars are in it, for we should need to know first whether we are to count only those cars which are complete as they stand, or those we could reconstruct from the separate parts in the yard, or only those that are in running order. Moreover, we need to know how much of a car can be missing if it is still to count as a car, what is to count as a reconstruction or as 'in

[18] Wallace, 'Sortal Predicates and Quantification', p. 9.

[19] Frege fudges the issue in a different way when he rejects 'thing' as a sortal on the grounds that there is no finite number of things. The difficulty here is not that there is no end to counting them but that there is no beginning. In fact there is no *definite* number (finite or infinite) of things in any non-empty space. (Cf. *Foundations of Arithmetic*, p. 66.)

running order' before we can start counting. There are similar
and quite well-known problems with other paradigm sortals
such as 'man': when does a foetus become a man, and when do
Siamese twins cease to be twins and become one person with
supernumerary organs? Consider trying to count the number
of animals in each species on H. G. Wells's *Island of Dr. Moreau*.[20]
What this means is that open-texture as well as non-sortalhood
may be a cause of non-countability and that the present countability criteria fail to distinguish between the two.

Of course, we may make the necessary decisions to make
such things as cars countable even in a wrecker's yard. The
point is, however, that these decisions vitiate the first part of
Strawson's criterion, and undermine the spirit of the others,
for Strawson required that particulars grouped under sortals
be countable without antecedent principles of individuation or
additional conceptual decisions; that sortals carry around with
them, as it were, their own principles for counting. In this way
true sortals differ from dummy sortals such as 'thing' for which
we have to make further conceptual decisions as to what constitutes one thing. We could fall back on Wallace's criterion (c),
namely, that it makes sense 'to ask someone how many $\mathscr{A}$s there
are in such and such a space'. As it stands, however, this is subject to just the same objections about numbers, fractions, etc., as
the first part of his criterion. Wallace is right that the question
makes sense, the only trouble is it can never, in these cases, be
answered by counting. If the criterion is weakened further to
cope with this problem we will end up with some such version
as 'it makes sense to say there are so many $\mathscr{A}$s'. But this is the
criterion already given for +count nouns and we don't want that.

A more satisfactory solution is to weaken the counting
criterion in the way suggested by Sheehan:

> '[A necessary condition of "$\mathscr{A}$"'s being a sortal is that] "$\mathscr{A}$"
> is such that there *can* be cases in which "$\mathscr{A}$" provides,
> without further conceptual decision and without presuppos-
> ing other principles of individuation, principles adequate for
> counting $\mathscr{A}$s.'[21]

[20] It is just this sort of problem with borderline cases which leads Wallace to
exclude 'animal' as a sortal ('Philosophical Grammar', p. 74). It is surprising that
he doesn't see that the same problem exists with almost every general term.

[21] 'The Relativity of Identity', p. 20; my italics.

We need to provide some sort of gloss on the 'without further conceptual decision and without presupposing other principles of individuation' proviso. While it is fairly clear what prior conceptual decisions amount to (which is not to say that it is easy to see why they are relevant—I shall come to that in a moment) 'principles of individuation' might be a bit more obscure. It seems to me that the notion of principles of individuation is the most primitive idea on which we can start to build our account of relative identity. In order to be able to count $\mathscr{A}$s on any occasion one has to know, within broad limits, how much of what there is counts as one $\mathscr{A}$. When a general term supplies at least minimal principles, however vague they may be, which non-arbitrarily give this sort of knowledge then the term may be said to convey *principles of individuation*.[22] The trouble with this account is that it doesn't make the crucial distinction between when the term itself provides the principles of individuation or when it 'borrows' them from some other term. The idea behind Sheehan's criterion is that sortals should provide their own principles and not borrow them, but the distinction is not altogether clear.

We require the criterion to exclude dummy sortals like 'red thing' despite the fact that in certain circumstances (as when we're given a box of red balls) we can count red things— though only by utilizing the principles of individuation provided by 'ball'. Compare the situation in which we're given a box of red cubes and told to count the red things in the box: we can't because we don't know whether to utilize the principles of individuation appropriate to 'cube' or to 'surface'. This gives the rationale of the restriction against presupposing other principles of individuation. But consider the sortal 'white car', in counting white cars we plainly use the principles of individuation conveyed by 'car', thus in a weak sense the term borrows its principles of individuation. Can we define a stronger sense of borrowing in which we can none the less say that 'thing' borrows principles of individuation from 'ball' in our

---

[22] For material object sortals M. J. Woods introduces the helpful idea that principles of individuation for $\mathscr{A}$s enable one to draw the boundaries of an $\mathscr{A}$ in three dimensions. Cf. 'Identity and Individuation', in Butler (ed.), *Analytical Philosophy*, 2nd series, op. cit., p. 129. See also Perry's notion of 'placing' an object ('Identity', p. 84); and Wiggins's notion of an 'edge' ('The Individuation of Things and Places', pp. 190–1).

first example? The answer it seems to me is the following: a term conveys principles of individuation when there is only one set of principles of individuation which provides the individuative principles associated with the term on every occasion on which the term is literally used. That is, given any literal use of a term in which principles of individuation are associated with it then the term *conveys* those principles only if the term is associated with the same principles on every literal use. (We must exclude metaphorical uses in which terms conveying principles of individuation might well be associated with radically different principles of individuation—as, for example, when songs are called numbers.)

The trouble now is with certain ambiguous terms such as 'diner' which sometimes conveys the principles of individuation associated with 'person' and sometimes those associated with 'railway carriage' and where neither use could properly be called metaphorical. But, in view of the fact that we are classifying terms semantically, what we really have in this case are two different terms (which happen to have the same surface form). On our account a term will be said to borrow principles of individuation if in a certain literal use it is associated with principles of individuation conveyed by a term '$\mathscr{A}$' and in some other literal use it is associated with principles of individuation conveyed by a distinct term '$\mathscr{B}$'. Admittedly this is a somewhat strange use of 'borrows' but that expression was introduced merely as a metaphor.

In the light of this we can rewrite Sheehan's criterion thus:

> A term '$\mathscr{A}$' is a sortal iff there *can* be cases in which '$\mathscr{A}$' provides, without further conceptual decision and without borrowing other principles of individuation, principles adequate for counting $\mathscr{A}$s.

The point of adding the clause against 'further conceptual decisions' is that if we permitted them it would prove possible to take a term which borrowed principles of individuation and legislate that it in fact conveyed them.

Sheehan's criterion has certain advantages over the one proposed by Wallace. It has none of the problems with 'number' that Wallace's criterion had. It does not require that I can count how many numbers there are, or even how many

numbers there are in a certain 'space', nor that I can count
how many fractions there are between 0 and 1. And there are
certainly cases in which I can count numbers and fractions;
for example, I can count the fractions or numbers which satisfy
a certain equation. It seems to me that Sheehan's criterion will
admit all the terms we normally think of as sortals. It also
excludes some terms which we want to exclude: e.g. mass terms
and dummy sortals. Admittedly, there are cases in which we
can count things, as when, to use Sheehan's example, a furniture removalist asks how many things are to be moved—we
know the answer because in this circumstance 'thing' borrows
principles of individuation from 'piece of furniture'.

Sheehan presented his weak countability criterion as a necessary condition for sortalhood, but we have turned it into both
a necessary and a sufficient condition. How strong are Sheehan's
objections to treating it as a sufficient condition? Sheehan
claims that if it were sufficient for sortalhood it would admit
'official' in the sense in which to be the same official is just to
hold the same office. Let us call this sense 'official*'. 'Official*'
clearly passes the weak countability criterion, but why does
Sheehan think it is not a sortal? The answer lies in the preliminary gloss he puts on 'sortal' in which for '$\mathscr{A}$' to be a
sortal implies that '$\mathscr{A}$' could act as covering concept for an
identity statement. There are a number of terms of this type:
e.g. 'landmark' in the sense in which to be the same landmark
is nothing more than to mark conspicuously the same position;
'church' in the sense in which to be the same church is nothing
more than to be a place of worship for the same congregation;[23]
'milkman' in the sense in which to be the same milkman is
simply to have the same milkround; and many others. Wiggins[24]
urges that 'a is the same official* as b' is paraphraseable as 'a
holds the same office as b' which is not an identity statement
and, therefore, neither is the original. But, as I shall argue in
detail later,[25] Wiggins's argument is not only invalid as it
stands but every attempt to reconstitute it into a valid argument seems to employ principles which are either implausible or undermine Wiggins's own theory of identity. If 'a' and

[23] Cf. Hume's *Treatise*, Bk. I, Part 4, § 6 (Penguin edn., pp. 305–6).
[24] *Identity and Spatio-Temporal Continuity*, p. 13.
[25] See below, § 10.3.

'*b*' are the names of official*s then there seems to be every reason to regard '*a* is the same official* as *b*' as an identity statement—even on Wiggins's terms. These issues I shall discuss later on. At the moment I am insufficiently persuaded of the validity of this line of thought to reject 'official*' as a sortal.

3.4 *The Structure of Sorts*

Sortals are a type of general noun, that is, they are entirely linguistic things. To each sortal, however, corresponds a class, or sort, which is non-linguistic. The members of the sort form the extension of the sortal. The sort which corresponds to the sortal '$\mathscr{F}$' may thus be defined as $\{x : \mathscr{F}(x)\}$, and I shall say that $\{x : \mathscr{F}(x)\}$ is the sort named by '$\mathscr{F}$'. If an item a is a member of the sort named by '$\mathscr{F}$' then a will be said, following Frege, to *fall under* '$\mathscr{F}$'. A singular term 'a' will be said to *refer under* a sortal '$\mathscr{F}$' iff either (i) 'a' is a proper name of which '$\mathscr{F}$' gives the sense; or (ii) 'a' is a definite description of the form 'the $\mathscr{F}$' or 'the $\mathscr{F}$ which . . .'; or (iii) 'a' is an ostensive expression containing a demonstrative together with '$\mathscr{F}$' (e.g. 'that $\mathscr{F}$'). Thus 'the man who broke the bank at Monte Carlo' refers under 'man', while the man who broke the bank at Monte Carlo falls under 'man', 'human being', 'animal', and 'gambler'. Where sortal subscripts are added to individual constants (e.g. '$a_{\mathscr{F}}$') it is thereby made explicit that the referring expression '$a_{\mathscr{F}}$' refers under '$\mathscr{F}$'. When sortal subscripts are added to individual variables (e.g. '$x_{\mathscr{F}}$') it indicates that the variable takes values from the range of items falling under '$\mathscr{F}$'.

Now one of the most obvious things about sorts which this brings out is that one item falls under many sortals. Moreover, of the many sorts into which an item might fall some will include others and some will only intersect with others. For example, the sort named by 'man' is included in that named by 'animal', the one named by 'gambler' in that named by 'human being'. But, if we suppose that the man who broke the bank at Monte Carlo was a clergyman, the sort named by 'gambler' only intersects with that named by 'clergyman'. It is desirable to make these relations precise and introduce some terminology with which we can express the relations between sorts. The terminology chosen will be familiar from its somewhat different use in the traditional logic of terms.[26] A sortal '$\mathscr{F}$' will be said to be *superordinate* to a sortal '$\mathscr{G}$' iff

$$(\forall x)(\mathscr{G}(x) \to \mathscr{F}(x)) \;\&\; \sim (\forall x)(\mathscr{F}(x) \to \mathscr{G}(x)).$$

A sortal '$\mathscr{F}$' will be said to be *subordinate* to a sortal '$\mathscr{G}$' iff '$\mathscr{G}$' is superordinate to '$\mathscr{F}$'. We could give a purely extensional account of these expressions in terms of material implication rather than entailment but this would not capture the sense we want. Moreover, it would lead to problems with un-exemplified sortals (e.g. 'winged horse')[27] which would, on an extensionalist account, be subordinate to every sortal. For similar reasons we need to use entailment rather than strict implication: strict implication would ensure that any necessarily unexemplified sortal (e.g. 'round square') was subordinate to every sortal. We can prove that

$$\sim (\exists x)(\mathscr{F}(x)) \supset (\forall x)(\forall g)(\mathscr{F}(x) \supset g(x))$$

and thus

$$\Box \sim (\exists x)(\mathscr{F}(x)) \supset \Box(\forall x)(\forall g)(\mathscr{F}(x) \supset g(x))$$

and, since (converse Barcan formula)

$$\Box(\forall x)(\forall g)(\mathscr{F}(x) \supset g(x)) \supset (\forall x)(\forall g)\Box(\mathscr{F}(x) \supset g(x)),$$

we obtain

$$\Box \sim (\exists x)(\mathscr{F}(x)) \supset (\forall x)(\forall g)(\mathscr{F}(x) \dashv3 g(x)).{}^{[28]}$$

It would be difficult and implausible to exclude necessarily unexemplified sortals and since the converse Barcan formula can be proved within the weakest system of quantified modal logic (LPC+T), the paradox is not easy to avoid within the framework of a strict implication system. One way of so avoiding the paradox would be to interpret the quantifiers as ranging over non-existent and necessarily non-existent items as well as over entities.[29] In fact it will prove desirable to adopt both the

[26] Cf. H. W. B. Joseph, *Introduction to Logic* (Oxford: Oxford University Press; 2nd edn., 1916), p. 116.

[27] 'Winged horse' is certainly a sortal, for we can count the number of winged horses in the legend of Bellerophon.

[28] I owe this argument to an unpublished paper by Leslie Stevenson, 'Extensional and Intensional Logic for Sortal-Relative Identity'.

[29] L. Goddard and R. Routley, *The Logic of Significance and Context* (Edinburgh: Scottish Academic Press, 1973), vol. i, pp. 123–52; R. Routley and V. Routley, 'Exploring Meinong's Jungle: Items and Descriptions' (unpublished).

Routley–Goddard interpretation of the quantifiers and entailment in formulating a theory of relative identity. Systems of
entailment are sufficiently widely accepted[30] to need no further
justification, while Geach's slogan 'No identity without entity'[31]
is surely just wrong as far as the use of identity relations in
natural language is concerned. We clearly need to be able to
quantify over items we might wish to assert an identity relation
between.

Two sortals '$\mathscr{F}$' and '$\mathscr{G}$' will be said to be *co-ordinate* iff being
an '$\mathscr{F}$' entails being a '$\mathscr{G}$' and vice versa; or:

$$(3.3) \qquad \mathscr{F} \approx \mathscr{G} =_{df} (\forall x)(\mathscr{F}(x) \leftrightarrow \mathscr{G}(x)).$$

Two sortals '$\mathscr{F}$' and '$\mathscr{G}$' will be said to *intersect* iff

$$(\exists x)(\mathscr{F}(x) \mathbin{\&} \mathscr{G}(x));$$

or:

$$(3.4) \qquad \mathscr{F} \mid \mathscr{G} =_{df} (\exists x)(\mathscr{F}(x) \mathbin{\&} \mathscr{G}(x)).$$

(3.4) ignores one complication, for a butcher may be a baker
in one of two ways: a single man might simultaneously be both
a butcher and a baker, or a single man might change his pro-
fession and become a baker after ceasing to be a butcher.
Certain sortals, e.g. 'boy' and 'man', are necessarily related in
this second way. Whether or not we wish to call such a relation
'intersection', it seems desirable to define a broader relation
which captures this:

$$(3.5) \qquad \mathscr{F} \mid_\tau \mathscr{G} =_{df} (\exists t, t')(\exists x)[R_t(\mathscr{F}(x)) \mathbin{\&} R_{t'}(\mathscr{G}(x))]$$

which leaves it open whether a single individual is simultane-
ously or successively an $\mathscr{F}$ and a $\mathscr{G}$. Given this distinction (3.4)
could be represented:

$$(3.6) \qquad \mathscr{F} \mid \mathscr{G} =_{df} (\exists t)(\exists x)[R_t(\mathscr{F}(x)) \mathbin{\&} R_t(\mathscr{G}(x))].$$

A sortal '$\mathscr{F}$' will be said to *restrict* a sortal '$\mathscr{G}$' iff '$\mathscr{F}$' is subordinate to or co-ordinate with '$\mathscr{G}$'; or:

$$(3.7) \qquad \mathscr{F} \subseteq \mathscr{G} =_{df} (\forall x)(\mathscr{F}(x) \rightarrow \mathscr{G}(x)).$$

We can also define the notion more widely so that it is not
restricted to sortals: A general term '$\mathscr{A}$' restricts a general

---

[30] See e.g. A. R. Anderson and N. D. Belnap, *Entailment* (Princeton: Princeton
University Press, 1975).
[31] 'Ontological Relativity and Relative Identity', p. 288.

term '$\mathscr{B}$' iff $(\forall x)(\mathscr{A}(x) \to \mathscr{B}(x))$. Similar extensions of the notions of superordination, subordination, co-ordination, and intersection can also be defined. In our present sense of 'restricts' in the limit case every general term restricts itself (allowing this will be useful later). It will also be useful to define a sense of 'restricts' in which this is excluded. A sortal '$\mathscr{F}$' will be said to *restrict a more general sortal* '$\mathscr{G}$' iff '$\mathscr{F}$' is subordinate to '$\mathscr{G}$'. A sortal '$\mathscr{F}$' will be said to be *ultimate* iff there is no sortal superordinate to '$\mathscr{F}$'.

Finally, a sortal '$\mathscr{F}$' will be called a *phase sortal* iff it is a temporal restriction of some more general sortal. Thus 'boy' is a phase sortal restricting 'man'.[32]

---

[32] Cf. Wiggins, *Identity and Spatio-Temporal Continuity*, pp. 7, 29.

4

Criteria of Identity

4.1 The Concept of Identity Criteria

Criteria of identity are often appealed to but little discussed.[1] Geach characterizes the notion as that 'in accordance with which we thus judge as to . . . identity'.[2] There is, however, a difficulty here: It is not clear whether we should take the criteria of identity for an identity claim to be a set of conditions satisfaction of which *logically guarantees* the truth of the identity claim and failure of which logically guarantees its falsity; or as a set of conditions satisfaction of which constitutes *good evidence* for the truth of the claim and failure of which constitutes good evidence for its falsity. The difference can be illustrated by an example: that two cars should have the same registration number constitutes good evidence that they are the same car, but does not logically guarantee it; whereas the fact that they are spatio-temporally continuous (given certain conditions) is not merely good evidence for the identity but actually constitutes it. The term 'criterion', at least since Wittgenstein popularized it, does not give much assistance in deciding which way to take 'criteria of identity';[3] and both ways have been

---

[1] The expression 'criterion of identity' goes back at least to Frege's *Grundlagen*, and reappears in Wittgenstein's *Philosophical Investigations*. Dummett, in his article on Frege in *The Encyclopedia of Philosophy*, ed. Paul Edwards (New York: Macmillan, 1967), vol. iii, p. 229, claimed that Frege's account of a criterion of identity was a 'cornerstone of Wittgenstein's whole later philosophy', though in his *Frege* (pp. 580–1) he is much less sweeping.

[2] *Reference and Generality*, p. 39. (The force of the 'thus' is not made clearer by Geach's context.)

[3] See Rogers Albritton's vacillations on the subject in 'On Wittgenstein's use of the Term "Criterion"', in Pitcher (ed.), *Wittgenstein: The 'Philosophical Investigations'*, op. cit., pp. 231–50. As usual Wittgenstein's remarks in *The Blue and Brown Books* (Oxford: Blackwell, 1958), pp. 24–5, 49–50, 63–4; and *Philosophical Investigations*, Part I, 51, 56, 141–2, 239, 376–7 *inter alia*, are far from helpful. For further references see the massive bibliography which follows W. Gregory Lycan's review article, 'Noninductive Evidence: Recent Work on Wittgenstein's "Criteria"', *American Philosophical Quarterly*, 8 (1971), 122–5.

accepted in the literature: Geach, Perry, and Wiggins take it that criteria of identity logically constitute the identity;[4] Strawson uses the term in a way that implies that criteria of identity provide good evidence only.[5] I shall follow Geach, Perry, and Wiggins mainly because if we don't take the criteria as providing logically necessary and sufficient conditions it is not clear how we are to take them. There is an additional reason in that one of the intuitions behind relative identity theories is that identities of different types are differently constituted. If identity criteria are to be relevant at all to relative identity then they must be more than mere symptoms.

In accepting this strong account of what identity criteria are we have to reject another claim which appears tempting: the claim that when we in fact judge identity we must use identity criteria. Clearly we do, on a large number of occasions, judge merely by symptoms of identity or distinctness. We do, on frequent occasions, judge whether two cars are identical by whether they have the same number-plate rather than by judging whether they are spatio-temporally continuous. Another claim we must reject (but for independent reasons) is that identity criteria enable us to assign a truth-value to any identity claim. In this identity criteria do not differ from any other type of criteria. We have, for example, perfectly good criteria for the application of the term 'brother', but we do not know whether this term is applicable to Plato. That we do not simply indicates our ignorance, not the inadequacy of our criteria for brotherhood. Clearly this view of what criteria can do is untenable however we cash 'criterion' out.

Different criteria of identity are associated with different general terms. There is nothing in this which conflicts with absolute identity,[6] which is as well for the classical theory since

---

[4] Geach, 'Ontological Relativity and Relative Identity', p. 288; Perry, 'Identity', pp. 8–10; Wiggins, *Identity and Spatio-Temporal Continuity*, p. 43. Shoemaker also takes it this way: see his helpful account in *Self-Knowledge and Self-Identity* (Ithaca: Cornell University Press, 1963), pp. 3–5.   [5] *Individuals*, pp. 31–4.

[6] Cf., for example, Terence Penelhum, 'Hume on Personal Identity', *Philosophical Review*, 64 (1955), pp. 580–1. Wiggins, Perry, Herbst, and Dummett all accept some version of (LL) but wish to supplement it with an account of identity criteria. M. R. Ayers, 'Individuals without Sortals', *Canadian Journal of Philosophy*, 4 (1974), 113–48, is almost alone in rejecting even this concession to relativism. His success is limited as I've argued in 'Ayers on Relative Identity', *Canadian Journal of Philosophy*, 6 (1976).

the point seems incontrovertible. We can see this if we consider how we would go about deciding whether two plays were written about the same character, or had the same author, whether two cars were the same colour, whether two books had the same title or were on the same topic, or whether two calculations gave the same result. It is not just that the symptoms of identity are different in each case, but that the identity is differently constituted. Nor can we absorb each case under some umbrella account such as (LL). Moreover, following Dummett,[7] it is reasonable to claim that identity criteria are not only associated with certain general nouns but actually constitute part of their meaning. Dummett draws attention to words like 'book' which have different senses which depend entirely upon changes in identity criteria and not on changes in criteria of application (the sense of 'book' in which we can use two books to prop a table up and that in which an author may have written two books).[8]

Two questions now arise which I shall attempt to answer in the remainder of this chapter. Firstly, which general nouns convey identity criteria? Secondly, under what conditions, if any, do two distinct nouns convey the same identity criteria?

4.2 Sortals and Criteria of Identity

Since sortals, by definition, satisfy the weak countability criterion it follows that they must have criteria of identity associated with them. For if the items falling under a particular general term can, on some occasions, be counted it follows that on some occasions we know what it is to be the same item of that sort again. Counting presupposes identity, for we must have principles which protect us from counting the same one twice.

The identity criteria associated with a sortal '$\mathcal{F}$' tell us what it is for a and b to be the same $\mathcal{F}$. This account is both perfectly general for sortal-relative identity and also reasonably intelligible. It might help, however, to have the notion fleshed out a bit with some specific principles and some particular examples. The difficulty here is that both principles and examples are likely to be contentious and I don't want anything I say about

[7] Frege, pp. 73–4; see also M. J. Woods, 'Identity and Individuation', p. 121.
[8] Frege, p. 74.

identity criteria in general to depend on a particular view of, say, personal identity or the role of spatio-temporal continuity. The examples I use will be examples only and may be replaced by others which agree with alternative (and possibly better) philosophical intuitions. My aim is not to advocate a particular theory of the identity of material objects, or persons, or psychological states or anything else, but merely to present a general theory of identity with which most of the various alternative accounts of these issues are compatible.

The identity criteria conveyed by a sortal are best regarded as a bundle of principles. One such principle must clearly be relational. If the concept of $\mathscr{F}$-identity can be analysed and if a and b are the same $\mathscr{F}$ it follows that there is some relation, apart from '$\zeta =_{\mathscr{F}} \eta$', which they satisfy. Even within the framework of absolute identity theory quite a lot of work has been done formulating such relational principles for different categories of items. For example, for material bodies the relation of spatio-temporal continuity is often proposed; for persons sameness of memory; for universals similarity; for what Strawson calls 'private particulars' (for example, thoughts and sensations) exact similarity and sameness of person (on a Strawsonian account); and so on. In some cases we see that we may analyse $\mathscr{F}$-identity in terms of some other sortal identity, but this will then be subject to a further analysis. In each case there is a basic relational condition constitutive of $\mathscr{F}$-identity for a given sortal '$\mathscr{F}$', though this does not exhaust the identity criteria conveyed by '$\mathscr{F}$'. Let us express this two-place relation thus '$R_{\mathscr{F}}(\zeta,\eta)$' so that we have:

$$(4.1) \qquad\qquad a =_{\mathscr{F}} b \to R_{\mathscr{F}}(a,b).$$

If we add to this the requirements that a and b both fall under '$\mathscr{F}$' we get a principle which in some cases (e.g. colour-identity construed in terms of similarity) exhausts the identity criteria associated with a sortal. The sortal 'yellow' (the sense of 'yellow' in which a paint chart might have three yellows in it) is such that we can say of two patches of colour that they are the same yellow if they are both yellow and they are both similar in respect of colour. In other cases problems still crop up. Sometimes we still lack a sufficient condition for $\mathscr{F}$-identity; sometimes we have a sufficient condition but one which is still not criterial. As an example of the first type, given that a and b are both men and are both spatio-temporally continuous it does not follow that they are the same man—for they might be Siamese twins. A way of coping with this difficulty would be to stiffen our analysis of spatio-temporal continuity so that mere contiguity at some point was no longer sufficient but that (say) contiguity of each place occupied by a with some place occupied by b (and vice versa) was required.[9] On a materialist view of men, it seems plausible to maintain that we could make such an account (given enough subtlety) give both necessary and sufficient conditions for being the same man. Such conditions would not, however, be criterial for we would not be able to judge whether two objects were spatio-temporally continuous. A solution to the first type of problem thus leaves the second type untouched, and it is the second type that we are mainly concerned with here.

The additional principles we need to make the relation criterial are provided by locating the objects in question under a sortal. The sortal provides the principles of individuation which make it possible to pick out the object from its environment. What I have so far said about principles of individuation may suggest that they are purely spatial—serving to tell us how much of space is occupied by a given $\mathcal{F}$—(albeit in an extended, metaphorical sense of 'space'). This impression should now be corrected. Principles of persistence may also be included among the individuative principles conveyed by a sortal. These express what constitutes the coming into being and passing away of the sort of object in question, and determine what changes may or may not befall it in the meantime.[10] It is only when we can thus isolate an individual $\mathcal{F}$ both spatially and temporally from its environment that we can judge whether it is spatio-temporally continuous with some $\mathcal{F}$ and therefore that they are the same $\mathcal{F}$.

Of course, not every part of this analysis fits every case. There are some items which are not spatial, and some which are not temporal and some which are neither. Numbers, for example, may be regarded as being individuated by the

---

[9] For elaboration of this move see Richard Swinburne, *Space and Time* (New York: St. Martins Press, 1968), pp. 22–3. The details do not concern us.

[10] See Herbst, 'Names and Identities and Beginnings and Ends', pp. 44–5.

successor-of relation: no number is its own successor. There may be items which though both spatial and temporal have extremely loose principles of spatial individuation and somewhat unusual principles of persistence. For example, a vampire may change from a man into a bat and even (at least in Bram Stoker's novel) into a patch of mist and remain but one vampire.[11] There are even some cases in which we can supply identity criteria though the (non-sortal) general noun in question conveys no principles of individuation. In such cases we have to make clear (usually fairly stipulatively) what is to count as one such $\mathscr{A}$ for the particular case in hand. Cases of this sort are considered in § 4.4. All sortals however convey principles of individuation and those under which temporal items fall usually convey principles of persistence. Where such principles apply they should be included among the criteria of $\mathscr{A}$-identity together with the basic relational condition and the requirement that both items fall under '$\mathscr{A}$'.[12]

There are a number of sortal terms in natural language for which the criteria of identity are hard to state, vague, or subject to confusion. Certain sortals have very indeterminate criteria of identity, e.g. 'wave', 'cloud', and 'theme'. It is, in general, difficult to judge when we have the same wave, cloud, or theme but this is not to say that it is never possible nor that there is anything necessarily wrong with a sortal which conveys vague identity criteria. In other cases, the vagueness extends in one direction only, as in a number of technical terms (e.g. 'virus') for which identity criteria are quite difficult.[13] Other examples of this sort are what Wiggins terms 'porous sortals', typically names of types of animals where it is left open whether, for porous sortal '$\mathscr{F}$', animals which are $\mathscr{F}$ form a separate species or simply a stage in the life histories of animals in some other

---

[11] See Joseph Margolis's entertaining account 'Dracula the Man: An Essay in the Logic of Individuation', *International Philosophical Quarterly*, 4 (1964), 541–9; also Wiggins's introduction of the sortal 'Proteus-creature' ('The Individuation of Things and Places', fn. 2, p. 191) to cope with problems raised by the *Odyssey*, IV, lines 453–63.

[12] The general account of identity criteria just given owes a great deal to Wiggins's account in *Identity and Spatio-Temporal Continuity*, pp. 34–6; and to Perry's in 'Identity', pp. 84–90, 105–14, although I use 'criterion of identity' differently from Perry (cf. 'Identity', p. 107).

[13] For remarks along these lines see M. J. Woods, 'Identity and Individuation', pp. 121–2.

species.[14] Such porous sortals have indeterminate persistence conditions. Other terms may be more difficult in that they appear to have two sets of identity criteria which need not always coincide. A well-known example is 'person' for which requirements of spatio-temporal continuity and possession of a common memory seem equally appropriate but need not always be satisfied by the same individuals. In this case a more pressing worry is that the concept is not a unitary concept at all but two distinct, though related, concepts.[15] Less controversial examples of these 'dual' concepts are 'official' (with the distinct sense of 'official*'), 'landmark', 'church', and 'milkman' which were noted in § 3.3, and, of course, Dummett's two senses of 'book' mentioned in § 4.1.

If all sortals convey identity criteria, is it ever the case that two distinct sortals convey the same identity criteria? And, if so, under what conditions do they do so? Philosophers have generally agreed that some sortals do convey the same identity criteria as others but have usually disagreed on the conditions such sortals must satisfy. So far as I know the following conditions exhaust those that have been proposed: Two sortals convey the same criteria of identity

   (i) when one restricts the other;[16]
   (ii) when both restrict a common sortal;[17]
   (iii) when one is an ultimate sortal of which the other is a restriction.[18]

[14] *Identity and Spatio-Temporal Continuity*, pp. 59–60; fn. 37 (p. 69); and Wiggins, 'Reply to Mr Chandler', *Analysis*, 29 (1968/9), pp. 175–6.

[15] Cf. Wiggins's remarks on 'person' (*Identity and Spatio-Temporal Continuity*, pp. 43–4).

[16] This *seems* to be Geach's view. Cf. *Reference and Generality*, pp. 50, 152–3: Any term which conveys identity criteria '*either* is itself a term "$\mathscr{A}$" that can be related in the way described to a proper name "a" [i.e., in such a way as to give the sense of "a"], *or* is derived from such a term "$\mathscr{A}$" by . . . restriction' (p. 50). The quotation does not *entail* (i), however, and I shall show in § 6.3 that Geach's view is quite different from (i).

[17] Wiggins, *Identity and Spatio-Temporal Continuity*, p. 62: 'What does now receive a privileged status is the highest genuine sortal concept "$\mathscr{F}_n$" in any chain of restrictions "$\mathscr{F}_1$", "$\mathscr{F}_2$" . . . which carries with it an autonomous individuative force sufficient to determine without reference to lower sortals the persistence and coincidence conditions for any $\mathscr{F}$ [sic].' Also, Shoemaker, 'Wiggins on Identity', in Milton K. Munitz (ed.), *Identity and Individuation* (New York: New York University Press, 1971), p. 113: 'They will share the same criterion of identity if they restrict a common sortal.'

[18] Leslie Stevenson, 'A Formal Theory of Sortal Quantification', p. 187: 'An

Since all sortals restrict themselves, (i) and (iii) each entail (ii).

Before we consider (i)–(iii) it will be desirable to have some notation for criteria of identity. For a sortal '$\mathscr{F}$' let the two-place relation '$C_{\mathscr{F}}(\zeta,\eta)$' represent the identity criteria it conveys. Thus we have

$$(4.2) \qquad\qquad C_{\mathscr{F}}(a, b) \leftrightarrow a =_{\mathscr{F}} b$$

and, additionally, the requirement that $C_{\mathscr{F}}(a, b)$ be criterial for $a =_{\mathscr{F}} b$. '$C_{\mathscr{F}}(\zeta,\eta)$' should not be confused with the relation '$R_{\mathscr{F}}(\zeta,\eta)$' for we have $R_{\mathscr{F}}(\zeta,\eta) \subseteq C_{\mathscr{F}}(\zeta,\eta)$ but not vice versa. Now consider (i) and assume two sortals '$\mathscr{F}$' and '$\mathscr{G}$' such that $\mathscr{F} \subseteq \mathscr{G}$. One way of establishing (i) would be to adopt the principle that, if $\mathscr{F} \subseteq \mathscr{G}$,

$$(4.3) \qquad\qquad a =_{\mathscr{F}} b \to a =_{\mathscr{G}} b.$$

I shall argue in § 6.3 that (4.3) is, in fact, false but for the moment let us assume that it is correct since it looks as if it might appeal to Geach[19] and, in any case, it appears plausible and seems to give an argument for (i). It is with this argument alone that I want to deal here. The argument runs as follows: If $C_{\mathscr{F}}(a,b)$ holds then, by (4.2), so does $a =_{\mathscr{F}} b$ and hence, by (4.3), so does $a =_{\mathscr{G}} b$. Therefore, it is concluded, what is criterial for $\mathscr{F}$-identity is criterial for $\mathscr{G}$-identity. But this conclusion doesn't follow, for if $C_{\mathscr{F}}(a, b)$ failed then so would $a =_{\mathscr{F}} b$ but this would tell us nothing about $a =_{\mathscr{G}} b$. In other words, in the case envisaged, the identity criteria of '$\mathscr{F}$' are criterial sufficient conditions for $\mathscr{G}$-identity but not criterial necessary conditions.[20] So $C_{\mathscr{F}}(\zeta, \eta)$ is not identical with $C_{\mathscr{G}}(\zeta,\eta)$, but rather

ultimate sortal may be said to give the criterion of identity of everything it applies to, and of all sortals subordinate to it.' Wiggins 'surmises' that his 'highest genuine sortal' 'may possibly be nothing other than a concept which is ultimate' (*Identity and Spatio-Temporal Continuity*, p. 62). But note that Wiggins's notion of an ultimate sortal is wider than mine (cf. ibid., p. 32).

[19] Geach, 'A Reply', *Review of Metaphysics*, 22 (1968/9), 556. (In fact, it is not the principle Geach has in mind, but that must wait until § 6.3. The passage in question is deleted from the reprint in *Logic Matters*.)

[20] If, instead of (4.3) we had:

$$a =_{\mathscr{F}} b \supset a =_{\mathscr{G}} b$$

the argument would not even get this far, for while $C_{\mathscr{F}}(a,b)$ would still be a sufficient condition for $a =_{\mathscr{G}} b$ it would certainly not be a criterial sufficient condition.

$C_{\mathscr{F}}(\zeta,\eta) \subseteq C_{\mathscr{G}}(\zeta,\eta)$. And from this we can show that two sortals have the same criteria of identity when they are co-ordinate. In this case we have:

$$(4.4) \qquad\qquad a =_{\mathscr{F}} b \leftrightarrow a =_{\mathscr{G}} b$$

and thus $C_{\mathscr{F}}(a, b)$ would provide necessary as well as sufficient criteria for $a =_{\mathscr{G}} b$. Although this manner of proving that co-ordinate sortals carry the same identity criteria depends on the false premiss (4.3) the conclusion is not in doubt. If $\mathscr{F} \approx \mathscr{G}$, (4.4) is true since no two $\mathscr{F}$s could be a single $\mathscr{G}$ or vice versa. And to prove our claim all we need is (4.4).

We have said very little about the nature of ultimate sortals and until we do so (in Chapter 5) it will be difficult to see what plausible arguments might be mounted in favour of (iii). However, in dealing with (ii) it is possible to find objections which will hold against (iii) as well. Suppose that there is some sortal which '$\mathscr{F}$' and '$\mathscr{G}$' both restrict. Then we can define a relation '$R(\gamma, \delta)$' over sorts (where 'γ' and 'δ' are place-holders for sortal terms) such that:

$$(4.5) \qquad\qquad R(\mathscr{F},\mathscr{G}) =_{df} (\exists h)(\mathscr{F} \subseteq h \ \& \ \mathscr{G} \subseteq h)$$

intuitively, the relation 'γ restricts some same sortal as δ'. Now if '$R(\gamma, \delta)$' is an equivalence relation it will turn out that there is only one sortal which '$\mathscr{F}$' and '$\mathscr{G}$' both restrict.[21] Thus all sortals which '$\mathscr{F}$' and '$\mathscr{G}$' both restrict will have the same criteria of identity for there will be only one such sortal. But this will only give the result that '$\mathscr{F}$' and '$\mathscr{G}$' have the same criteria of identity if it is the case that two sortals share criteria of identity if one restricts the other. Let '$\mathscr{H}$' be the sortal which '$\mathscr{F}$' and '$\mathscr{G}$' both restrict. Then we can prove nothing about the identity criteria of '$\mathscr{F}$' and '$\mathscr{G}$' unless we assume that $C_{\mathscr{F}}(\zeta,\eta) = C_{\mathscr{H}}(\zeta,\eta)$ and $C_{\mathscr{G}}(\zeta,\eta) = C_{\mathscr{H}}(\zeta,\eta)$. Given this, $C_{\mathscr{F}}(\zeta,\eta) = C_{\mathscr{G}}(\zeta,\eta)$ is obvious, but there seems to be no way of proving what is wanted without that assumption—an assumption we have already argued is false.

I see no other way to justify the second answer except by this appeal to the first. Moreover, the approach does seem intuitively

---

[21] The question of whether '$R(\gamma, \delta)$' is an equivalence relation will be discussed in Chapter 5 where it will be argued that it is not since it fails transitivity.

implausible. Suppose '$\mathscr{F}$' and '$\mathscr{G}$' have the same identity criteria then it follows, given $\mathscr{F}(a)$ & $\mathscr{F}(b)$ & $\mathscr{G}(a)$ & $\mathscr{G}(b)$, that $a =_{\mathscr{F}} b \leftrightarrow a =_{\mathscr{G}} b$ which would rule out any case of (R) occurring within a sortal hierarchy. But there do seem to be cases of (R) which satisfy these conditions. For example, the poet C. Day Lewis wrote detective novels under the name of Nicholas Blake. Now clearly, C. Day Lewis is the same man as Nicholas Blake while they are not the same writer (though both are writers) despite the fact that 'man' and 'writer' both restrict 'person'.

Moreover, this second position will run into the difficulties which Brody has pointed out in connection with Locke's theory of identity. According to (ii) for $\mathscr{F}$s which are $\mathscr{H}$s $C_{\mathscr{F}}(\zeta,\eta)$ holds iff $C_{\mathscr{H}}(\zeta,\eta)$ does. But there seems to be no *a priori* guarantee that this will be so. Moreover, there is little reason for supposing that what is *criterial* for $\mathscr{H}$-identity is also criterial for $\mathscr{F}$-identity and $\mathscr{G}$-identity. These last three objections also apply to (iii).

A number of the issues adverted to here will be discussed further in Chapter 5. But, at least until those who believe otherwise provide better arguments, the conclusion that only co-ordinate sortals have identical criteria of identity seems to be intact.

4.3 Mass Terms and Criteria of Identity

It is clear that as far as identity criteria are concerned mass terms are very different from sortals. In the first place, they don't divide their reference and thus provide no principles of individuation for those items that fall under them. It is, of course, true that a mass term such as 'gold' does serve to distinguish gold from those parts of its environment which are not gold, but it fails to distinguish one thing which is gold from another. Mass terms can 'individuate' one *type* of stuff from another but 'type of stuff' is, as we shall see, a sortal and it is this sortal rather than the mass term 'gold' which isolates the type of stuff which is gold from other types of stuff. Certainly a mass term marks no distinctions within a type of stuff, though this can be done by sortals which are derived from the mass term by a method to be described in this section.

The same is true of principles of persistence. There is a sense in which we can talk of what constitutes the coming into being or passing away of snow (namely, the freezing of water and the melting of snow) but it is the sense conveyed by the sortal 'type of stuff' rather than that conveyed by 'snow' itself. Principles of persistence associated with mass terms have to do with the transmutation of one type of stuff into another. In other cases, as when we might say that music is created by being composed, the principles are those conveyed by 'piece of music' not 'music' itself. In the sense of 'exist' appropriate to 'music' (as distinct from that appropriate to 'piece of music') it seems to me that music cannot be said to have been brought into existence by human activity. If we shrink from this then it seems inevitable that the persistence criteria we have in mind are those conveyed by 'piece of music'.

It seems that mass terms do not convey principles of individuation or of persistence. In cases where we find such principles attached to a mass term they turn out, in fact, to be borrowed (in the sense of § 3.3) from some associated sortal. When we turn to the relational component of identity criteria we find a similar situation. When we talk of the same music there seems to be no one relation which is at stake: is it the same performance or the same piece of music, for example? Similarly with 'the same metal': the same type of metal or the same piece of metal? Even 'the same sugar' seems a prey to this fundamental difficulty: the same spoonful, or the same packet? We cannot judge until we know. As Quine says: 'A mass term like "water" or "sugar" does not primarily admit "same" or "an". When it is subjected to such particles, some special individuating standard is understood from the circumstances. Typically, "same sugar" might allude to sameness of shipment.'[22] Given our account of identity criteria it seems fair to conclude that mass terms do not convey them.

But now we seem to have a problem for at least one of the (D)-theses of § 1.4, namely (D$_4$) which limited completing concepts to terms conveying identity criteria. Mass terms lack identity criteria and yet may appear as covering concepts in relative identity statements. We thus have covering concepts in natural language which are not completing concepts in a (D$_4$)-relative identity theory. However, there is a technique which turns

---

[22] Quine, review of *Reference and Generality*, *Philosophical Review*, 73 (1964), 102.

mass terms into sortals, or occasionally dummy sortals, when they occur in contexts of the form:

(4.6) a is the same $\mathcal{M}$ as b

or

(4.7) $a =_{\mathcal{M}} b$.

Consider

(4.8)   This snow is the same snow as that snow.

Our task is to reformulate (4.8) in such a way as to meet the requirements of (D_4) without changing its sense. Now clearly there are cases in which we can judge whether (4.8) is true or false and thus criteria of identity must be available but they are not conveyed by the covering concept as it stands. If (D_4) is to have any plausibility at all mass terms, when used as covering concepts, must be functioning as disguised sortals, or as some other type of term which does convey identity criteria. In fact, every mass term covering concept can be replaced by either a sortal or a dummy sortal. On the theory I advocate what (4.8) amounts to is an assertion that this snow is the same lump (ball, heap, or block) of snow as that snow. Unless we understand that in (4.8) the second use of 'snow' is to be read in this way the sentence provides us with no criteria by which we can judge it.[23]

   This theory is not new and, in fact, has some distinguished precursors. Strawson, for example, writes: 'The *general* question of the criteria of distinctness and identity of individual instances of snow or gold cannot be raised or, if raised, be satisfactorily answered. We have to wait until we know whether we are talking of *veins*, *pieces* or *quantities* of gold or of *falls*, *drifts* or *expanses* of snow.'[24] There are, in fact, a whole range of what might be termed 'sortalizing auxiliary nouns', hereafter called

---

[23] Anscombe and Geach seem to be arguing this point opaquely in 'Aristotle', *Three Philosophers* (Oxford: Blackwell, 1961), pp. 17, 47–8.

[24] P. F. Strawson, 'Particular and General', *Proceedings of the Aristotelian Society*, 54 (1953/4), 242; also *Individuals*, pp. 202–9. Quinton goes further and says that such considerations 'always' apply when mass terms are used to refer (cf. *The Nature of Things* [London: Routledge and Kegan Paul, 1972], p. 46). I am not concerned to defend this stronger thesis which anyway seems open to counter-examples of the type noted by Quine (e.g. 'Gold is a chemical element') where a mass term is used apparently as a singular term. On the weaker version, see also Geach, *Reference and Generality*, p. 44.

'*sans*' (such as 'vein', 'piece', 'heap', 'volume', 'expanse', 'kind', 'type', 'area', 'lump', etc.) whose main (and possibly in some cases, whose only) purpose is to operate with a mass term and convert it into a sortal or dummy sortal.[25] It is perhaps better to talk of a noun's having a *use* as a sortalizing auxiliary noun for many nouns have more than the one use. In what follows I shall take it that a noun, 'N', has a use as a sortalizing auxiliary noun iff there is a phrase of the form 'N of M' which is $^+$count where 'M' is a mass term.[26] On the theory which I take Strawson and Quine to be suggesting and which I am supporting, in any statement, S, of the form (4.6) for which there are identity criteria the *san* is understood and suppressed. If this is so, then it must be possible to rewrite S to include a *san* in such a way as to preserve the intended sense of S.

To establish the theory, however, we have to defend it against some powerful attacks made by Tyler Burge and Helen Cartwright. Burge[27] objects to Strawson's treatment by means of a dilemma. He claims that Strawson is saying either (i) that we are barred by grammar from asking or answering questions of the form

(4.9)   Is a a single M?

or (ii) that we have no grammatical sentences which express identity or distinctness of instances of snow, except those which employ sortalizing auxiliary nouns before the mass term, and if we did we would have no understanding of the conditions under which they would be true. Burge argues that (i) is, of course, unexceptionable but need not be taken to show that mass

[25] Vendler notes these constructions but uses the term 'measure nouns' for what I've called sortalizing auxiliary nouns. (Cf. Z. Vendler, *Linguistics in Philosophy* [Ithaca: Cornell University Press, 1967], p. 40 n.) This term is as inappropriate as mine is cumbersome. Stephen Voss also recognizes these usages and has coined the happier term 'parcel words' with a Lockean derivation.

[26] It is interesting to note that the same sort of constructions are permissible with pluralized sortals: e.g. 'herd of cows', 'packet of peas', 'parcel of toys', etc., but not with singular sortals—further evidence for Laycock's thesis (mentioned in § 2.4) that pluralized sortals are mass terms. Since plural sortals can cover identity statements (e.g. 'These are the same cows as we saw last week') and since plural sortals do not convey identity criteria they should be treated in the same way as mass term covering concepts (e.g. 'This is the same collection of cows as we saw last week').

[27] 'Truth and Mass Terms', *Journal of Philosophy*, 69 (1972), 272–4.

terms do not divide their reference. I expect *that* much is true, though it would surely be odd to have a term '$\mathscr{M}$' which did divide its reference but for which we couldn't ask or answer questions of the form (4.9). However, it is clear that Strawson is making a stronger claim than (i).

In reply to (ii) Burge correctly points out that there are grammatically well-formed sentences expressing identity or distinctness of snow and gold which don't involve a sortalizing auxiliary. He gives (4.8) as an example. He further argues that we understand them, and we can confirm or disconfirm them as easily as we can 'This star is the same star as that star' in which only sortals are involved. Again, this can scarcely be denied; but it none the less misses the essential point which is that in assessing them we require criteria of identity according to which we can make our judgement. The fact that it isn't difficult to assess such statements is neither here nor there: it does not show that we can obtain identity criteria for snow without employing sortals. Indeed, if Strawson's theory is correct, the fact that we can so easily verify or falsify (4.8) indicates no more than the extreme naturalness with which we sortalize the mass term allegedly acting as a (D_4)-completing concept.

Burge gives the game away on the next page where he writes: 'Ordinary usage seems to resist one's counting the objects which a mass term is true of. Yet we can quantify over these objects . . . and express identity and difference between them.'[28] Given identity and quantification we should be able to count snows by the following device (where '$\mathscr{M}$' is the mass term 'snow'):

$$(4.10) \quad (\exists x^1,...,x^n)\,[\mathscr{M}(x^1) \ \& \ ... \ \& \ \mathscr{M}(x^n) \ \& \ x^1 \neq x^2 \ \& \ ... \ \& \ x^{n-1} \neq x^n \ \& \ (\forall y)(\mathscr{M}(y) \supset . \ y = x^1 \vee ... \vee y = x^n)].$$

However, it is clear, as Burge admits, that with this we would not be counting snows but things that are snow. But we still haven't got criteria of identity because 'thing that is snow' no more provides them than does 'snow'. What we need is a sortal as covering concept.

Further objections to the theory are raised by Helen Cartwright.[29] Firstly, she argues, in many cases more than one *san*

[28] 'Truth and Mass Terms', p. 274.
[29] 'Heraclitus and the Bath Water', *Philosophical Review*, 74 (1965), 476–9.

will be applicable. In such cases which will be chosen? For example, in (4.8) such *sans* as 'block', 'piece', 'volume', 'lump', 'ton', 'ball of five feet diameter', etc. could all act as an appropriate sortalizer for 'snow'. I fail to see why having this choice should embarrass a follower of Quine and Strawson. It is not as though each different *san* is going to give a different answer to the question 'Is this snow the same as that?' and in many cases even the method of finding the answer will remain the same. Where the method is different, the choice will be pragmatically determined. As we might expect, similar things happen with counting, as J. M. E. Moravcsik notes.[30] We understand 'The King is counting his gold' because we know which term provides the principles of identity and distinctness according to which the King individuates his gold. We know he is counting his pieces of gold rather than his ounces of gold. In such cases the correct *san* can be discovered from the circumstances. On the other hand, if the choice of *san* is going to make a difference to the answer we give, then there is all the more reason for putting the *san* in, for without the *san* the question will be ambiguous and (if we are prudent) we will refrain from answering it until the intended sortalization is given. The possibility that conflicting criteria of identity might be involved lies at the very core of the motivation for introducing *sans* explicitly.

Cartwright's second objection is the following: '[S]uppose that the [snow] in question is melted—so that there no longer *is* a set of [blocks] or lumps; or . . . that the water Mary wiped up might have been *spilled*. A puddle of water is not the sort of thing which can be spilled; and what can be spilled—say, a glass of water—is not the sort of thing one can wipe up.'[31] In these cases we do not have an embarrassing choice of *sans*, but rather the context rules out so many of them that we have difficulty in finding one which would be appropriate. Suppose the snow we started with melts, we cannot therefore say:

(4.8a)   This snow is the same block of snow as that snow.

because now there is no snow for 'that snow' to refer to. Nor could we say:

(4.8b)   This snow is the same block of snow as that water.

[30] 'Subcategorization and Abstract Terms', *Foundations of Language*, 6 (1970), 475.   [31] 'Heraclitus and the Bath Water', p. 476.

for 'block of snow' does not refer to an expanse of water. Yet we want to say that in an important sense the snow before it melted and the water afterwards are the same, but we want to know 'the same what?' An obvious answer would be: the same collection of H_2O molecules, so that we'd have:

(4.8c)   This snow is the same collection of H_2O molecules as that water.

I fail to see what problems (4.8c) poses. Cartwright's second example poses a similar difficulty for our analysis. Suppose Mary spills a glass of water and then wipes up the puddle of water which resulted. We would want to hold:

(4.11)   The water Mary spilled is the same water as the water Mary wiped up.

But which *san* could we use? Clearly, 'glass of water' will not do (because Mary couldn't wipe up a glass of water) nor will 'puddle of water' (because Mary couldn't spill a puddle of water). But this does not leave us entirely bereft of resources: we could use 'collection of water molecules' or 'volume of water'.

Cartwright goes on to introduce a new problem by considering chemical as well as physical changes. Suppose we dissolve some metal in an acid and later reclaim it. In a solution molecules of metal become dissociated and, on reclamation, the atoms re-associate in a different way—thus, not even the molecules of the metal which was dissolved are the same as those which are reclaimed. However, I'm not sure that we would want to say that it was the same metal throughout[32] for that implies that a quantity of metal can suffer a spatio-temporal discontinuity and still remain the same quantity of metal. On Cartwright's treatment, during the solution's existence there was no metal, and afterwards the same metal as before sprang back into existence. It seems to me that a quantity of metal is not the kind of thing that can come into being twice and lapse from existence in between.

None the less there is clearly something which is the same before, during, and after the dissolution but what this is seems

[32] Although it is, of course, the same type of metal, which is one way of sortalizing 'metal'.

to me to be not metal but a collection of atoms. Those who claimed that the same metal was reclaimed would, I think, retreat to the claim that what they meant was that the collection of atoms remained the same. Thus it appears as if 'collection of atoms' has by proxy rights to act for 'metal' as a completing concept. But this is mistaken. There can be occasions on which a is the same collection of atoms as b, but a is not the same metal as b, though both are metals. (For example, if a is a metal which, by some chemical process, can be transformed into a different type of metal by just a rearrangement of atoms.) Thus if we permitted:

$$\text{metal} \rightarrow \text{collection of atoms}$$

as a transformation for covering concepts, we would not preserve intended sense and truth-value. Moreover, we would go beyond the transformation I propose, which is:

$$(4.12) \qquad\qquad \mathcal{M} \rightarrow san + of + \mathcal{M}.$$

(Using 'collection of water molecules', as I did in the case of the water Mary spilled, does not go beyond (4.12) since it is equivalent to 'collection of molecules of water' where 'collection of molecules' is a composite san.)

It might be held that in any case where a sortalized mass term was needed to cover an identity statement 'quantity of $\mathcal{M}$' was at hand to provide the requisite completion. Cartwright seems to reject all, or at least many, $sans$ in favour of 'quantity'.[33] There are limits to its use: for example, 'quantity of hunger', or 'quantity of music' are odd. However, it could still be urged that 'quantity' is more widely applicable than any of its brothers. A further qualification must be introduced for we could, in ordinary language, say of two distinct lumps of gold that they were the same quantity of gold. The difficulty can be resolved by Russell's distinction between a quantity and a magnitude: 'When two quantities are equal, they have the same magnitude.'[34] However, all possibility of confusion on this issue could be avoided, without loss of generality, by the use of Locke's term 'parcel' instead of Russell's 'quantity'.[35] However, as

---

[33] Helen Morris Cartwright, 'Quantities', *Philosophical Review*, 79 (1970), 32–3.
[34] Russell, *The Principles of Mathematics* (London: Allen and Unwin; 2nd edn., 1937), § 151, p. 159. Cartwright uses 'amount' in preference to Russell's 'magnitude'.   [35] *Essay*, Bk. II, Ch. 27, § 2 (Fraser, vol. i, p. 441).

Burge has rightly pointed out,[36] 'quantity of gold' and 'parcel of gold' are not sortals, and we can no more count parcels (or quantities) of gold than we can count things.[37] We can however replace 'parcel of gold' with a sense-preserving alternative which fits (4.12), namely, 'collection of molecules of gold', and, more generally, 'parcel of $\mathcal{M}$' by 'collection of parts of $\mathcal{M}$'.[38] Neither of these substituted phrases is a sortal (since we can never say how many collections we have unless we make some decision as to what is to count as one collection) but, as we shall see in § 4.4, the first does convey identity criteria while the second may do so if we can replace 'parts of $\mathcal{M}$' by a pluralized sortal.[39] And, as we shall also see in § 4.4, even 'parcel of gold' and 'quantity of gold' may, in appropriate contexts, supply identity criteria.

Thirdly, Cartwright argues that, from the fact that we may have many appropriate *sans* to choose from, we will (depending upon which we choose) get different truth-values for any identity statements taking a mass term as covering concept: 'Some water or sugar might, in various circumstances, fail to be the same water or sugar—that there is no way of telling, apart from a particular context, whether some water or sugar is or is not to be counted the same.'[40] This is, of course, exactly what the (D_4)-relativist is claiming: we have to have a completing concept before we can assess an identity statement, and our assessment will depend upon which completing concept we choose. Anyone who takes this talk about completing concepts seriously will say that this problem is exactly the reason for doing so.[41]

---

[36] 'Truth and Mass Terms', p. 272.

[37] It is significant that Chappell, who also favours the Lockean terminology, lists criteria which distinguish 'parcel of $\mathcal{M}$' from sortals. These criteria are those which have been (in some cases mistakenly) used to distinguish mass terms from sortals. (Cf. V. C. Chappell, 'Stuff and Things', pp. 71–3.)

[38] 'Amount of $\mathcal{M}$' would require some alternative reading, though it is difficult to suggest one which is foolproof. Consideration of this issue would take us into the curiously unexplored area of quantitative identity. Fortunately, we are here only concerned with parcels.

[39] Cartwright's reasons for preferring 'quantity' to other *sans* are briefly discussed in Appendix 2.

[40] 'Heraclitus and the Bath Water', p. 477. We have already mentioned this as a special case of her first argument.

[41] Cp. the use Geach makes of this point in arguing for (R), 'Identity', p. 244. He uses the same example as Cartwright.

However, as Cartwright goes on to admit with her examples, this problem (if it exists) is not peculiar to mass terms but infects sortals as well. 'Word' is a sortal and yet, as Cartwright notes, is subject to just the same ambiguity.[42] For example, we have both 'óbjèct' and 'öbjéct' which 'have little more in common than their spelling'.[43] Is 'óbjèct' the same word as 'öbjéct' or not? In other words, do we take whether *a* is the same word as *b* to be determined graphically or phonetically?[44] Presumably Cartwright would agree that 'word' can function as a covering concept despite this ambiguity,[45] if so the ambiguity would give no argument for excluding similarly ambiguous sortalized mass terms.

However, the ambiguity of 'word' is not quite parallel to the sort of ambiguity Cartwright was trying to get at in her original objection, namely that 'snow' in (4.8) is ambiguous *before* it is sortalized. Two points that I made in reply to her first criticism are relevant here: (i) We may hope that the context in which (4.8) is uttered will help us unambiguously to decide which *san* to use (i.e. which gives the intended sense of the utterance). (ii) If (i) fails to narrow the choice down to one *san* we may hope that all those left in by (i) will result in our giving the same truth-value to (4.8). To these two points we may add: (iii) If (i) leaves in more than one applicable *san* and if some of those that are left in result in the assignment of different truth-values to (4.8), then this shows no more than the inadequacy of using the mass term 'snow' as a completing concept in (4.8)— which is the very point I was arguing for. In this case we have to list the possible *san*-transformations of 'snow' and in doing this we are doing no more than making explicit the ambiguities of (4.8) as it stands. Moreover, if we are to be able to judge (4.8) true or false we have to do just this. For Cartwright to claim that 'apart from a particular context' we have no way of knowing which *san* to choose concedes exactly the point I'm trying to make. Given a context we may hope that the *san* is uniquely determined; or, if it is not, that the choice doesn't

---

[42] 'Heraclitus and the Bath Water', p. 478.   [43] Ibid., p. 471.

[44] The relativist here claims another example of (R): 'óbjèct' is the same sequence of letters as 'öbjéct', but not the same sequence of sounds. Cf. Geach, 'Identity', p. 244.

[45] Other sortals such as 'theist' (believer in theism, or tea addict) exhibit similar ambiguities which are easier to spot and therefore less confusing.

make a difference to judgements of the identity (cases (i) and (ii) above). Apart from a context which settled the matter we can only hope to judge the identity if the *san* is explicit (case (iii)). (It is also possible that even with a context the choice of *san* is neither uniquely determined nor indifferent as far as the judgement is concerned—a case Cartwright doesn't consider— in this case also it is essential to make the *san* explicit.)

Cartwright seems half to recognize this for she suggests uses of mass terms with 'same' in which, as she puts it, 'there is . . . something suspicious in the use of the word "same" ':[46] 'He showed some intelligence on that occasion (he did not show the same *intelligence* today).' 'When the drug wears off you may have some pain (the same *pain* Mrs. Jones had after her operation).' 'Let us hear some opinion on the subject (the same *opinion* that was heard last night).' 'From where I sit, I can see some blue (can you see the same *blue*?).' If there is something suspicious about the use of 'same' with these mass terms it is because in these cases we *obviously* wouldn't know which criteria of identity were intended.[47] My point is that the inadequacy of the mass terms as completing concepts (which is obvious in some of these statements) is present, but less obvious, in all statements in which mass terms are supposed to act as completing concepts.

How come, then, if sortals can also be ambiguous, we don't have to get rid of sortals as covering concepts? The answer to this is that we *do* have to get rid of the ambiguous sortals as covering concepts, but we do *not* have to get rid of *all* sortals as covering concepts since not all sortals are ambiguous as to identity criteria. If '$\mathcal{F}$' is an ambiguous sortal, we must expose its ambiguity by listing the different dictionary entries for '$\mathcal{F}$'. For example, we cannot assign a truth-value to:

(4.13) François-Marie Arouet is the same theist as Voltaire.

if we are in doubt as to whether 'theist' here means 'believer in theism' or 'tea addict'. However, we can list the two alternative readings of (4.13) and assign the value *true* to the first and *false* to the second.

Perhaps it is worth while summing up the points so far made

[46] 'Heraclitus and the Bath Water', p. 478.
[47] In some cases Cartwright's suspicion seems somewhat unjustified. In the case of 'same intelligence', for example, it seems clear that 'degree of intelligence' is the required sortalization.

in this argument. Firstly, Cartwright claims that there may be
an abundance of *sans* and we won't be able to choose between
them. In reply I would argue that either the choice of one
particular *san* rather than another makes a difference or it does
not. If it does, then our choice may be made for us by the context; if it does not then the choice is indifferent. Secondly,
Cartwright argues that there may be cases where it is not
possible to find a *san* at all. I can't prove that there will not be
such cases but I think it highly unlikely that there will be when
we are in genuine need of a completing concept. Thirdly,
Cartwright argues that there is no way of telling (in some
cases) whether some water is or is not the same water. This, it
seems to me, concedes exactly the point I want. It is not
possible on some occasions to judge whether this is the same
water as that because we need to know whether we are considering tubfuls, glassfuls, pools, oceans, or drops of water
before we can decide questions like these—at least in some
cases.

Finally, Cartwright has an argument which she considers
'perhaps most important'.[48] She urges that the question
whether what is some water is the same water is *logically prior*
to the question as to whether it is the same tubful of water or
aggregate of water molecules. I'm far from clear what she
means by a 'logically prior question' but I suspect that at
least part of what it involves is either that if X is a logically
prior question to Y then it is impossible to ask Y without
asking, or having previously asked, X (but not vice versa); or
that it is impossible to answer Y without answering, or having
previously answered, X (but not vice versa). If this is what she
means, then I think she is mistaken. I can see no reason for
assuming that in order to ask (a) 'Is this the same pool of
water as that?' one has to ask (b) 'Is this the same water as
that?', let alone that to be able to answer the first question
one must have already answered the second. It seems to me
that, most usually, (a) will be just one of the glosses that may
be put on the radically ambiguous (b). If this is the case then
(a) will surely be logically prior (in the sense of 'logically prior'
just suggested) to (b), rather than vice versa. On the other
hand, it may be just that, in context, (a) is the only gloss to put

[48] 'Heraclitus and the Bath Water', p. 479.

on (b). In such a case to ask (a) is simply being more explicit than to ask (b). In such circumstances neither question is logically prior to the other.

4.4 Dummy Sortals[49] and Criteria of Identity

We have seen so far that while sortals convey identity criteria, mass terms do not. However, mass term covering concepts can be removed, by means of (4.12), in favour of either a sortal or, sometimes, a dummy sortal. Cases where (4.12) yields sortals give no cause for alarm to the (D_4)-relativist, but what about cases where dummy sortals result? There are cases in which we really do need dummy sortals such as 'collection of molecules' as covering concepts (e.g. the water Mary spilled/wiped up case). Moreover, we will need such covering concepts quite apart from the sortalization of mass terms issue: we need to be able to talk of things being, for example, the same collection of planks or bits.

In the case of 'collection of molecules' it is perfectly possible to define criteria of identity which are genuinely criterial, namely:

(4.14) a is the same collection of molecules as $b \equiv .\ (\forall x: \text{mole-} \\ \text{cule}(x))(x \in a \equiv x \in b)$

which corresponds to the standard definition of set identity.[50] Clearly we can define identity criteria for other dummy sortals (e.g. 'collection of planks', 'collection of atoms', 'collection of molecules of water', and so on) in exactly the same way. We can, moreover, adapt (4.14) to deal with 'ζ is the same parcel of matter as η'. The conditions expressed in (4.14) are criterial for both identity and distinctness for we can (at least in principle, under ideal conditions) judge whether the left-hand side is true by running through molecules to see whether they are members of a or b, once we have decided what we are going to count as collection a and collection b. And, of course, the reason we can do this is that 'molecule' (like 'atom', and 'plank' and 'molecule of water') is a sortal.

---

[49] Dummy sortals include all non-sortal +count nouns.

[50] I use 'collection' rather than 'set' because formulae like (4.14) are needed most frequently in contexts such as (4.11) and it is not clear that sets of molecules are the sort of things that can be wiped up and spilt. Collections of molecules, in the sense in which I use the term, are.

The cases so far considered in which dummy sortals convey criteria of identity are commonly of the form 'collection of $\mathscr{F}$s' where '$\mathscr{F}$' is a sortal. In some cases 'collection' doesn't appear: in different circumstances 'set', 'amalgam', 'concourse', 'crowd', 'aggregate', etc. may take its place. If we represent all these usages by '$Coll(\mathscr{F})$'[51] we may define general identity criteria for crowds and collections of $\mathscr{F}$s thus:

(4.15) a is the same $Coll(\mathscr{F})$ as $b \equiv (\forall x_{\mathscr{F}})(x_{\mathscr{F}} \in a \equiv x_{\mathscr{F}} \in b)$.

Here the '$\mathscr{F}$' which appears subscripted to bound variables acts as a range-restrictor on the quantifier, indicating that the variable ranges only over the sort named by '$\mathscr{F}$'.

Our account so far is sufficient to give identity criteria for 'a is the same collection as b' provided two conditions are met: (i) that we can replace 'collection' by '$Coll(\mathscr{F})$' for some sortal '$\mathscr{F}$'; and (ii) that the context enables us to decide what is to count as a and b. The second condition is needed because 'collection' conveys no principles of individuation and it is thus impossible to know where one collection ends and another begins. This is one of the few things that Ayers gets right in his paper 'Individuals Without Sortals': 'The limits of a "collection" . . . are intrinsically arbitrary, . . . If a cock stands on a dunghill, the particles of its feet form as genuine a "collection" with the particles of the dunghill as they do with the particles of its legs or body.'[52] However, although the limits of a collection are intrinsically arbitrary a context might make them clear—typically, by providing a sortal which serves to distinguish them (e.g. collection of particles in the *dunghill*).

We can now extend our account by generalizing and liberalizing these two conditions. We can judge whether a is the same set as b in contexts which make it clear, e.g., that a and b are sets of numbers (provided, of course, we know which sets of numbers a and b are). But we can go further than this for we can judge that the set of the cat and the fiddle is the same set as the set of the fiddle and the cat. In other words, for judgements as to set-identity it is not necessary to locate every member of the sets in question under a single sortal, it is sufficient if we can

---

[51] Cases in which we have (e.g.) 'parcel of gold' may, as I've suggested, be properly replaced by '$Coll$(gold molecule)'.

[52] 'Individuals Without Sortals', p. 128.

locate each member under some sortal. This extends identity criteria in two directions: to sets formed from the union of other sets (e.g. the set of things which are either cats or fiddles) and to sets whose members are known by enumeration. While 'set' does not always convey identity criteria it is clear that in certain contexts particular uses of it do. The technique used here for making statements of set-identity criterial is similar to that used in § 4.2 for making statements of spatio-temporal continuity criterial. In each case the need is to identify the items designated by the singular terms of the statement under one or more sortals. Further extensions are now obvious.

Utilizing the principle that no two material objects can occupy exactly the same place at the same time (a principle on which spatio-temporal continuity conditions are grounded) we could define identity criteria for material objects thus:[53]

(4.16) a is the same material object as $b \equiv (\forall t, r)(a$ occupies r at $t \equiv b$ occupies r at $t)$

(where 'r' and 't' are variables taking regions and times as values). There are no problems with the criteriality of (4.16) so long as we can in principle identify spaces and times and provided that we can locate a and b under some sortal (not necessarily the same one for each) so that we know what is to count as a region occupied by a or b.[54] But now, surely, we can impose requirements of this type in order to make

(4.17) a is the same item as $b \equiv (\forall \phi)(\phi(a) \equiv \phi(b))$

yield identity criteria. The additional requirements we need are obvious enough: firstly, we need to be able, at least in principle, to identify properties and secondly, we need to be able to locate a and b under some sortal (not necessarily the same one for each) so that we know what it is for a predicate to apply to a or b. This second requirement obviates the difficulties with Leibniz's Law raised by Dummett and Herbst and

---

[53] This develops a suggestion originally due to Stephen Voss, to whom I am grateful for criticism of my earlier views on these questions.

[54] This corresponds, I think, to Geach's admission that identity criteria are conveyed by one sense of 'thing': 'meaning roughly "piece of matter that moves around with its own proper motion and all together", so that . . . a watch . . . would be a "thing", but an undetached part [of a watch] would not count as a distinct "thing"'. (*Reference and Generality*, p. 145.)

discussed briefly above in § 1.2. The essential problem was a circularity: If (LL) defines our only concept of identity, then our only way of using it to judge whether any identity statement, '$a = b$', is true is to establish that all and only predicates true of a are true of b. But this requires our knowing what a and b are and, hence, what they are or are not identical to. On our new account this circle can be broken since we have relative identities as well as those defined by (LL). In particular, in locating a and b under a sortal we use sortal-relative identity to determine what a and b are and then, if we discover that they are the same $\mathcal{F}$ we can go on to inquire whether they are the same item or identical absolutely. This opens up the possibility of a useful reconciliation between absolute and relative identity which will be explored further in Chapters 6 and 7.

It is worth while considering the objections Ayers makes to claims similar to these about the role sortals play in individuation.[55] Ayers thinks that dummy sortals or, to use his term, categorial concepts, are sufficient for individuation, since they provide principles of individuation or unity. The trouble is that in explicating his notion of a principle of unity Ayers is continually forced to retreat towards the relativist position, since it turns out that not every category has a single principle of unity. Ayers recognizes this and tries to block this retreat by claiming that individuation is possible without principles of unity.[56] This view strikes me as plainly implausible, and it is not the one that Ayers has been arguing for. Moreover, the account he does give of his principles of unity is scarcely very convincing and in the case of the category of physical objects consists mainly of the principle that they cohere despite (in some cases) the possibility of change of parts and (in others) the possibility of dispersal.

While the individuative resources of a language are supplied by its sortal terms we have seen in this section that this does not force us to adopt a (D_2)-relative identity theory. Indeed, (D_2) is too restrictive for natural language not only because syntax allows other than sortal general nouns in covering

[55] Ayers, 'Individuals Without Sortals', especially pp. 113–17, 128–31, 135–42. For more detailed criticisms see my 'Ayers on Relative Identity'.
[56] Ibid., p. 136.

concept position, but also because in some contexts some of these nouns cannot (sense-preservingly) be replaced by a sortal. Such identity statements are still assessible if (sortal-based) identity criteria are supplied by the context or built into the singular terms of the statement.[57] This accounts for what I take to be the obvious truth that we cannot assign a truth-value to '*a* is the same set as *b*' outside a context which tells us what *a* and *b* are, while we can assign a truth-value to 'The set of featherless bipeds is the same set as the set of men', despite the fact that the covering concept is not a sortal. This has to do with the fact, noted most radically in the Tractarian theory of identity, that the singular terms of an identity statement and the identity sign are complementary. We shall consider it again in Chapters 6 and 7 when we consider whether the (D)-thesis isn't more restrictive than it ought to be. However, nothing so far said and nothing to be said later leads us to doubt that sortals contain the individuative resources of a language, nor that they are the prime bearers of identity criteria. What comes into question in Chapters 6 and 7, and has, to some extent, already been questioned in this section, is whether (D) is the correct way to formulate this insight.

This is a good place to tie up a few loose ends before moving on. We see that (D_2) is too restrictive; and so is (D_3), which limits completions to sortals and mass terms. As we have seen, in certain contexts dummy sortal completing concepts are indispensable. Of the remaining (D)-theses, (D_1), which permits any general noun as completing concept, is the version which fits the actual syntax of natural language best. There is no general noun '$\mathscr{A}$' such that '*a* is the same $\mathscr{A}$ as *b*' is syntactically deviant in English (where '*a*' and '*b*' are replaced by appropriate English singular terms). (The syntax for pluralized general nouns is slightly different.) Thus any general noun is acceptable as a covering concept in English. But the notion of a completing concept is a bit grander than that of a covering concept, and it is difficult to see what sort of incompleteness the use of certain general nouns (e.g. 'item') could be removing when they are employed as covering concepts. It is certainly

[57] I shall term 'substantival' a covering concept used in circumstances which make the identity statement it covers assessible. Thus sortal (and certain dummy sortal) covering concepts are always substantival.

not the kind of incompleteness which has motivated relative identity theorists or which will help us in any way to achieve our aim of a theory which does justice to the way we actually think about identity. (It is, in fact, a rather uninteresting kind of incompleteness which will be considered—and dismissed—in § 6.1.) That leaves just (D$_4$), which limits completions to general nouns conveying identity criteria, and (D$_5$), which limits completing concepts to ultimate sortals. (D$_4$) we reserve for Chapters 6 and 7. To (D$_5$) we turn in the next chapter.

5

Ultimate Sortals

5.1 The Structure of Ultimate Sorts

The notion of an ultimate sortal is an important one. We have a version of (D), (D$_5$), which restricts completing concepts to ultimate sortals and the question will arise as to whether we can have examples of (R) if completing concepts are restricted in this way. The questions to be answered here will make that question relatively easy. The main argument which follows is concerned with two principles which may be stated as follows:

(I) *The Restriction Principle*: If an individual *a* falls under two distinct sortals '$\mathscr{F}$' and '$\mathscr{F}_1$' in the course of its history then there is at least one sortal which '$\mathscr{F}$' and '$\mathscr{F}_1$' both restrict.

(II) *The Uniqueness Principle*: If an individual *a* falls under two distinct sortals '$\mathscr{F}$' and '$\mathscr{F}_1$' in the course of its history then there is only one ultimate sortal which '$\mathscr{F}$' and '$\mathscr{F}_1$' both restrict.

With the formalism introduced in § 3.4 we can express the Restriction Principle as

$$(5.1) \qquad \mathscr{F} \mid_\tau \mathscr{F}_1 \supset (\exists g)(\mathscr{F} \subseteq g \,\&\, \mathscr{F}_1 \subseteq g)$$

or as:

$$(5.2) \qquad \mathscr{F} \mid_\tau \mathscr{F}_1 \supset R(\mathscr{F}, \mathscr{F}_1)$$

where '$R(\mathscr{F}, \mathscr{F}_1)$' is as in (4.5); and the Uniqueness Principle as:

$$(5.3) \quad \mathscr{F} \mid_\tau \mathscr{F}_1 \supset (\exists g)[\mathscr{F} \subseteq g \,\&\, \mathscr{F}_1 \subseteq g \,\&\, (\forall g_1)(g \subseteq g_1 \supset g \approx g_1) \\ \&\, (\forall h)(\mathscr{F} \subseteq h \,\&\, \mathscr{F}_1 \subseteq h \,\&\, (\forall h_1)(h \subseteq h_1 \supset h \approx h_1) \supset. \\ h \approx g)].$$

If the Restriction Principle and the Uniqueness Principle are both true then there can be no case of (R) with ultimate sortals as covering concepts in both conjuncts. It will be as well to

spell out the relations between these two principles and ultimate sortals in a little detail. Let us suppose the Restriction
Principle true, and let '$\mathscr{G}$' be a sortal which '$\mathscr{F}$' and '$\mathscr{F}_1$' both
restrict. Now either '$\mathscr{G}$' restricts only itself or it restricts some
other sortal as well. If '$\mathscr{G}$' restricts only itself then '$\mathscr{G}$' is an
ultimate sortal. If '$\mathscr{G}$' restricts some further sortal as well then
either that sortal restricts only itself (in which case it is ultimate)
or it restricts some other sortal as well, in which case . . . Since
any classificatory hierarchy in natural language can have only
a finite number of levels, we eventually arrive at a sortal which
restricts only itself and is therefore ultimate. Because of the
transitivity of 'γ restricts δ', the Restriction Principle entails that
there is at least one ultimate sortal which '$\mathscr{F}$' and '$\mathscr{F}_1$' both
restrict. The Uniqueness Principle entails, in addition, that
there is only one such ultimate sortal, that of all the sortals
which '$\mathscr{F}$' and '$\mathscr{F}_1$' both restrict only one will be ultimate.

Wiggins accepts both the Restriction Principle and the
Uniqueness Principle and seeks to validate them by an argument of great length and astonishing complexity.[1] This is
supported and amplified by one of comparable complexity
from Shoemaker.[2] Fortunately, the two arguments are parallel
in strategy. Both fall into two parts: the first an argument (in
Wiggins's case the trace of an argument) for the Restriction
Principle; the second an argument for the Uniqueness Principle
on the basis of the Restriction Principle. The second part of the
argument is largely concerned with proving that 'γ restricts the
same sortal as δ' (the relation '$R(\gamma, \delta)$') is an equivalence relation. I shall argue that neither Wiggins's nor Shoemaker's
argument is valid, that '$R(\gamma, \delta)$' is not an equivalence relation,
and that there is no reason to suppose that either principle is
true nor, indeed, that either has even pre-theoretical plausibility. But before moving on to that part of my enterprise I want
to show that Wiggins's argument is a little surprising in the
context in which it occurs.

Wiggins supposes the truth of the principle:

(5.4) $(\forall x)(\forall t)[\text{exists}(x, t) \supset (\exists f)(f(x, t))].$

That is, for every item x and for every instant of x's existence

[1] *Identity and Spatio-Temporal Continuity*, pp. 30–4.
[2] 'Wiggins on Identity', in Munitz (ed.), *Identity and Individuation*, pp. 108–13.

there is some sortal under which x falls at that instant; or, as Wiggins puts it, 'everything is something or other.'[3] Now Wiggins claims[4] to be arguing from (5.4) to the conclusion:

$$(5.5) \qquad (\forall x)(\exists f)(\forall t)[\text{exists}(x,t) \supset f(x,t)]$$

which is stronger than (5.4). But what he in fact argues for is the conclusion:

$$(5.6) \quad (\forall x)(\exists f)(\forall t)[(\text{exists}(x,t) \supset f(x,t)) \,\&\, (\forall g)(g(x,t) \supset g \approx f)]$$

which is stronger still.[5] He urges, for example, that 'what remains to be disproved is the possibility that a should coincide with b under $\mathscr{F}$, b with c under $\mathscr{F}_1$, c under $\mathscr{F}_2$ with d . . ., where $\mathscr{F}$, $\mathscr{F}_1$, $\mathscr{F}_2$ . . . are not related by being qualifications of some *one* sortal.'[6] Now (5.5) does not, as I shall show, require either the Restriction Principle or the Uniqueness Principle, whereas (5.6) requires them both.

It is important to see why there are very real penalties for Wiggins if (5.5) is not met, and that there are no real penalties for him if (5.6) fails. Wiggins holds that every genuine identity statement can be covered by a sortal. If we have a case in which one individual successively falls under a series of sortals '$\mathscr{F}$', '$\mathscr{F}_1$', etc. and there is no sortal under which it falls throughout its career then we have, on (D_2)-relativist principles, no grounds for saying that the *same* individual falls successively under '$\mathscr{F}$', '$\mathscr{F}_1$', etc. for we have no sortal completing concept for that individual throughout its career. Thus the (D_2)-relativist needs (5.5). What he doesn't need, however, is the stronger claim Wiggins argues for, namely that '$\mathscr{F}$', '$\mathscr{F}_1$', etc. must *restrict one and only one* sortal under which the individual falls throughout its career. For, while Wiggins does attempt an argument to show that there could be only one such sortal, he

---

[3] *Identity and Spatio-Temporal Continuity*, p. 29.

[4] Ibid., pp. 29–30, 34.

[5] I am sceptical of Wiggins's restricting the claim that items must fall under some sortal to items which exist. If we pursue Wiggins's line of thought about the connection between sortals and individuation then surely every individuable item must fall under some sortal. (Cf. *Identity and Spatio-Temporal Continuity*, p. 27 for further remarks on this issue.)

[6] Ibid., p. 30; my italics. In *Identity and Spatio-Temporal Continuity* Wiggins is (as the title suggests) concerned almost exclusively with material object identity (cf. p. 25). His notion of 'coincidence' in this context is quite easy to understand. In other contexts, however, it is, as he admits, 'hardly more than a metaphor'. (Cf. 'The Individuation of Things and Places', p. 179.)

completely ignores the possibility that the sortal under which an individual falls throughout its career may only intersect with '$\mathscr{F}$', '$\mathscr{F}_1$', etc. and assumes that in order for an individual to fall continuously under a single sortal and successively under a number of sortals, the latter must all restrict the former. But this assumption needs arguing for.

Without actually providing him with an argument, Wiggins's terminology clearly leads him towards the stronger assumption. Wiggins refers to the sortals '$\mathscr{F}$', '$\mathscr{F}_1$', etc. under which an individual successively falls as 'phase-sortals' and, as he remarks, 'all phase-sortals are of their very nature . . . *restrictions* of underlying more general sortals'[7] which he calls 'substance-sortals'.[8] Now clearly, if he assumes that '$\mathscr{F}$', '$\mathscr{F}_1$', etc. are phase sortals the Restriction Principle is, though not proven, at least made plausible, for we would know then that '$\mathscr{F}$' restricted some sortal and that '$\mathscr{F}_1$' did, and so on, and we would also know that there must be some sortal to satisfy the requirement (5.5) of (D$_2$). We would still *not* have, what the Restriction Principle requires, that '$\mathscr{F}$', '$\mathscr{F}_1$', etc. restrict the same sortal and that *that* sortal satisfies (5.5). None the less, we can see Wiggins's appeal to phase sortals as a persuasive move in support of the Restriction Principle. However, even this move must be disallowed because on the present definition of 'phase sortal' there is no guarantee that each member of a series of sortals under which an individual finds itself is a phase sortal. For example, a car might successively find itself under the sortals 'white car' and 'red car' neither of which is, on the definition of § 3.4, a phase sortal. On the other hand, if we widen the definition of phase sortal to let in these terms there seems no reason to suppose that each member of such a series of sortals is a restriction of some more general sortal. For example, a twig may, in appropriate circumstances, become a work of art (viz., an *objet trouvé*) without there being any sortal which 'twig' restricts nor any sortal which 'work of art' restricts. To secure the fact that it is one individual which is first the twig and then the work of art it is sufficient to ensure that 'twig' and 'work of art' intersect over this particular twig.[9]

---

[7] Ibid., p. 30.　　　　　　　　　　　　　　　　　　[8] Ibid., p. 7.

[9] It might be objected that Wiggins's notion of an ultimate sortal differs from my own. However, Wiggins's definition (ibid., p. 32) includes my own as its

5.2 *The Restriction Principle*

Although Wiggins's talk about phase sortals and restriction sortals was congenial to the Restriction Principle, Wiggins never regarded it as a proof of the Principle. Indeed, Wiggins argues so sketchily for the Principle that one wonders whether he thinks it needs arguing for at all. In fact the most substantial parts of the argument below are due to Shoemaker. Wiggins imagines[10] a circumstance in which an individual goes through a succession of stages a, b, c, d, each characterized by different sortals, '$\mathscr{F}$', '$\mathscr{F}_1$', and '$\mathscr{F}_2$' so that we have:

$$(5.7) \qquad a =_{\mathscr{F}} b \ \& \ b =_{\mathscr{F}_1} c \ \& \ c =_{\mathscr{F}_2} d.$$

Now Wiggins seeks to prove that '$\mathscr{F}$', '$\mathscr{F}_1$', and '$\mathscr{F}_2$' must all be restrictions of some one sortal. My own position is that the claims of (D_2) would be adequately met by showing:

$$(5.8) \qquad (\exists g)(a =_g b \ \& \ b =_g c \ \& \ c =_g d)$$

which would leave open the possibility that, instantiating '$\mathscr{G}$' for 'g', '$\mathscr{G}$' might only intersect with '$\mathscr{F}$', '$\mathscr{F}_1$', and '$\mathscr{F}_2$' and that there might be more than one instantiation for 'g' which would result in a true proposition. That is, it is possible that:

$$(5.9a) \qquad a =_{\mathscr{G}_1} b \ \& \ b =_{\mathscr{G}_1} c \ \& \ c =_{\mathscr{G}_1} d$$

$$(5.9b) \qquad a =_{\mathscr{G}_2} b \ \& \ b =_{\mathscr{G}_2} c \ \& \ c =_{\mathscr{G}_2} d$$

$$(5.9c) \qquad \sim (\mathscr{F} \subseteq \mathscr{G}_1 \vee \mathscr{F}_1 \subseteq \mathscr{G}_1 \vee \mathscr{F}_2 \subseteq \mathscr{G}_1)$$

$$(5.9d) \qquad \sim (\mathscr{F} \subseteq \mathscr{G}_2 \vee \mathscr{F}_1 \subseteq \mathscr{G}_2 \vee \mathscr{F}_2 \subseteq \mathscr{G}_2)$$

are all true. In this section I shall be concerned with Wiggins's arguments against (5.9c) and (5.9d), in the section which follows with (5.9a) and (5.9b).

Wiggins's first move is to establish that when the individual comes to the end of its $\mathscr{F}$-phase, say, it is not the case that any old sortal will serve to continue it into its $\mathscr{F}_1$-phase. 'That', he rightly says, 'would be wrong because it would fail to distinguish sufficiently between a thing's being *replaced* and its *continuing to exist*.'[11] Having established that, he is concerned to mark out the subset of sortals which would continue it in

first disjunct. It will not therefore exclude any of the examples on which my own case rests.

[10] Ibid., pp. 30–1.　　　　　　　　　　　　　　[11] Ibid., p. 31.

existence and to argue that it is the (unit) set of (ultimate) sortals which '$\mathscr{F}$', '$\mathscr{F}_1$', and '$\mathscr{F}_2$' restrict.

(III) [S]uppose there were even as many as two . . . sortals, '$\mathscr{G}_1$' and '$\mathscr{G}_2$', competing respectively to make b coincide under '$\mathscr{G}_1$' with c^1 and coincide under '$\mathscr{G}_2$' with c^2. Since by the prohibition on branching not both can secure b, why should either? If there is to be any such thing as individuation then there must be some basis on which putative rival claims can be distinguished, and the only basis there could be is this. A thing is legitimately individuated and singled out as one thing through a chain of phases if and only if the chain is so organized that the sortals '$\mathscr{F}$', '$\mathscr{F}_1$', . . . describing a thing in adjacent phases, phase $\mathscr{F}$, phase $\mathscr{F}_1$, . . . are *restrictions of the same sortal*. Now if the relation ' "$\mathscr{F}$" restricts the same sortal as "$\mathscr{F}_1$" ' is an equivalence relation, then this relation will secure that some one underlying sortal extends from any adjacent pair of phases throughout the whole chain back to the beginning and forward to the end of this particular individual's existence.[12]

This argument seems fairly confused: branching it seems to me has little to do with the question in hand, and that little mainly concerns the Uniqueness Principle. The only remark that Wiggins here makes which supports the Restriction Principle is that a thing can be 'legitimately individuated and singled out as one thing through a chain of phases' only when the Restriction Principle is satisfied. To secure (D_2) all we need is (5.8) which leaves open the possibility that (5.9) is true. To secure (5.8) all we need is:

$$(5.10) \qquad (\exists x)(\mathscr{F}(x) \,\&\, \mathscr{F}_1(x) \,\&\, ... \,\&\, \mathscr{G}_1(x))$$

not the much stronger

$$(5.11) \qquad (\forall x)[(\mathscr{F}(x) \to \mathscr{G}_1(x)) \,\&\, (\mathscr{F}_1(x) \to \mathscr{G}_1(x)) \,\&\, ...]$$

which seems to be what Wiggins thinks we need. An example might make it clear why we do not need (5.11). Suppose we

---

[12] Ibid. (I have changed Wiggins's choice of letters for sortal constants in the interests of clarity.)

have a man (let's call him 'J. S. Mill') who was a civil servant and subsequently became an M.P. We could, of course, use 'person' as covering concept, in which case (5.11) *would* hold —for being a civil servant and being an M.P. both entail being a person. On the other hand, we could use 'husband of Harriet Taylor' as covering concept in which case (5.10) would be adequate—for neither being a civil servant nor being an M.P. entails being a husband of Harriet Taylor. Moreover, there seems little doubt that J. S. Mill is thus legitimately singled out and individuated, and without reference to 'person'. Moreover, there are cases in which, so far as I can see, no sortal superordinate to the phase sortals exists. For example, a bookshelf may be turned into a box, and although 'plank of wood' may be an adequate concept for identifying the two it is plainly not superordinate to either 'bookshelf' or 'box' but merely intersects with them. Surely the items involved—the box, the book-shelf, and the plank—are all legitimately individuated.

Shoemaker attempts to remedy the gap in Wiggins's argument. Wiggins takes no account of an object whose chequered career may consist of an $\mathcal{F}$-phase followed by a phase in which it fell under both '$\mathcal{F}$' and '$\mathcal{F}_1$' (intersection in the sense of (3.6)), followed by an $\mathcal{F}_1$-phase. This is indeed a possibility and Shoemaker makes room for it by an extension of the Restriction Principle to the effect that an individual can simultaneously fall under two sortals (i.e. in Shoemaker's terminology the 'two sortals are (or can be) simultaneously satisfied') only if there is some sortal which both restrict.[13] (Here, again, the possibility of mere intersection is ignored.) But this extension is a comparatively minor matter, and apart from it Shoemaker considers much the same case as Wiggins.

Shoemaker concludes that we 'would have a basis for [claiming that the $\mathcal{F}_1$ continues the former $\mathcal{F}$ rather than replaces it] if we knew that "$\mathcal{F}$" does . . . restrict a common sortal with "$\mathcal{F}_1$".'[14] Clearly restriction of a common sortal would be sufficient, but we so far have nothing to show that it would be necessary. Shoemaker now attempts to provide the missing link:

If it is true that an $\mathcal{F}_1$-phase can . . . , continue a former $\mathcal{F}$ in existence, presumably this must be a conceptual truth, and pre-

[13] Shoemaker, 'Wiggins on Identity', p. 110.   [14] Ibid., p. 111.

sumably it must be true in virtue of the nature of the sortal concepts '$\mathcal{F}$' and '$\mathcal{F}_1$' and their relationship to one another. It is relatively easy to see how this would be a conceptual truth if '$\mathcal{F}$' and '$\mathcal{F}_1$' were restrictions of a common sortal '$\mathcal{G}$' for then '$\mathcal{F}$' and '$\mathcal{F}_1$' would share a common criterion of identity; the principle for tracing $\mathcal{F}$s through time would be the same as the principle for tracing $\mathcal{F}_1$s through time. But it is difficult to see how any other relationship between '$\mathcal{F}$' and '$\mathcal{F}_1$' would make it a conceptual truth that an $\mathcal{F}_1$-phase can . . . continue a former $\mathcal{F}$ in existence.[15]

As Shoemaker admits, the argument is 'plausible though hardly conclusive'.[16] It seems to me, however, that its plausibility is also fairly limited unless one is prepared to accept the Restriction Principle (or something very like it) in the first place.

Shoemaker's argument depends upon two claims: (1) That it must be a conceptual truth about '$\mathcal{F}$' and '$\mathcal{F}_1$' which enables an $\mathcal{F}_1$ to keep a former $\mathcal{F}$ in existence; (2) That '$\mathcal{F}$' and '$\mathcal{F}_1$' only share a common criterion of identity when they restrict a common sortal. The latter claim, as I've argued in § 4.2, is most likely false and further comment is unnecessary until better arguments are produced in its favour. The first claim, however, is surprising and, I think, also false. Wiggins, in fact, seems to reject just such a claim, when he says: '[N]othing in the proof [of the Restriction Principle] must depend upon a certain conceptual conservatism into which no philosophical inquiry into substance and identity should find itself forced, viz., the supposition that one can tell *a priori* for any given sortal . . . whether or not it is a substance-sortal or merely a phase-sortal.'[17]

Now clearly it is a conceptual matter about two sortals whether either restricts the other and thus, if we could be sure that '$\mathcal{F}$' and '$\mathcal{F}_1$' did restrict some common sortal, we could be sure of Shoemaker's claim (1). But, in fact, we have to argue the other way: from claim (1) to the claim that '$\mathcal{F}$' and '$\mathcal{F}_1$' restrict some common sortal, and this is presumably why Shoemaker admits that his argument is plausible but not conclusive. However, its plausibility is due solely to the fact that the intersection of sortals has been neglected, for it is not a conceptual matter that two sortals intersect. It may be the

---

[15] Ibid.   [16] Ibid.
[17] *Identity and Spatio-Temporal Continuity*, fn. 37 (p. 69).

merest contingent fact that there is a sortal with which both
'$\mathscr{F}$' and '$\mathscr{F}_1$' intersect and yet, from the point of view of (D_2),
there is no reason why such a sortal, '$\mathscr{G}$', say, shouldn't be
sufficient to continue the former $\mathscr{F}$ in existence as an $\mathscr{F}_1$, the
same $\mathscr{G}$ as the former $\mathscr{F}$. Moreover, there are cases in which
'$\mathscr{F}$' and '$\mathscr{F}_1$' both *restrict* a sortal '$\mathscr{G}$' and yet we don't have
among these three sortals a covering concept which permits
the $\mathscr{F}_1$ to continue the former $\mathscr{F}$ in existence. We can easily
give an example of both cases (although an example Wiggins
would disallow for different reasons): It is possible for a bookshelf to continue a former desk in existence in the case in which
they are both the same plank of wood. Now this is certainly not
a conceptual truth for it is merely a contingent fact that the
desk and the bookshelf are made of a plank of wood (i.e. 'desk'
and 'bookshelf' both intersect, but do not restrict, 'plank of
wood'). What is a conceptual truth about 'desk' and 'bookshelf' is that they both restrict 'piece of furniture', but neither
'desk' nor 'bookshelf' nor 'piece of furniture' can be used as
covering concept to permit the bookshelf to continue the former
desk in existence. Perhaps Shoemaker means something weaker
by 'conceptual truth': for the possibility that the bookshelf
permits the former desk to continue in existence (under the
covering concept 'plank of wood') certainly depends upon its
being conceptually possible that 'desk' and 'bookshelf' intersect
with 'plank of wood'. But if this is all he means, then this
conceptual truth is easily explained without the Restriction
Principle.

It seems to me that neither Wiggins's nor Shoemaker's
arguments are correct. In fact we do not need the Restriction
Principle but rather what we might analogously call the Intersection Principle. Neither Wiggins nor Shoemaker do anything
to make us doubt the adequacy of the Intersection Principle.
The Intersection Principle, it seems to me, has much intuitive
appeal while the Restriction Principle is in fact too strong.[18]

[18] In dealing with sortals subordinate to ultimate sortals Wiggins is prepared to
avoid 'unrealistic and absurd prohibitions on cross classification' (*Identity and
Spatio-Temporal Continuity*, p. 33). In a footnote he admits that dichotomous division would ensure a classificatory system such that every class would either be
disjoint from every other class or else either restricted by or restricting some other
class. But such a classificatory system would not consist of sorts, for the complement
of a sortal is not a sortal. He also gives an example from Chomsky's *Aspects of the*

5.3 The Uniqueness Principle

In the second part of his argument Wiggins seeks to prove the Uniqueness Principle on the basis of the Restriction Principle. His major effort in this direction is to try and show that 'γ restricts the same sortal as δ' is an equivalence relation. But before we consider that argument it is worth considering Wiggins's earlier remarks quoted in (III) above which may help to put it in perspective. In (III) Wiggins argues, first, that if there were two sortals '$\mathcal{G}_1$' and '$\mathcal{G}_2$' competing to continue a former $\mathcal{F}$ in existence then branching would occur. But if an individual branches at b into c^1 and c^2 then it cannot be identical with both and thus it is identical with neither. Thus neither '$\mathcal{G}_1$' nor '$\mathcal{G}_2$' can provide the (D_2)-completing concept necessary to preserve the former $\mathcal{F}$ in existence. Then Wiggins successively deploys the Restriction Principle and the Uniqueness Principle. The Restriction Principle implies that what is required to continue the former $\mathcal{F}$ in existence through an $\mathcal{F}_1$-phase is a sortal which both '$\mathcal{F}$' and '$\mathcal{F}_1$' restrict. The Uniqueness Principle then ensures that there is not more than one such ultimate sortal and thus that branching is prohibited. This is not (and does not, I think, profess to be) a logically valid argument for the Restriction and Uniqueness Principles, but rather a persuasive appeal to the principles as principles which avoid undesirable results. (Wiggins has done nothing so far to show that they are the only such principles.) But I doubt that Wiggins's argument gets us even this far. I cannot see that allowing a choice of sortals for continuing the former $\mathcal{F}$ in existence commits one to branching, for surely we might have $b_{\mathcal{F}_1} =_{\mathcal{G}_1} c$ and $b_{\mathcal{F}_1} =_{\mathcal{G}_2} c$, even though $\sim (\mathcal{G}_1 \approx \mathcal{G}_2)$, and no case of branching results here. Branching is, I think, an entirely illusory penalty for the failure of the Uniqueness Principle.

The main part of Wiggins's argument for the Uniqueness Principle is his attempt to prove that '$R(\gamma, \delta)$' is an equivalence relation. Given that, and the Restriction Principle's requirement that '$\mathcal{F}$', '$\mathcal{F}_1$', and '$\mathcal{F}_2$' all restrict the same sortal, he can prove the Uniqueness Principle, i.e. that they cannot all restrict more than one sortal. To prove that '$R(\gamma, \delta)$' is an

Theory of Syntax (Cambridge, Mass.: M.I.T. Press, 1965), p. 80, to illustrate cross-classification among sorts (ibid., fn. 39 [pp. 70–1]). It is surprising that he assumes, without argument, that such features do not extend to ultimate sortals.

equivalence relation he has to prove that it is reflexive, sym-metrical, and transitive. Proving symmetry and reflexivity is easy: If '$\mathscr{F}$' restricts the same sortal as '$\mathscr{F}_1$' then '$\mathscr{F}_1$' restricts the same sortal as '$\mathscr{F}$'; and '$\mathscr{F}$' restricts the same sortal as '$\mathscr{F}$'. Transitivity gives more trouble. The case Wiggins has to rule out is that in which '$\mathscr{F}$' restricts the same sortal as '$\mathscr{F}_1$', namely '$\mathscr{G}_1$', and '$\mathscr{F}_1$' restricts the same sortal as '$\mathscr{F}_2$', namely '$\mathscr{G}_2$', where $\sim (\mathscr{G}_1 \approx \mathscr{G}_2)$ and $\sim (\exists h)(\mathscr{G}_1 \subseteq h \,\&\, \mathscr{G}_2 \subseteq h)$. The situation may be represented

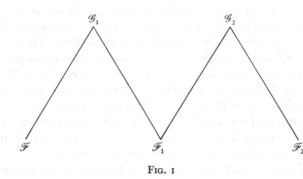

Fig. 1

We can immediately rule out dummy sortals and the disjunc-tive term '$\mathscr{F}_1 \vee \mathscr{F}_2$' as sortals superordinate to '$\mathscr{F}_1$' and '$\mathscr{F}_2$'. Again, I quote Wiggins's argument at length, it is impressive in its obscurity:

To be an $\mathscr{F}_1$ is on present suppositions to be a $\mathscr{G}_1$ which is ϕ or a $\mathscr{G}_2$ which is ψ, for some ϕ and ψ or other. Now either the sortals '$\mathscr{G}_1$', '$\mathscr{G}_2$' are so related that

$[\alpha]$ $\qquad (\forall x)(\forall y)[(\mathscr{G}_1(x) \,\&\, \mathscr{G}_2(x)) \supset (x =_{\mathscr{G}_1} y \equiv x =_{\mathscr{G}_2} y)]$

or they are not. If they are not, and if '$\mathscr{F}_1$' were nevertheless allowed the status of legitimate sortal and were a possible covering concept, then nothing would have been done to exclude the possibility of an object a's being classified as an $\mathscr{F}_1$, found to coincide under '$\mathscr{G}_1$' with b, and found to coincide under '$\mathscr{G}_2$' with an object c such that $(\forall f) \sim (b =_f c)$ . . . So if we reject the logical possibility of branch-ing, this option obliges us to reject '$\mathscr{F}_1$' altogether as a sortal . . . But we had supposed it was a sortal.[19]

[19] Ibid., p. 33. Again, I have altered some of the letters Wiggins used for sortals in the interests of clarity. The first 'or' in the first sentence of the quoted passage should read 'and' for we are supposing that '$\mathscr{F}_1$' restricts both '$\mathscr{G}_1$' and '$\mathscr{G}_2$'.

It is difficult to see quite what role $[\alpha]$ has to play in this argument, except as a formal principle prohibiting branching.[20] However, we should try and piece together the argument a bit at a time. Let's consider, first, why branching is bad. As far as I can see, Wiggins must have something like the following *reductio* argument in mind. ($[1]$–$[3]$ are the conditions for branching.)

$$[1] \quad a =_{\mathscr{G}_1} b \qquad\qquad \text{(premiss)}$$
$$[2] \quad a =_{\mathscr{G}_2} c \qquad\qquad \text{(premiss)}$$
$$[3] \quad (\forall f) \sim (b =_f c) \qquad\qquad \text{(premiss)}$$
$$[4] \quad (a =_{\mathscr{G}_2} c) \supset \mathscr{G}_2(a) \qquad\qquad \text{(premiss)}$$
$$[5] \quad \mathscr{G}_2(a) \supset a =_{\mathscr{G}_2} a \qquad\qquad \text{(premiss)}$$
$$[6] \quad a =_{\mathscr{G}_2} b \qquad ([1],\ \text{subst. of } '\zeta =_{\mathscr{G}_1} \eta',\ [2]\ [4]\ [5],\ \text{M.P.})$$
$$[7] \quad b =_{\mathscr{G}_2} c \qquad\qquad ([6]\ [2],\ \text{Symm. Trans., M.P.})$$
$$[8] \quad b =_{\mathscr{G}_2} c\ \&\ \sim (b =_{\mathscr{G}_2} c) \qquad ([3],\ \text{U.I. } \mathscr{G}_2/f,\ [7],\ \text{Conj.})$$

Lines $[4]$ and $[5]$ are plainly unexceptionable theses of any relative identity theory. However, in the derivation of $[6]$ we have used a principle of substitutivity of relative identity which has not been made explicit. The principle Wiggins probably intends is the one he's used earlier in the book[21] and which we rendered as (DLL). But as we noted in § 1.5, if (DLL) holds then (R) is ruled out. The (R)-relativist, as we shall see, is perfectly happy to admit the logical possibility of splitting. Wiggins makes it clear that his argument presupposes the denial of (R)[22] yet if the conclusion to his argument is correct there will certainly be a temptation to use it as a means of dismantling those cases of (R) which result from employing ultimate sortals as covering concepts. Moreover, we cannot lessen the dependence of Wiggins's argument on the denial of (R) by employing $[\alpha]$, rather than (DLL), to rule out splitting since $[\alpha]$ is true only if (R) is false. But, for the sake of argument, let's grant Wiggins's prohibition on splitting: can he now prove the transitivity of '$R(\gamma, \delta)$'?

Suppose that we have some individual a such that

$$(5.12) \qquad\qquad \mathscr{F}_1(a)$$

---

[20] Cf. Shoemaker's puzzlement on the same issue, 'Wiggins on Identity', p. 112.
[21] Namely, his formula (1) on p. 3 of *Identity and Spatio-Temporal Continuity*.
[22] Ibid., pp. 30, 34.

is true. Since '$\mathscr{F}_1$' restricts both '$\mathscr{G}_1$' and '$\mathscr{G}_2$' we have:

(5.13) $\mathscr{G}_1(a)$ & $\mathscr{G}_2(a)$

which gives us the condition for intersection:

(5.14) $(\exists x)(\mathscr{G}_1(x)$ & $\mathscr{G}_2(x))$.

If a is a $\mathscr{G}_1$ then it must be the same $\mathscr{G}_1$ as some $\mathscr{G}_1$, and similarly for '$\mathscr{G}_2$'. This gives:

(5.15) $(\exists x)(x =_{\mathscr{G}_1} a)$

(5.16) $(\exists x)(x =_{\mathscr{G}_2} a)$

and thus:

(5.17) $b =_{\mathscr{G}_1} a$

(5.18) $c =_{\mathscr{G}_2} a$

which are the first two conditions for splitting. Now presumably Wiggins's argument is that the situation envisaged in Fig. 1 *requires* splitting. That is, requires in addition to (5.17) and (5.18):

(5.19) $(\forall f) \sim (b =_f c)$.

The rest of his argument is a *reductio*. The situation in Fig. 1 requires splitting, splitting can be ruled out, therefore the situation in Fig. 1 can be ruled out. But the fact that things are as presented in Fig. 1 doesn't force us to accept (5.19), for it may be that b and c lie in the intersection of '$\mathscr{G}_1$' and '$\mathscr{G}_2$' and, moreover, may be such that either

(5.20) $b =_{\mathscr{G}_1} c$

or

(5.21) $b =_{\mathscr{G}_2} c$

is true. In either case the need to accept (5.19) and consequently the allegedly undesirable case of splitting is avoided. Thus even if we prohibit splitting it is still possible to get situations in which a sortal '$\mathscr{F}_1$' restricts both '$\mathscr{G}_1$' and '$\mathscr{G}_2$' which are neither co-ordinate nor restrict a common sortal.

Shoemaker has an alternative argument which seeks to prove the Uniqueness Principle on the basis of the Restriction Principle. For this argument he employs a very obscure premiss:

(IV)   Where two sortals '$\mathscr{F}$' and '$\mathscr{G}$' are such that an $\mathscr{F}$ and a $\mathscr{G}$ can exactly coincide at a given time, that is, can occupy exactly the same place at the same time, what will show them not to be cosatisfiable will be the fact that a particular $\mathscr{F}$ and a particular $\mathscr{G}$ can coincide at one time without coinciding throughout their histories.[23]

Given (IV) Shoemaker's argument proceeds as follows (the sortals involved are related as shown in Fig. 1 and Shoemaker's aim is to prove that '$\mathscr{G}_1$' and '$\mathscr{G}_2$' restrict some one common sortal):

[(IV)] implies that if sortals '$\mathscr{G}_1$' and '$\mathscr{G}_2$' are cosatisfiable [i.e. are such that a single individual may simultaneously fall under both] they must be such that it is necessarily the case that a $\mathscr{G}_1$ and [a] $\mathscr{G}_2$ cannot coincide at one time without coinciding throughout their histories. And this can be so only if '$\mathscr{G}_1$' and '$\mathscr{G}_2$' share the same criterion of identity, the same principle for tracing their instances through space and time. They will share the same criterion of identity if they restrict a common sortal (as was noted in the argument for [the Restriction Principle]) and it is difficult to see how else they could do so.[24]

Now much here depends upon whether my gloss on 'cosatisfiable' is correct. It seems to me that it must be.[25] But on this reading (IV) is plainly false. Consider the sortals 'BMC car' and 'yellow car', according to (IV) these are not cosatisfiable because cars may be resprayed and thus, though a yellow car and a BMC car may coincide at a certain time, it doesn't follow that they coincide throughout their histories. Thus there cannot be one individual which is simultaneously a yellow car and a BMC car. But this is simply false. On the other hand, to strengthen the notion of cosatisfiability to ensure the truth of (IV) would require: '$\mathscr{F}$' and '$\mathscr{G}$' are cosatisfiable iff

$$(\forall x)(\forall t)[(\mathscr{F}(x,t) \ \& \ \mathscr{G}(x,t)) \supset (\forall t')(\mathscr{F}(x,t') \supset \mathscr{G}(x,t'))].$$

But if we use (IV) with this sense of 'cosatisfiability' in Shoemaker's subsequent argument, we are not entitled to assume

[23] 'Wiggins on Identity', p. 113.   [24] Ibid.
[25] Cf. Shoemaker's remark, ibid., p. 112: '"$\mathscr{G}_1$" and "$\mathscr{G}_2$" . . . could fail to be so related that something can be, at one and the same time, both a $\mathscr{G}_1$ and a $\mathscr{G}_2$. Or, as we might put it, they could fail to be "cosatisfiable". But in that case they could not both be restricted by "$\mathscr{F}_1$". . . .' This plainly suggests that '$\mathscr{F}$' and '$\mathscr{G}$' are cosatisfiable iff $(\exists t)(\exists x)[R_t(\mathscr{F}(x)) \ \& \ R_t(\mathscr{G}(x))]$, i.e. the intersection relation given by (3.6).

that '$\mathcal{G}_1$' and '$\mathcal{G}_2$' are cosatisfiable simply because both are restricted by '$\mathcal{F}_1$'.

If we use Shoemaker's weak sense of 'cosatisfiable', *and* permit him (IV) *and* some unstated assumptions about criteria of identity then his argument would be valid. '$\mathcal{F}_1$' restricts both '$\mathcal{G}_1$' and '$\mathcal{G}_2$' and hence '$\mathcal{G}_1$' and '$\mathcal{G}_2$' are cosatisfiable by definition (for every $\mathcal{F}_1$ must coincide with a $\mathcal{G}_1$ and a $\mathcal{G}_2$). But if a $\mathcal{G}_1$ and a $\mathcal{G}_2$ ever coincide then, by (IV), they always coincide. He then needs two assumptions: (1) That a $\mathcal{G}_1$ and a $\mathcal{G}_2$ always coincide only when '$\mathcal{G}_1$' and '$\mathcal{G}_2$' convey the same criteria of identity; (2) That '$\mathcal{G}_1$' and '$\mathcal{G}_2$' can only convey the same criteria of identity when they restrict some common sortal. This will give him his conclusion as stated, but not the Uniqueness Principle which he hoped for. That would require a third principle about criteria of identity, possibly: (3) No two ultimate sortals share a criterion of identity. Whether or not he can hold both (IV) and his weak definition of 'cosatisfiability', of his three assumptions about criteria of identity only the third is correct.

The devious arguments employed by Wiggins and Shoemaker to pass from the Restriction Principle to the Uniqueness Principle are, however, unnecessary. Given (5.2) there is a straightforward proof that '$R(\gamma, \delta)$' is an equivalence relation and thence to the Uniqueness Principle.[26] Suppose that $R(\mathcal{F}_1, \mathcal{F}_2)$ and $R(\mathcal{F}_2, \mathcal{F}_3)$ then, for some sortal '$\mathcal{G}_1$', $\mathcal{F}_1 \subseteq \mathcal{G}_1$ and $\mathcal{F}_2 \subseteq \mathcal{G}_1$ and, for some sortal '$\mathcal{G}_2$', $\mathcal{F}_2 \subseteq \mathcal{G}_2$ and $\mathcal{F}_3 \subseteq \mathcal{G}_2$. But since all $\mathcal{F}_2$s are both $\mathcal{G}_1$s and $\mathcal{G}_2$s, we have $\mathcal{G}_1 |_\tau \mathcal{G}_2$ and hence by (5.2) $R(\mathcal{G}_1, \mathcal{G}_2)$. Thus, for some sortal '$\mathcal{H}$', $\mathcal{G}_1 \subseteq \mathcal{H}$ and $\mathcal{G}_2 \subseteq \mathcal{H}$ and so $\mathcal{F}_1 \subseteq \mathcal{H}$ and $\mathcal{F}_3 \subseteq \mathcal{H}$ (by transitivity of '$\gamma \subseteq \delta$') and thus $R(\mathcal{F}_1, \mathcal{F}_3)$, by (4.5). Hence '$R(\gamma, \delta)$' is transitive, and since it is also symmetrical and reflexive it is an equivalence relation.

What this proves is that (5.2) as well as (5.3), the Restriction Principle as well as the Uniqueness Principle, is false, for:

$$(5.22) \qquad R(\mathcal{F}, \mathcal{F}_1) \ \& \ R(\mathcal{F}_1, \mathcal{F}_2) \supset R(\mathcal{F}, \mathcal{F}_2)$$

is simply false. It is an easy matter to construct a counter-example with Euler diagrams (see Fig. 2). Thus '$R(\gamma, \delta)$' cannot be an

---

[26] The argument is due to Stevenson, 'Extensional and Intensional Logic for Sortal-Relative Identity', p. 10.

equivalence relation, and hence we may not assume that if '$\mathscr{F}$' and '$\mathscr{F}_1$' restrict '$\mathscr{G}_1$', and '$\mathscr{F}_1$' and '$\mathscr{F}_2$' restrict '$\mathscr{G}_2$' there must be just one sortal which both '$\mathscr{F}$' and '$\mathscr{F}_2$' restrict. There may, indeed, be none or there may be more than one. Of course, Fig. 2 is just what the Restriction Principle was designed to exclude, but since we have no valid argument for the Restriction Principle this is hardly a matter of concern.

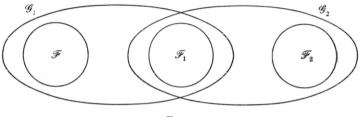

Fig. 2

Let me try and summarize the results of this tortuous discussion. In the first place Wiggins thinks that in order to secure (5.5) he needs to show that there can be only one ultimate sortal under which any individual falls and that it falls under that sortal throughout its career. In fact, (5.5) only requires that there be at least one sortal under which an individual falls throughout its career. Moreover, (D$_2$) does not require anything more than (5.5). Secondly, Wiggins thinks that all the sortals under which an individual successively falls must restrict some sortal under which it falls throughout its career. But this, also, is too strong: all that is required is that they intersect with an appropriate sortal. His acceptance of the Restriction Principle is largely unargued and plainly mistaken. Thirdly, his argument that '$R(\gamma, \delta)$' is an equivalence relation is based on the rejection of splitting which in turn relies upon the denial of (R). Fourthly, even if we agree to ban splitting as well as accepting the Restriction Principle there is nothing in the situation we are seeking to avoid (Fig. 1) which entails a violation of that ban. Thus a mere ban on splitting will not help us to avoid the situation shown in Fig. 1. Finally, the relation 'γ restricts the same sortal as δ' is plainly not an equivalence relation since it fails transitivity. Thus, I see no objection to holding that a single individual may successively fall under '$\mathscr{F}$',

'$\mathscr{F}_1$', '$\mathscr{F}_2$', ... where there is no sortal which they all restrict. Nor do I see any objection to holding that a given sortal '$\mathscr{F}$' may restrict two (or more) ultimate sortals which intersect but are not co-ordinate. Sortals in natural language do not, in fact, behave in the neat way Wiggins (and Shoemaker) suppose.

6

(D)-Relative Identity Theory

6.1 Two Irrelevant (D)-Theses

It is now time to consider the second of the two questions raised in § 1.4. What (if anything) is wrong with absolute identity claims which makes them incomplete in a way which can be remedied by the addition of a general noun? In this section I want to note two ways in which absolute identity statements are *not* incomplete, at least not in the way we're interested in.

In the first place the incompleteness we are concerned with is not syntactic, at least as far as English is concerned. There may, as Nelson points out,[1] be some ungrammaticality in saying 'Cicero is the same as Tully' but such ungrammaticality is certainly marginal, and even if we think that this sentence is ungrammatical we can certainly think of others of the same form which cannot be objected to on this ground. Thus what incompleteness there is in English statements having this form must be semantic incompleteness. Of course, in a formal theory of identity neither '$a = b$' nor any other string of symbols expressing absolute identity need be a wff but this would be a disadvantage if the theory was intended as a canonical language for natural language identity statements, *unless* we had grounds for thinking the natural language analogues of '$a = b$' in some way defective.

The second point, also due to Nelson,[2] is that the incompleteness of 'a is the same as b' cannot wholly be on account of the ambiguity that this sentence has between qualitative and numerical, or between type and token, identity. The reason is not that just the same sort of ambiguity infects 'a is identical with b' for this sentence, in ordinary language, just as often

[1] Jack Nelson, 'On the Alleged Incompleteness of Certain Identity Claims', *Canadian Journal of Philosophy*, 3 (1973), 106.   [2] Ibid.

conveys qualitative as numerical identity. In the two best known relative identity theories, those of Geach and Wiggins, the incompleteness remains in sentences such as '*a* is the same thing as *b*' where numerical identity is plainly intended. It may be possible to fashion some third theory in which such sentences weren't incomplete and for such a theory the incompleteness of '*a* is the same as *b*' may be wholly or in part due to its ambiguity between qualitative and numerical identity. It is this sort of incompleteness which could be rectified by (D_1), which allows completion by any type of general noun. But it is not the sort of incompleteness we are interested in.

6.2 The Relation between (R) and (D)[3]

Whether we claim that there's anything wrong with '*a* is the same as *b*' or not we have to admit that in ordinary English statements of this form are expansible into statements of the form '*a* is the same $\mathscr{A}$ as *b*'; we can expand 'Cicero is the same as Tully' into 'Cicero is the same man as Tully'. Indeed, we can claim that for any such true statement there is such an expansion, and in general there will be more than one such. Thus, in general,

(6.1)   *a* is the same as *b*

may be expanded either as

(6.2)   *a* is the same $\mathscr{A}$ as *b*

or as

(6.3)   *a* is the same $\mathscr{B}$ as *b*.

Now, if (R) is true there is no reason to assume that (6.2) and (6.3) have the same truth-value. So let us assume that (6.2) is true and (6.3) is false. Then it is often argued that (6.1) as it stands has no determinate truth-value because it could be read either as (6.2) or as (6.3). This, then, seems to be one way of establishing a type of incompleteness of sentences of the form (6.1). If the argument is valid, then (R) entails (D).[4]

---

[3] I am grateful to Richard Routley for many important points in this section.

[4] This view has been accepted by both (R)-relativists and (D)-relativists. Cf. for example, Peter Sheehan, 'The Relativity of Identity', p. 27, and '*De Re*

The argument, however, is not valid. Firstly, we have done nothing to show that (6.1) does not have a truth-value of its own. From the fact that 'James is reading a book' can be expanded either to 'James is reading a book by Lytton' or to 'James is reading a book by Virginia' we can't infer that the original has no determinate truth-value (despite the fact that here the two expansions must differ in truth-value and it could not be the case that James is reading a book which isn't by somebody or other). Even in cases of sentences of clearly indeterminate truth-value (e.g. 'I was shocked by the shooting of the Marines') the indeterminacy is not proved simply by the fact that there are two readings of the original. Of course, if there were not the possibility of the two readings then there would be no indeterminacy but that merely shows that if there is an indeterminacy then there is the possibility of two readings;[5] *not* that if there is a possibility of two readings then there is an indeterminacy. Secondly, the (R)-relativist is not claiming that (6.2) and (6.3) will always differ in truth-value but only that they sometimes may do so. Accordingly, even if the inference pattern were valid, the relativist is only entitled to infer from (R) that (6.1) is *sometimes* indeterminate as to truth-value. On those occasions on which the possible expansions do not conflict in truth-value we have shown no indeterminacy in (6.1).

There are at least three ways in which we can analyse '$a = b$' in a way consistent with (R), and the first two are also consistent with (LL). The first is simply to define '$a = b$' by (LL). Even in a classical, applied, second-order logic it is possible to introduce definitions for both absolute and relative identity such that (R) is satisfiable and the consistency of the logic preserved.[6] The second way, is to say that $a = b$ iff a and b are the same in all respects. This is *not* captured by:

$$(6.4) \qquad a = b \equiv (\forall a)(a =_a b)$$

Modality' (Unpublished, 1972). Also Wiggins, *Identity and Spatio-Temporal Continuity*, p. 1. Geach, it should be noted, does not employ this argument. Indeed, he seems rather to argue from (D) to (R), but sometimes it looks as if he only does this because he feels that (D) would be inexplicable without (R). See his somewhat grudging admission of (R) in *Reference and Generality*, p. 157.

   5 This seems to be Geach's argument. Cf. *Reference and Generality*, p. 157.
   6 See Routley and Griffin, 'Towards a Logic of Relative Identity'.

for the right-hand side of (6.4) is always false, since a and b do not fall under every general noun. Instead we need:[7]

$$(6.5) \qquad a = b \equiv (\forall a)[(a(a) \ \& \ a(b)) \supset a =_a b]$$

that is, if a and b are the same then they are the same with respect to every general noun under which both fall. I shall call this the $(\forall a)$-account of '$a = b$'. Clearly, even if '$a = b$' were indeterminate in truth-conditions if expansions with different truth-values were available this would not affect the case where '$a = b$' was glossed by (6.5) for no conflicts of truth-value among possible expansions could arise in that case. Moreover, $(\forall \phi)(\phi(a) \equiv \phi(b)) \supset (\forall a)(a(a) \ \& \ a(b) \supset. \ a =_a b)$. (The converse, however, would require additional assumptions.) Thus the second policy is a weaker form of the first and its consistency within classical second-order logic is guaranteed by that of the first.[8]

It may be objected that (6.5) is not a natural interpretation to place on a statement of the form (6.1). If someone says, for example, 'John's car is the same as Bill's', it may seem more natural to say that there is some respect in which John's car and Bill's car are the same. This third view may be generally stated thus:[9]

$$(6.6) \qquad\qquad a = b \supset (\exists a)(a =_a b).$$

Together with the converse implication we get (the $(\exists a)$-account of '$a = b$'):[10]

$$(6.7) \qquad\qquad a = b \equiv (\exists a)(a =_a b)$$

which would enable us to assign definite truth-conditions to statements of the form (6.1). The trouble with (6.6) and (6.7) is that if we run them in conjunction with (LL) we can derive Wiggins's formula (DLL) which rules out (R). We might,

---

[7] In (6.5) there may still be problems with the range of the second-order quantifier. If it includes intensional general nouns (e.g. 'object of Bill's thought') it may well impose too strong a condition on '$a = b$'.

[8] On either of these two policies, of course, given that $a = b$ we cannot form a case of (R) using a and b. But this does not matter since the (R)-relativist is not claiming that for every true $\mathcal{A}$-identity statement, '$a =_{\mathcal{A}} b$', there is a true $\mathcal{B}$-distinctness statement, '$\sim (a =_{\mathcal{B}} b)$'.

[9] Wiggins, *Identity and Spatio-Temporal Continuity*, p. 28 adopts (6.6) but limits covering concepts to sortals.

[10] Odegard, 'Identity Through Time', p. 30 adopts (6.7) but, like Wiggins, limits covering concepts to sortals.

however, keep (6.6) or (6.7) and (R) so long as we do not interpret '$\zeta = \eta$' as it is interpreted in the absolute theory but as an (unspecified) relative identity relation.[11] There is still, of course, an indeterminacy in (6.1) when it is interpreted in this way for it does not tell us in which respect a and b are the same, but this is not as damaging as an indeterminacy of truth-conditions. It amounts merely to the fact that (6.1) is not so informative as (6.2) or (6.3), but there is no reason why every statement should attain some arbitrary standard of informativeness. (Compare 'James is reading a book' and 'James is reading a book by Lytton'.)

Moreover, even this lack of informativeness in (6.1) may be remedied by context. Geach makes allowance for cases in which (6.1) appears in a context which makes clear in which respect the identity is intended.[12] If a formal theory of relative identity is to be completely adequate for natural language it will have to be placed within a context logic. The technical details of such a programme, however, are very difficult,[13] and in what follows I shall largely ignore context and concentrate on a context-free theory of relative identity (which will be difficult enough).

It may be, however, that this discussion misses the relativists' main point. Perhaps there is a third thesis which helps bridge the gap between (D) and (R). Dummett suggests a candidate. Even if (6.1) is ambiguous this does not mean that 'same' is ambiguous; any more than the ambiguity of 'I was shocked by the shooting of the Marines' shows that 'shooting' is ambiguous. Dummett argues that 'same' and other polygamous terms such as 'good' and 'real' are univocal but 'represent a kind of operator which forms, from a given general term, another general term whose sense is uniformly related to that of the original general term.'[14] Now if we can treat 'ζ is the same . . . as η' as a function from general nouns to relations, we can treat 'a is the same . . . as b' as a function from general nouns to truth-values. Let us call this second view the *function thesis*. The function thesis clearly entails (D) and is consistent with (R).

11 See Odegard's non-(LL) account of the indiscernibility of identicals in 'Identity Through Time', p. 36; and my discussion in § 8.2.
12 For example in 'Identity', p. 238.
13 See Goddard and Routley, *The Logic of Significance and Context*.
14 Dummett, *Frege*, p. 550.

Dummett attributes the function thesis to Geach but Geach, in a personal communication, has disowned it. At one time, however, he did adopt a similar thesis concerning 'good'. He compared 'ζ is good' with 'ζ is the square of':

There is no one number by which you can always multiply a number to get its square: but it does not follow either that 'square of' is an ambiguous expression meaning sometimes 'double of', sometimes 'treble of', etc., or that you have to do something other than multiplying to find the square of a number; and, given a number, its square is determinate.[15]

But even if the function thesis does not have Geach's support it is still worth considering on its own merits. It does have the advantage of yielding (in conjunction with some plausible assumptions about sense) Geach's (D)-thesis that absolute identity statements lack clear sense. The function thesis directly gives us a strong (D)-thesis, namely:

(D. I)   Absolute identity statements are indeterminate in truth-conditions.

And from (D. I) we can derive an even stronger version of (D) if we are prepared to accept certain views about meaning. In particular, if we accept Davidson's theory that 'to give truth conditions is a way of giving the meaning of a sentence'[16] we can get from (D. I) to Geach's claim that absolute identity statements lack clear meaning or fully determinate sense. This is not implausible but largely depends upon what view of meaning one has. There is a sense in which 'a is the same as b', like '625 is the square of', is significant, for it is composed of significant units correctly concatenated.

The function thesis plainly derives its plausibility from (R). Again using the analogy with 'ζ is the square of': '$(\zeta)^2$' is a function since it yields different values as it takes different numbers as arguments. Similarly, if (R) is true, $a =_\gamma b$ yields different truth-values as different general nouns fill its argument place. But (R) is neither necessary nor sufficient for the function thesis. It is not necessary because we could still hold that $a =_\gamma b$ was a function even if it always yielded the same truth-value what-

---

[15] Geach, 'Good and Evil', *Analysis*, 17 (1956), 38. The point could be generalized to any polygamous predicate.
[16] Donald Davidson, 'Truth and Meaning', *Synthese*, 17 (1967), 310.

ever general noun it took as argument. (Just as we treat $(\zeta)^0$ as a function even though it always yields the same value whatever argument it takes.) A function is not identical with its value even if its value is constant. (R) is not sufficient for the function thesis because we might hold (as Geach in fact does) that in '$a =_{\mathscr{A}} b$' we cannot separate the '$=$' and the '$\mathscr{A}$' any more than we can separate the 'of' and the 'brother' in 'Lytton is brother of James'. In this case it couldn't be that '$a =_\gamma b$' is a function from general nouns to truth-values. This alternative will be considered in the next section.

6.3 The Fregean Analysis

If '$\phi_{\mathscr{A}}(\zeta^1,...,\zeta^n)$' is an n-ary polygamous predicate it cannot, in general, be analysed as '$\phi(\zeta^1,...,\zeta^n)$ & $\mathscr{A}(\zeta^1)$ & ... & $\mathscr{A}(\zeta^n)$'. For example, 'ζ is a good burglar' cannot be analysed as 'ζ is good & ζ is a burglar'. Frege clearly recognized this in connection with 'ζ is one $\mathscr{A}$', which certainly cannot be analysed as 'ζ is one & $\mathscr{A}(\zeta)$'.[17] But, equally clearly, he did hold that the relative identity relation 'ζ is the same $\mathscr{A}$ as η' could be analysed as '$\mathscr{A}(\zeta)$ & $\mathscr{A}(\eta)$ & $\zeta = \eta$'.[18] In his honour, therefore, I shall call this the Fregean analysis of relative identity relations. Now the Fregean analysis does not work for all relative identity relations: for example

(6.8) John's car is the same colour as Bill's car.

cannot be analysed as:

(6.9) John's car is a colour & Bill's car is a colour & John's car is the same as Bill's car.

So we can't uphold the Fregean analysis as a general principle, and we need to be clear about its scope. In view of (6.8) it has been claimed[19] that the analysis fails for common-property statements as distinct from 'genuine' identity statements. This then requires some account of what a 'genuine' identity statement is. The matter is not easy[20] and one is tempted to suppose that we can mark off 'genuine' identity statements by the alleged fact that the Fregean analysis works for them and not

---

[17] Frege, *The Foundations of Arithmetic*, p. 40.
[18] Frege, *Grundgesetze der Arithmetik*, vol. ii, p. 254.
[19] For example, Perry, 'Identity', p. 22.
[20] I shall return to it in § 10.3.

for common-property statements. This approach, of course, does not help us get clear about the scope of the Fregean analysis.

If the Fregean analysis is not always applicable, is it ever applicable? Whether we are relativists or not the relative identity relations 'ζ is the same car as η' and 'ζ is the same number as η' are different both in content and extension, for:

(6.10)   John's car is the same car as Bill's but they are not the same number.

can surely be true. The Fregean analysis seeks to analyse both in terms of the same relation and this has a certain amount of initial implausibility, which might, however, be entirely superficial and could scarcely be more worrying than the univocity of 'same' in the function thesis. The relations 'ζ is a left-handed brother of η' and 'ζ is a red-haired brother of η' are different in content and extension and yet both may be similarly analysed: the first as 'ζ is left-handed & ζ is a brother of η' and the second as 'ζ is red-haired & ζ is a brother of η'. As Perry puts it: 'If we take the relation to be what is expressed by any open sentence having more than one argument position, then different relations are involved [in (6.10), for example]. But if we recognize that many such open sentences express something complex, only part of which is relational in a straight-forward sense we may claim the relations expressed are the same.'[21] For contrast Perry considers 'ζ is a better golfer than η', and 'ζ is a better swimmer than η' both of which are different in content and extension and which do not analyse into 'ζ is a golfer & ζ is better than η' and 'ζ is a swimmer & ζ is better than η'. The question is: Which is 'ζ is the same $\mathscr{A}$ as η' more like, 'ζ is a left-handed brother of η' or 'ζ is a better golfer than η'?

One test which Perry gives to help us decide is the following (though I'm not sure how much weight he wishes to place on it): 'it does not follow from "x is a better golfer than y" and "x is a swimmer" that "x is a better swimmer than y" ' whereas 'it follows from "x is a left-handed brother of y" and "x is red-

[21] 'Identity', p. 24. The examples are from ibid., pp. 24–5; see also Perry, 'The Same F', *Philosophical Review*, 79 (1970), 183–4. Interestingly enough, although Perry is arguing against (R), his comments generate a case of (R): for in his first sense of 'relation' there are two relations in (6.10), while (if he's right about the Fregean analysis) in his second sense of 'relation' there is only one.

haired" that "x is a red-haired brother of y".'[22] Does the parallel inference for 'a is the same $\mathscr{A}$ as b' go through or not? There are strong grounds for saying that it does not: from 'a is the same type word as b' and 'a is a token word' it does not follow that 'a is the same token word as b'. Clearly the inference fails if (R) is true, but not if it is false.

If we accept absolute identity theory and wish to encompass the relative identity statements of natural language within it then we have to accept either the Fregean analysis or some comparable principle to analyse relative identity statements into absolute ones.[23] If the absolute theory has to rely on the Fregean analysis, this will surely count against the theory since, as we've seen, the Fregean analysis at best is not universally applicable and thus we won't be able to use it to fit all relative identity relations into the absolute theory, and, moreover, there seems to be no non-arbitrary way to fix the limits of its applicability. Perry, for example, clearly accepts the principle but only argues for it through an argument in favour of the absolute theory.

On an (R)-relative identity theory the Fregean analysis has to be rejected on pain of contradiction. For if we can analyse '$a =_{\mathscr{A}} b$' as '$\mathscr{A}(a)$ & $\mathscr{A}(b)$ & $a = b$' then, for reasons of symmetry, we should be able to analyse '$a \neq_{\mathscr{A}} b$' as '$\mathscr{A}(a)$ & $\mathscr{A}(b)$ & $\sim (a = b)$'.[24] (We do not, however, have to accept it as an analysis of '$\sim (a =_{\mathscr{A}} b)$' which could be analysed as '$\sim \mathscr{A}(a)$ $\vee \sim \mathscr{A}(b) \vee \sim (a = b)$'.) Indeed, if we wish to use the Fregean analysis to reduce relative identity statements to absolute identity statements we shall have to employ both halves of the analysis. Failure to do that would simply show that the absolute identity theory was inadequate for expressing natural language identity statements. There is no difficulty in doing this with a case of (R) such as '$a =_{\mathscr{A}} b$ & $\sim (a =_{\mathscr{B}} b)$' since this might be analysed as '$\mathscr{A}(a)$ & $\mathscr{A}(b)$ & $a = b$ & $(\sim \mathscr{B}(a) \vee \sim \mathscr{B}(b))$' which gives rise to no contradiction. But if we have

$$(6.11) \qquad\qquad a =_{\mathscr{A}} b \ \& \ a \neq_{\mathscr{A}} b$$

[22] 'Identity', p. 25; 'The Same F', p. 185.

[23] The only alternative known to me will be considered in § 7.4.

[24] It will be helpful to introduce here a notational distinction due to Stevenson ('A Formal Theory of Sortal Quantification', p. 195) between '$\sim (a =_{\mathscr{A}} b)$' for '$a$ is not the same $\mathscr{A}$ as b' where possibly '$\sim \mathscr{A}(a) \vee \sim \mathscr{A}(b)$' and '$a \neq_{\mathscr{A}} b$' for '$a$ is a different $\mathscr{A}$ to b' where '$\mathscr{A}(a)$ & $\mathscr{A}(b)$'.

as our example of (R), both halves of the Fregean analysis give:

(6.12) $\mathscr{A}(a)$ & $\mathscr{A}(b)$ & $\mathscr{B}(a)$ & $\mathscr{B}(b)$ & $a = b$ & $\sim (a = b)$.

Moreover, even if we only accept the first half of the Fregean analysis as a means of converting relative identity statements into absolute identity statements a contradiction arises. If the first half of the Fregean analysis holds, we have '$a =_{\mathscr{A}} b$' implies '$a = b$'. But if (LL) defines absolute identity then this gives us Wiggins's formula (DLL) which is incompatible with (R). On the other hand, if (LL) does not give an account of the '$a = b$' produced by the first half of the Fregean analysis then the Fregean analysis has been used in vain, since it does not produce absolute identity statements out of relative ones. To avoid the contradiction, the (R)-relativist has to avoid the proposed analysis by adding the principle:[25]

(D₀) Statements of the form '$a =_{\mathscr{A}} b$' do not analyse into '$\mathscr{A}(a)$ & $\mathscr{A}(b)$ & $a = b$'.

Now it looks as if the relativist who accepts (D) will object to the Fregean analysis solely because he rejects statements of the form '$a = b$'. This is what Wiggins does as we shall see in the next chapter.[26] But Geach's view is a bit more complex. Geach distinguishes predicative uses of sortals, as formalized by '$\mathscr{F}(a)$', from their use as covering concepts in relative identity statements, and proposes to define the former in terms of the latter:

(6.13) $f(x) =_{df} (\exists y)(y =_{f} x)$.

Moreover, he maintains that a reverse definition is incoherent.[27] This clearly fits our earlier claim that identity criteria form part of the sense of sortals. It also creates new problems for the Fregean analysis since he holds that the *analysans* contains (albeit disguised) exactly the same sort of statement that it was the purpose of the analysis to remove from the *analysandum*. Writing out in full the Fregean analysis of '$a =_{\mathscr{F}} b$' would give on this view:

(6.14) $(\exists x)(a =_{\mathscr{F}} x)$ & $(\exists y)(b =_{\mathscr{F}} y)$ & $a = b$.

---

25 Cf. Geach, *Reference and Generality*, p. 151.

26 *Identity and Spatio-Temporal Continuity*, p. 28.

27 *Reference and Generality*, p. 191, 'Ontological Relativity and Relative Identity', p. 291.

Clearly (6.14) is no good for getting rid of relative identity statements.

Two questions now arise: Is Geach's claim about the analysis of predicative uses of sortals correct? and Does he really need his objection to '$a = b$' in addition to his objection to '$\mathscr{F}(a)$' and '$\mathscr{F}(b)$'? Geach argues for his doctrine by means of an analogy. He claims his definition 'is formally just like defining "is a brother" (say) as "is a brother of somebody" ', that the definition 'could not proceed the other way around' because ' "brother of" is logically prior to "brother" '.[28] The point is that there is no being a brother without being somebody's brother and it is this feature of the logic of 'brother' that Geach hopes his definition will capture. Similarly, he holds that there is no being an item of a certain sort without satisfying the identity criteria appropriate to the sort. $\mathscr{F}$-identity tells us what it is to be a single $\mathscr{F}$. Identity is not a relation between the members of a domain but a relation that constitutes the members of the domain, that tells us what members we've got. Failure to recognize this fact tempts us to claim (as Quine once did) that 'to say that x and y are identical is to say that *they are* the same *thing*.'[29]

We see from our discussion of sortals and criteria of identity why sortals are chosen for this task. We could, I suppose, amend (6.13) so it defined a predicative use of any type of general noun, but this would not capture the important philosophical features I think Geach has in mind. It is only when the general noun in question conveys not only the principles necessary for judging whether two items are identical with respect to it but also provides the principles necessary for individuating the items in the first place that its predicative uses become dependent on its uses as a covering concept. Predicating a sortal '$\mathscr{F}$' of an item a cannot form part of the analysis of a relative identity statement since the coherent use of the singular term 'a' presupposes a relative identity statement, namely '$(\exists x)(a =_{\mathscr{F}} x)$', and this because '$a$' cannot be coherently used unless a can in principle be individuated.

The second question is whether Geach needs to object also to '$a = b$'. Since he holds (R) he must either reject '$a = b$' as

<hr>

[28] 'Ontological Relativity and Relative Identity', p. 291.
[29] *Methods of Logic*, p. 208 (my italics).

part of the analysis of '$a =_{\mathscr{A}} b$' or '$\sim (a = b)$' as part of the analysis of '$a \neq_{\mathscr{A}} b$'. And since there is no reason to prefer one to the other it seems he must reject them both. But the important question is whether Geach's view about the analysis of predicative uses of sortals gives him any argument against '$a = b$' in places where it is not part of a Fregean analysis. It seems to me that it doesn't and that Geach's objections to '$a = b$' are very weak. After his account of the predicative uses of sortals, Geach says that he will 'treat "the same" in "is the same $\mathscr{F}$ as" not as a syntactically separable part, but as an index showing that we have here a word for a certain sort of relation'.[30] This thesis certainly doesn't follow from his account of the predication of sortals since that, at most, shows that you can't use the Fregean analysis to separate 'the same' from the sortal which follows it, and from this it hardly follows that the two can never be separated. Moreover, even if we treat 'the same' as an inseparable part of 'ζ is the same $\mathscr{F}$ as η', it still does not follow that we cannot assign sense to 'a is the same as b' where this does *not* result from decomposition of 'a is the same $\mathscr{F}$ as b'. In particular, there is no reason to reject (LL) as an analysis of '$a = b$' even if we hold that '$a = b$' is never a part of any correct analysis of any relative identity statement.

Geach's analogy with 'ζ is brother of η' breaks down at this point. He writes: ' "of" in "is brother of" does not signify a relation by itself . . . but serves to show that the whole, "is brother of", stands for a relation.'[31] The argument works for 'ζ is brother of η' since 'a is of b', after appropriate substitutions of singular terms, does not give a sentence of English. (Some inappropriate substitutions do give an English sentence, e.g. 'John is of the opinion that life is dull.') On the other hand, this claim fails for 'ζ is the same $\mathscr{F}$ as η' since 'a is the same as b' does give a wff of English.

It seems that Geach has not got a good argument against '$a = b$' and, consequently, has not got one against '$a =_{\mathscr{A}} b$' where '$\mathscr{A}$' is not a sortal. (The project of trying to show that '$a = b$' is acceptable while '$a =_{\mathscr{A}} b$' is not is one which, rightly I believe, has not commanded attention.) (R), even when supplemented by Geach's account of sortal predication, does not, therefore, give us any argument for (D) nor any

[30] 'Ontological Relativity and Relative Identity', p. 291.   [31] Ibid.

argument against any form of relative identity. The most that (R) gives us is that '$a = b$' cannot form part of the analysis of '$a =_{\mathscr{A}} b$', *contra* the Fregean analysis. The most we so far assert is the claim that certain (uses of) absolute and (certain types of) relative identity statement fail to provide identity criteria (at least, outside a context) and thus may not be judged true or false.[32] The important point implied by Geach's account of sortal predication is that the identity relations which individuate the items of a domain are sortal-relative identity relations since only these provide principles of individuation. The failure of absolute identity to do this is related to the incoherence of the view that the items of our domain are bare particulars,[33] for the items 'individuated' by absolute identity alone are bare particulars. This does not show that absolute identity is incoherent, merely that it is incoherent to use absolute identity as the fundamental kind of identity which tells us what items we have. But this is important enough, as we shall see.

Whilst dealing with the Fregean analysis we may note a concession to it made by Dummett. Dummett rejects the Fregean analysis[34] but is prepared to concede that if '$\mathscr{A}$' and '$\mathscr{B}$' convey the same criterion of identity then '$a =_{\mathscr{A}} b$' can be analysed as '$\mathscr{A}(a)$ & $\mathscr{A}(b)$ & $a =_{\mathscr{B}} b$'.[35] I shall call this the Dummett analysis. This is entirely acceptable since it is difficult to see how the analysis could fail when '$\mathscr{A}$' and '$\mathscr{B}$' convey the same criteria of identity (i.e. are co-ordinate). But Dummett believes that two terms convey the same criteria of identity when one restricts the other. While this seems to me to be false it does suggest the following principle, analogous to (4.3), and independent of the thesis about when terms convey the same identity criteria:

(6.15) $(\mathscr{A} \subseteq \mathscr{B}$ & $a =_{\mathscr{A}} b) \rightarrow (a =_{\mathscr{B}} b$ & $\mathscr{A}(a)$ & $\mathscr{A}(b))$.

(6.15) has some plausibility for we would be inclined to agree that 'a is the same philosopher as b' is correctly analysed as 'a is a philosopher & b is a philosopher & a is the same person as b'.

Even Geach might have something like (6.15) in mind when

[32] I shall argue in Chapter 7 that this fact gives no support to a strong (D)-thesis such as (D. I).

[33] See Geach, 'Ontological Relativity and Relative Identity', p. 290; G. E. M. Anscombe, 'The Principle of Individuation', p. 84.

[34] *Frege*, p. 74.   [35] Ibid., pp. 75, 552.

he says: 'I did not give "is the same Greek as" and "is the same man as" as expressions for two different forms of relative identity; . . . Naturally not; for "is the same Englishman as y" (say) simply means "is the same man as y and is English".'[36] Geach cannot mean that 'ζ is the same Greek as η' and 'ζ is the same man as η' are the same relative identity relation for they have different extensions. Moreover, the analysis he gives implies that they are distinct, for relations '$R_1(\zeta,\eta)$' and '$R_2(\zeta,\eta)$' must be distinct if '$R_1(\zeta,\eta)$' analyses as '$R_2(\zeta,\eta)$ & p' (for non-tautologous 'p'). Finally, (6.15) cannot be what Geach has in mind because (6.15) is false and some of the counter-examples raised against it are due to Geach.[37] We have already defined the sense of 'official*' (in which to be the same official* is just to hold the same office). Now official*s are persons (not longer-lived things of which persons are parts) and thus 'official*' restricts 'person', yet it is not the case that 'a is the same official* as b' entails 'a is the same person as b'. Similarly, to use one of Geach's examples, we may define 'a is the same surman as b' as 'a and b are men and a has the same surname as b'.[38] It follows, despite denials from Perry and others,[39] that 'surman' restricts 'man' (it does not follow, incidentally, that they are co-ordinate for being a man does not entail having a surname) yet clearly being the same surman does not entail being the same man. What Geach must have intended in the passage just quoted is that we do not get different answers to the question 'Is this the same as that?' if we use 'Greek' as covering concept or if we use 'man'.[40]

---

[36] 'A Reply', *Review of Metaphysics*, 22 (1968/9), p. 556. (The passage is deleted in the abridged version of the article printed in *Logic Matters*, pp. 247–9.)

[37] With the case of 'ζ is a good $\mathscr{A}$' Geach explicitly rejects the equivalent of (6.15): 'tennis stroke' restricts 'human action' but 'a is a good tennis stroke' does not entail 'a is a good human action'. (Cf. 'Good and Evil', p. 40.) There is every reason for an (R)-relativist to reject such an account in the case of identity also. It is for this reason that I'm inclined to doubt whether Geach believes that two sortals convey the same identity criteria when one restricts the other—although he may hold, as I do, that such restriction is a necessary condition for their conveying the same identity criteria. (See above, pp. 55–7.)

[38] 'Identity', p. 245; 'Ontological Relativity and Relative Identity', p. 294. See § 8.3 for a fuller discussion of this example.

[39] Perry, 'Identity', p. 55; 'The Same F', pp. 195–6; Leslie Stevenson, 'Relative Identity and Leibniz's Law', p. 157. See also Geach's rejection of their interpretation in 'Ontological Relativity and Relative Identity', p. 295.

[40] This is the conclusion that Carl Calvert comes to after a long and careful discussion. Cf. his 'Relative Identity: An Examination of a Theory by Peter

6.4 *Alternative (D)-Theses*

Amongst those philosophers who reject (R) but accept (D) there is little uniformity of opinion as to the type of incompleteness suffered by absolute identity statements and its consequences. In this section I shall deal with some miscellaneous versions of (D) mainly to get them out of the way in order to deal with what might be called Wiggins's 'developed' theory in the next chapter. None the less, several of the theses considered here are due to Wiggins, though it's clear that he gives them very much less weight than the thesis to be considered in Chapter 7.

Wiggins once accepted only a very weak version of (D) which he expressed as follows: 'After an assertion that *A* is the same as *B* we can usually ask "the same *what*?".'[41] Ten years later he expressed the point more strongly: 'If someone tells you that *a = b*, then you should always ask them 'the same *what* as *b*?".'[42] The earlier version is too weak to be properly counted a form of (D), for (D) must, I think, imply that any identity statement which wasn't backed by the appropriate general noun—for which the 'same *what*?' question couldn't be answered—would be defective. The second version is equally unenlightening. Despite the fact that Wiggins says at the outset of *Identity and Spatio-Temporal Continuity* that this is what he will call (D), it can scarcely be an adequate characterization of the doctrine. As M. C. Bradley says, (D) is not a categorical imperative.[43]

In a section entitled 'The Rationale of the "Same What?" Question' Wiggins gets a bit closer to turning his version of (D) into a serious logical thesis. He writes: '[T]here [is] something radically wrong with any putative assertion of identity

Geach' (Unpublished Doctoral Dissertation, University of Washington, 1973), pp. 63–76.

[41] Wiggins quoted by Prior, 'Report on the *Analysis* "Problem" No. 11'. *Analysis*, 17 (1957), 123.

[42] *Identity and Spatio-Temporal Continuity*, p. 1. See also G. E. M. Anscombe, 'Aristotle', in Anscombe and Geach, *Three Philosophers*, p. 33. But compare Wiggins, 'The Individuation of Things and Places', p. 178, where he says that the covering concept needn't give 'a natural or idiomatic answer to the question "same what?"' —which, I suppose, leaves it open that it must none the less give *some* answer to that question.

[43] M. C. Bradley, Critical Notice of Wiggins's *Identity and Spatio-Temporal Continuity*, *Australasian Journal of Philosophy*, 47 (1969), 70.

for which *in principle* no such answer [as '$(\exists f)(a =_f b)$' to the question 'a is the same what as b?'] could be provided.'[44] This leads him to the claim that[45]

$$(6.16) \qquad a = b \supset (\exists f)(a =_f b).$$

Of course, if a and b are the same they must be the same something and we can ask 'the same what?' and there *would* be something radically wrong with an identity claim for which no answer to this question could in principle be given.[46] At best, however, this gives us (6.6) and not (6.16), for to get to the latter we need also some account of why only a sortal is fit to answer the 'same what?' question. Moreover, if we adopt the strong (D)-thesis of Wiggins's 'developed' theory, according to which absolute identity statements are senseless, then (6.16) and (6.6) will alike be senseless since they are truth-functional compounds with a senseless component. Probably Wiggins hopes to counter this problem by some distinction between relative and absolute identity languages, but he doesn't make this clear.

Wiggins's (6.16) is related to a (D)-thesis Odegard rejects, namely:

(6.17)   The statement '$a = b$' is [always] elliptical for a statement of the form '$a =_f b$'.[47]

It is a thesis he ascribes, with slight inaccuracy, to Geach. Odegard objects to (6.17) on the grounds that it is not the case that

... everyone who truly (or even knowingly) asserts '$(\mathcal{G}(a)$ & $\mathcal{G}(b))$ & $(a = b)$' either says or means '$(\mathcal{G}(a)$ & $\mathcal{G}(b))$ & $(a =_{\mathcal{G}} b)$'. For example, he might accept the [third] conjunct on authority, without knowing whether its truth is based on '$a =_{\mathcal{G}} b$'. And he could at least raise the question of whether this is so, which is something he could not do if '$a = b$' simply *meant* '$a =_{\mathcal{G}} b$'. Thus, according to Locke's theory, if '$(\mathcal{G}(a)$ & $\mathcal{G}(b))$ & $(a = b)$' is to yield '$a =_{\mathcal{G}} b$',

---

[44] *Identity and Spatio-Temporal Continuity*, p. 27.   [45] Ibid., p. 28.

[46] We may, of course, allow for the introduction of new general nouns for use as covering concepts; there is no reason why our conceptual scheme should be static.

[47] 'Identity Through Time', p. 30. There is textual support for my addition of 'always'. Odegard says, e.g., that the theory he is espousing 'recognises that "$\mathcal{G}(a)$ & $\mathcal{G}(b)$ & $a = b$" may be elliptical' (ibid.). And all his arguments are against the stronger thesis. Without the amendment (6.17) is scarcely a (D)-thesis.

it must be *augmented* by either '$a =_\mathscr{G} b$' or an instance of '$a =_f b$' in which the value of f is semantically tied to $\mathscr{G}$, whereas for Geach the [third] conjunct must be understood as meaning one of these two things.[48]

There are a number of points here which need disentangling. First, has Odegard got Geach right? What Geach presents is not just one account of absolute identity statements but two alternatives: either they are meaningless, or, if they have a meaning, the meaning is some instance of '$a =_f b$'.[49] However, Odegard's point about ordinary usage, if correct, will also work against this disjunctive version of (D). For Odegard supposes that someone truly asserts '$a = b$' but does not say or mean some instance of '$a =_f b$'. Thus the second disjunct of Geach's account is failed; but so, also, is the first because if '$a = b$' is *truly* asserted then it is not meaningless. Thus the speaker, when he truly asserts '$a = b$', neither asserts something meaningless nor says or means some instance of '$a =_f b$'. To this Geach will have to reply that there could be no such case: that if the speaker did not say or mean some instance of '$a =_f b$' then what he said was meaningless, and therefore not truly said.

On Odegard's side we can surely agree that people can, on occasion, sensibly assert '$a = b$' without thereby intending an instance of '$a =_f b$'—indeed most philosophers did this before reading Geach (and many of them afterwards). Whether such asserters of '$a = b$' could, none the less, *mean* an instance of '$a =_f b$' depends on the possibility of meaning something without intending to mean it. Pursued this way Geach's version of (D) runs into dangerous territory. However, Geach cannot be saying merely that, although someone can significantly assert '$a = b$' without meaning or saying or intending to mean or say an instance of '$a =_f b$', none the less '$a = b$' can be written out as an instance of '$a =_f b$', for then this thesis merely collapses into (6.16). In fact the situation would be worse than this for (6.16) does not convey the lack of sense of '$a = b$' which Geach intended to convey—if (6.16) is to make sense itself, '$a = b$' must make sense. Moreover, on this interpretation there would

[48] Ibid.
[49] Cf., for example, 'Identity', p. 238; *Reference and Generality*, p. 39; *Mental Acts* (London: Routledge and Kegan Paul, 1957), p. 69.

be no quarrel with Odegard who accepts (6.16). So a more careful reading of Geach doesn't help him out of this difficulty. However, a more careful reading of Odegard might.

When Odegard implies that someone might truly and knowingly assert

(6.18) $\mathscr{G}(a)$ & $\mathscr{G}(b)$ & $a = b$

without meaning

(6.19) $\mathscr{G}(a)$ & $\mathscr{G}(b)$ & $a =_{\mathscr{g}} b$

he might be claiming that they can do so (i) without meaning that there is some sortal covering concept or other; or (ii) without meaning that there is some particular sortal covering concept (that is, without their having in mind some particular covering sortal). (He is plainly not making the trivial point that they do not mean (6.19) because they mean '$\mathscr{G}(a)$ & $\mathscr{G}(b)$ & $a =_{\mathscr{g}} b$'. This would give him no quarrel with Geach.) Odegard accepts the thesis:

(6.20) $a = b \equiv (\exists f)(a =_f b)$

and also:

(6.21)   [T]here is a reason for the truth of '$a = b$' and . . . a statement of the reason will take the form of '$a =_{\mathscr{g}} b$'.[50]

Now for each of (6.20) and (6.21) we can try and generate a difficulty for the first interpretation of what someone who truly asserts '$a = b$' means. How could one, it might be argued, truly assert '$a = b$' without thereby meaning '$(\exists f)(a =_f b)$' given that (6.20) is true and, moreover, is (presumably) a logical truth? But this argument involves a distribution fallacy. It is possible for x truly to assert p, where $\square (p \supset q)$, without x thereby meaning (or even truly asserting) q. So the attempt to use (6.20) to undo Odegard's argument is a failure, but the second difficulty is, I think, more successful. How could one knowingly assert '$a = b$' without thereby meaning '$(\exists f)(a =_f b)$', given that (6.21) is true? For surely knowingly to assert p is to know the reason for p's being true. Thus if x knowingly asserts '$a = b$' then x knows that '$(\exists f)(a =_f b)$' is true, and if he knows that then isn't that what he means all along? This might be disputed, but what we can surely agree on is that in this case substituting '$(\exists f)(a =_f b)$' for '$a = b$' would preserve intended sense, and it is this, as Odegard recognizes, which is crucial. However, the relativist who seeks to combine (R) with absolute identity is not forced to accept (6.21). Indeed, he might be more likely to hold that the reason for the truth of '$a = b$' is that $(\forall \phi)(\phi(a) \equiv \phi(b))$ and this gives no comfort to the (D)-relativist. An alternative would be to restrict the scope of (D) to all 'knowing assertions' of identity statements. It would not follow that '$a = b$' was meaningless but that it could always be expanded whenever it was knowingly asserted. (D) would then have less generality than Geach and other (D)-relativists would like but it would cover an important range of central cases—for 'unknowing' assertions of '$a = b$' must be secondary, we can't speak vacuously all the time. This approach will be considered in more detail in the next chapter.

On interpretation (i), Odegard also runs into another problem. His argument to show that '$a = b$' and some instance of '$a =_f b$', say '$a =_g b$', don't have the same meaning is invalid. Even if '$a = b$' and '$a =_g b$' do have the same meaning someone who truly asserts '$a = b$' may raise the question as to whether it was the case that '$a =_g b$'; just as someone (who didn't understand English very well) might inquire whether a certain bachelor was unmarried or someone decoding a cipher might inquire whether a certain ciphered phrase meant so-and-so. Of course, such questions turn out to be about meanings (although the questioner mightn't think so) but we don't know whether the question 'Is it true that $a =_g b$?' is a question about the meaning of '$a = b$' until the present problem is resolved. But even if meanings are the same there's nothing to stop the question's being raised. The possibility of raising the question does not show that the two statements must have different meanings. However, the failure of this bad argument against (D) scarcely makes us confident that (D) is true.

On interpretation (ii) Odegard is right, but he imposes much stronger conditions on the (D)-thesis than Geach would accept. People do on frequent occasions truly assert statements of the form (6.18) without having *in mind* any particular sortal covering concept. But (D) is a logical thesis about identity and not a thesis about the psychology of identity statement asserters. To truly assert p is not to have in mind all synonyms of p. I don't think this argument touches Geach's thesis. The most (D) can do is provide, for every meaningful assertion of '$a = b$' (however vague its meaning is), an identity statement which captures that meaning and satisfies the demand for a covering concept. Odegard does not manage to show that Geach's (D)-thesis fails to do this.

My discussion of Odegard's argument is necessarily inconclusive since neither Odegard nor myself have given any account of what we mean by 'meaning' and, in particular, neither of us have suggested distribution laws for the operators Odegard uses in his argument, such as 'x means' or 'x truly asserts'. All this would have to be done before we could be sure that Geach's claims held about natural language. But while Odegard's arguments against (D) are not as clear cut as he seems to think, we have so far found nothing very convincing in (D)'s favour despite its popularity.

7

Wiggins's (D)-Relative Identity Theory

7.1 Wiggins's Theory

It is Wiggins who takes most seriously the question of the independent justification of (D). However, in this enterprise, as throughout his book, the thesis he seeks to justify behaves like a poltergeist, mysteriously changing form from page to page. Wiggins's most general statement is: 'On pain of indefiniteness, every identity statement stands in radical need of the answer to the question *same what?*'[1] The trouble with this is that we want to know in what sense '$a = b$' is indefinite and, as Bradley says, 'what is painful about it?'[2] Bradley compares the alleged indefiniteness of '$a = b$' with the indefiniteness of 'Jack is to the right.'[3] But the analogy, on its own, doesn't get us far for while 'Jack is to the right' (when context provides no point of reference) is universally bewildering, it is not universally agreed that '$a = b$' (when context provides no covering concept) is bewildering at all. The (D)-relativist is certainly not short of analogies for the incompleteness of '$a = b$', what is so far lacking is the assurance that any of the suggested analogies are really analogous.

It becomes clear that Wiggins believes that absolute identity statements suffer from sense indefiniteness. However, it is much less clear whether his reasons for this belief are good ones. The argument (or arguments) he proposes in the second part of *Identity and Spatio-Temporal Continuity* are implicitly based on the verification principle. He presents three rather different, but related, theses about '$a = b$':

The following [is a] truth-condition, T, for an identity-statement

[1] *Identity and Spatio-Temporal Continuity*, p. 27.
[2] 'Critical Notice', p. 70.   [3] Ibid., p. 73.

'$a = b$'. If one locates each of the particulars a and b ((under covering concept or concepts)) and, where appropriate, sc. in the case of 'identity through time', traces a and b through space and time ((under covering concepts)), one must find that a and b coincide ((under some covering concept $\mathscr{F}$)) . . . What particularly needs to be shown is the essential character of the parts of T marked by [double] brackets.[4]

Knowledge of relevant $\mathscr{F}$ . . . is both necessary and sufficient for the simultaneous understanding of what a is, of the sense of the question 'is a the same as b?' and of what establishes or refutes the assertion that a is indeed the same as b.[5]

There is not, and there could not be, any *general* account of what it is for an arbitrary individual a to coincide or not to coincide with an arbitrary individual b, nor could there be any usable account of what it is, in general, to make a mistake or avoid a mistake in tracing a and tracing b to see whether they coincide. To trace a [and b and see whether they coincide] I must know what a is.[6]

The initial effect of these three quotations is more than a little puzzling. In the first place, the third quotation is concerned only with identity through time for items for whose identity spatio-temporal continuity is criterial (that is, presumably, for material objects), and this is the only sort of identity which the first quotation explicitly deals with (although it does leave room for the treatment of identities for which other conditions are criterial). Of course, the identity of material objects is what Wiggins is mainly concerned with—his title alone suggests this—but in formulating a theory of relative identity we will need to expand our scope beyond this if the theory is to command respect. In particular, no general conclusion about identity statements (such as (D)) will follow from considerations about material object identity through time.

Secondly, in the first quotation T is not a truth-condition in the usual sense of the term for it seems clear that Wiggins believes that a truth-condition for the statement 'S' should indicate the manner in which one might go about verifying or falsifying 'S'. In other words, in Wiggins's usage a truth-condition for 'S' must be criterial for 'S'. To avoid confusion let me call this a criterial condition for 'S'.

---

4 *Identity and Spatio-Temporal Continuity*, p. 35.
5 Ibid., p. 36.   6 Ibid., p. 35.

What Wiggins is talking about in the first and third quotations are criteria of identity, and we can generalize what he says so that the principle which results is not restricted to the identity of material objects. The result for the first quotation would be something like:

(7.1)   The criterial condition for '$a = b$' must provide an operational criterion by which we may (in ideal circumstances) judge whether $a = b$, *and this can only be done if we can provide a substantival covering concept for '$a = b$'*.

Without the claim in italics (7.1) is merely a tautology, to the effect that criterial conditions must be criterial. What the italicized phrase adds is the claim that Wiggins added in double brackets in the original quotation. A similar process for the third quotation gives us:

(7.2)   There is not, and there could not be, any general account of what it is for a to be identical with b, nor could there be any usable account of what it is, in general, to make a mistake or avoid a mistake in judging whether $a = b$.

What this amounts to is the old claim of Chapter 4 that identity is differently constituted for different types of items. From (7.2) we can move to (7.1), for if identity criteria are different for different types of item then we need to know what type of item a and b are before we can know the criterial condition for '$a = b$' and this is, of course, exactly what the provision of a substantival covering concept for '$a = b$' tells us. (In fact, however, we are not quite there, for (7.1) requires that provision of a substantival covering concept is the *only* way in which this can be done and we shall, in § 7.4, have reason to consider another possible method.)

We can set this principle up, quite properly, as a version of (D):

(D. II)   It is only possible to judge whether an identity statement, 'S', is true or false when 'S' is, or can be, supplied with a covering concept.[7]

(D. II) captures the idea that an identity statement cannot be

---

[7] Geach also accepts (D. II). See his claim: 'I maintain that it makes no sense to *judge* whether x and y are the "the same" . . . unless we can add or understand some general term—"the same $\mathcal{F}$."' (*Reference and Generality*, p. 39; my italics.)

assessed unless it has a covering concept which supplies it with criteria of identity.

In the second of the three quotations, however, Wiggins goes considerably beyond (D. II), for he claims there that knowledge of an appropriate covering concept is both *necessary and sufficient* for understanding what *a* is, and what the question 'Is *a* the same as *b*?' means, as well as resolving the indeterminacy of '*a* = *b*'. The first of these claims I shall discuss in more detail later, but it does seem to me that Wiggins is using a somewhat deviant sense of 'knowing what *a* is' when he claims that knowledge of some substantival covering concept for *a* is both necessary and *sufficient* for it. I think it would naturally be taken that knowledge of some covering general noun was necessary for knowing what *a* is, but I would be surprised if such knowledge was, in general, sufficient.

The second claim is equally curious. There has been, so far, no suggestion from Wiggins that we do not *understand the meaning* of '*a* = *b*', merely that we have no way of assessing whether it is true or false. Now standard English transformations should be sense-preserving and since 'Is *a* the same as *b*?' is a standard transform of '*a* is the same as *b*' we would expect the one to be significant if the other were. Wiggins is claiming that we do not understand the sense of the question unless we can provide a covering concept for the statement. It surely follows that we can't understand the statement either, unless we provide a covering concept.[8] It is plain from the context in which the second passage occurs that Wiggins thinks this claim is sufficiently supported by (D. II). If (D. II) gives him:

(7.3)   We can in principle judge whether '*S*' is true or false iff we can supply a covering concept for '*S*'.

then he can get

(7.4)   We can understand what '*S*' means iff we can supply a covering concept for '*S*'.

only if he has a second premiss:

(7.5)   We can understand what '*S*' means iff we can in principle judge whether '*S*' is true or false.

[8] Wiggins, so far as I can see, does not say as much in so many words, though other (D)-relativists have gone this far, e.g. Michael Durrant, 'Numerical Identity', p. 100. Quite a bit of what Wiggins does say, however, implies this position.

But (7.5) is a verification principle which Wiggins does not explicitly avow and which, I think, ought to be rejected.

Given that this appeal to the verification principle cannot be allowed we are left, at best, with (D. II) which imposes an assessibility condition on identity statements. I don't think it will be possible for Wiggins to move from (D. II) to a stronger (D)-thesis without introducing either a verification principle or some further relative identity principle, such as the function thesis. In §§ 7.2 to 7.4 I shall consider the objections which might be raised against even (D. II). I think Wiggins is right in asserting that identity statements cannot be assessed until some substantival term is given, but he is wrong (as will be shown in § 7.4) in thinking that it must be given as covering concept.

7.2 Bradley's Criticisms

In his critical notice of Wiggins, Bradley puts forward an argument which seems to trade (if I have understood it aright) on Wiggins's hovering between (D. II) and (7.4). Bradley effectively adopts as an 'obvious truth' the principle:

(7.6)   To decide whether $a = b$ we must know what the names in question refer to and this involves knowing that a is the $\mathcal{F}$ which . . . and b is the $\mathcal{G}$ which. . . .[9]

Bradley then goes on to object that if this leads to Wiggins's indefiniteness thesis then the indefiniteness affects not just identity statements but 'any sentence in which a predicate is attached to a proper name'.[10] This spread of indefiniteness is, he claims, 'intolerable' and thus he supposes that the 'obvious truths [viz. (7.6)] will not immediately yield' Wiggins's indefiniteness thesis.[11]

Bradley and Wiggins are at cross-purposes here. (7.6) effectively concedes (D. II) which is the most to which Wiggins is entitled. Moreover, if we accept (7.6) it does not seem 'intolerable' that this sort of indefiniteness (viz. indefiniteness of assessibility) should spread to sentences in which a predicate

---

[9] This principle is not stated by Bradley in so many words but it seems a fair generalization of his examples on p. 75 of his 'Critical Notice'. In fact (7.6), which requires *identification* of the relata of an identity statement, is stronger than (D. II) which merely requires knowledge of a sortal under which both relata fall.

[10] Ibid. Perry ('Identity', p. 81) has the same argument but uses it to different ends.   [11] Bradley, ibid.

is attached to a proper name, for statements of the form '$\phi(a)$' are generally not assessible unless we know what a is. But if we took (7.6) to commit us to the stronger version of (D), namely, the sense-indefiniteness thesis (7.4), then we would also expect this sense-indefiniteness to spread far and wide also; and this *would* be counter-intuitive for we would not normally say that '$\phi(a)$' was *meaningless* or lacked determinate *sense* simply because we did not know a sortal under which a fell. So when Bradley says that Wiggins's sense-indefiniteness thesis cannot follow from (7.6) he is, in an unnecessarily convoluted way, rejecting the verification principle which would get him from (D. II) to (7.4). If we reject the verification principle then there is no danger of sense-indefiniteness spreading throughout the language.

Let us now consider the assessibility-indefiniteness that is common ground to both Wiggins and Bradley as far as '$a = b$' is concerned, and which Bradley claims spreads elsewhere. Having accepted (7.6) there is, so far as I can see, no reasonable policy Bradley could adopt to stop it spreading, but then it is not clear why he needs to stop it spreading. To claim that '$\phi(a)$' cannot be assigned a truth-value until we know a sortal under which a falls, so far from being wildly counter-intuitive, has some plausibility. It is not, however, quite correct. We can obviously assign a truth-value to any predicational statement which is analytically true or false without knowing a sortal under which its subject falls. We know that 'This is either red or not red' is true without knowing what 'this' refers to. Exceptions of this sort, however, would not, I suspect, unduly trouble Bradley. But there are other exceptions which seriously limit Bradley's claim. For example, we can assign the value *false* to 'The object in the matchbox is a live elephant' without knowing any sortal under which the object in the matchbox falls.

In the light of this we need to reassess the whole of Bradley's argument. He holds that (7.6) is an obvious truth about the assessibility-indefiniteness of absolute identity claims and (by parity of reasoning to his original argument) it follows from this that assessibility-indefiniteness will spread to all predicational statements. Originally, this looked like a reasonable claim but we have now shown it to be false. If Bradley's argument is valid it would follow (*modus tollens*) that (7.6) and thus (D. II) are false also. He is saved from this unwelcome conclusion by the fact his argument is invalid. To make it valid would require the addition of some principle which enabled one to generalize from a claim about the criterial conditions of a certain type of statement to a claim about the criterial conditions of all types of statements. I am at a loss to know how such a principle might be formulated, or, supposing it formulated, why we should think it true. There thus seems little reason to fear an 'intolerable' extension of assessibility-indefiniteness and every reason to expect a slight one.[12]

Bradley has another argument against a claim which he takes from Wiggins and characterizes thus:

(7.7)   Coincidence can only be defined and therefore assessed by reference to a suitable sortal.[13]

Bradley proposes the following alternative assessment condition for '$a = b$':

(7.8) $(\forall t)[(\imath r)(a \text{ occupies } r \text{ at } t) = (\imath r')(b \text{ occupies } r' \text{ at } t)]$, provided that a is not a substance and b any genuine aggregate of its parts, nor vice versa.[14]

where 'r' and 'r''' are variables taking regions of space as values.

Wiggins has three arguments against the adequacy of (7.8):[15]

[H]ow can we know what it is to find a in a place unless we have *some* sortal specification of what a is?[16]

[T]he assertion that a and b coincide must come to something more than the stale assertion that the location of a = the location of b. It is the *occupants* . . . that must be the same. We must know not only what it is for location l to be occupied, but also what it is for l to be occupied by a.[17]

---

[12] This is a conclusion which Dummett accepts right from the start: 'If . . . I know that a river flooded last winter, but do not know what would establish that it was or was not the same river as that of which I am now being given the name [by being told, 'This is the River Windrush'], I shall not know, either, what would establish that it was true of the River Windrush that it flooded last winter.' (*Frege*, pp. 73-4.) It is precisely this sort of fact which makes identity criteria so important.

[13] 'Critical Notice', pp. 74-5; cf. Wiggins, *Identity and Spatio-Temporal Continuity*, p. 35; fn. 44 (p. 72).   [14] 'Critical Notice', p. 76.

[15] Similar objections to (7.8) are found in Perry, 'Identity', p. 107.

[16] *Identity and Spatio-Temporal Continuity*, fn. 44 (p. 72).   [17] Ibid.

The adequacy of (7.8) will depend upon the nature of the changes a and b can under-go. This in turn will depend upon what a and b are.[18]

Against each of these arguments Bradley repeats his argument about the generalizability of non-assessibility. He argues that if we need to know a sortal under which a falls before we can know what it is to find a in a place, or to distinguish a from the space it occupies, or to know what sort of changes a can undergo, we will have to know a sortal under which a falls 'to find whether a has a mass of 5·47 grms'.[19] But Bradley has yet to demonstrate that this follows. Moreover, while it will be possible to rig up cases in which we can tell whether a has a mass of 5·47 grms. without locating a under a sortal, in many cases this will not be possible. Bradley's argument is not very strong.

However, (7.8) is defective in quite other ways. It is not sufficient for identifying a and b to know that they occupy exactly the same place at the same time, even if you include the proviso that neither is a part of the other. In many cases distinct things can occupy the same place at the same time whether or not they are parts and wholes of each other. For example, the electromagnetic field within an atom is co-extensive with the atom but distinct from it. Ghosts and walls are frequently averred to occupy the same place at the same time without being identical. Wiggins advances the principle: 'No two things *of the same kind* (that is, no two things which satisfy the same sortal or substance concept) can occupy exactly the same volume at exactly the same time.'[20] But even this is too strong: two smells may fill the room simultaneously yet be distinct, the one of curry and the other of fish; two light rays may intersect in a given volume yet be the one of red light and the other of blue; shadows may overlap; different sounds may simultaneously fill the air.[21] Space occupation provides no

---

[18] Based on Wiggins's (D. vi), ibid., pp. 35–6.

[19] 'Critical Notice', p. 76.

[20] 'On Being in the Same Place at the Same Time', *Philosophical Review*, 77 (1968), 93. The principle comes from Locke's *Essay*, Bk. II, Ch. 27, § 1 (Fraser, vol. i, p. 439).

[21] Cf. David H. Sanford, 'Locke, Leibniz and Wiggins on Being in the Same Place at the Same Time', *Philosophical Review*, 79 (1970), 75–82. The shadow and light ray examples are from Leibniz, *New Essays Concerning the Human Understanding*, Bk. II, Ch. 27, § 1 (p. 238 of the Langley translation).

criterion for identification, even of physical items. However, the Leibnizian examples suggest that even providing a sortal under which both *a* and *b* fall and under which they spatio-temporally coincide is, generally, no sufficient condition for the assertion that *a* = *b*. None the less, it would seem to be a necessary condition for '*a* = *b*' as far as material objects are concerned.

7.3 *Nelson's Criticisms*

Nelson has two arguments against (D). First, he presents what he believes to be a counter-example to (D):

[I]t seems possible that I might hear my neighbours on various occasions, summon, scold, praise, curse and discuss Xantippe and Rufus, in such a way that it becomes clear that Xantippe is in fact identical with Rufus. And this might happen without its becoming clear what kind of a thing 'Xantippe' and 'Rufus' both name, i.e., whether that thing is a pet, child or poltergeist etc.[22]

Nelson's example is an extremely strange one and needs further elucidation. How, for example, did Nelson come to be able to identify Rufus with Xantippe? Did he hear one neighbour describing the exploits of Xantippe and the other describing similar exploits by Rufus? But that is not enough to warrant the identity claim: Rufus and Xantippe might have similar behaviour problems. In a conversation between the two neighbours it might become clear that both were talking about the same thing, but this would be because pronouns were used and would not connect Rufus with Xantippe. As soon as a sentence with 'Xantippe' as subject was introduced into the conversation it would be impossible to know whether the sentence was about Rufus or not. Of course, the neighbours might actually state that Rufus and Xantippe were identical without providing a covering concept, and Nelson could accept that piece of information without further grounds in the same way as he accepted all the other information about Rufus and Xantippe provided by his neighbours. But it would provide no real guarantee that the two were identical for the speakers might merely be trying to confuse an eavesdropping neighbour— saying doesn't make it so. In short, I am quite unpersuaded that

---

[22] 'On the Alleged Incompleteness of Certain Identity Claims', p. 112.

Nelson can set up his example convincingly. On the other hand, even if he can, it is not the case that he has no covering concept at all. As he admits later he would know that Rufus and Xantippe were the same topic of conversation.[23] But he can do better than this. The fact that both are summoned, scolded, praised, and cursed implies that both are animate, causal agents, both are (in a loose or extended sense) moral agents, and so on.

Nelson's second argument is stronger: '[F]rom the fact, if it be a fact, that every identity claim presupposes criteria of identity it does not follow that identity claims which do not themselves convey these criteria are semantically incomplete.'[24] The latter claim, Nelson says, 'is simply false'.[25] Consider the set, S, of prime numbers. Then being a prime number is the criterion for being a member of S. But from this it doesn't follow that '3 is a member of S' is semantically incomplete, though the sentence itself gives no clue as to what the membership criterion for S is. What's at issue here is what is meant by 'semantically incomplete'. If we mean the relatively weak claim, made about '$a = b$' by (D. II), that we cannot judge whether '3 is a member of S' unless we know the membership criterion of S then, in that sense, '3 is a member of S' is semantically incomplete. If we mean a stronger claim that '3 is a member of S' is meaningless then clearly it is not semantically incomplete (unless we adopt the verification principle) but then neither is '$a = b$' (unless we adopt the verification principle). But suppose we mean an intermediate claim that semantic incompleteness means having indeterminate truth-conditions (the claim made about '$a = b$' by (D. I)) then '3 is a member of S' is not semantically incomplete because we have the truth-condition: '3 is a member of S' is true if 3 is a member of S and false otherwise. But here the analogy between '3 is a member of S' and '$a = b$' breaks down. (D. I) gains what plausibility it has from (R) but Nelson's example about S doesn't mirror the situation we have concerning '$a = b$' if (R) is true. A closer analogy would be if 'S' were ambiguous between, say, the set of prime numbers and the set of numbers divisible by 3. In this case '3 is a member of S' has no determinate truth-conditions, and is semantically incomplete in the sense we are now con-

[23] Ibid.   [24] Ibid., p. 110.   [25] Ibid.

sidering. On the other hand, we could make '3 is a member of S' semantically complete by specifying the sense of 'S' intended each time '3 is a member of S' is uttered. Similarly, we can make '$a = b$' semantically complete by specifying in each use the respect in which identity is intended.

7.4 Perry's Criticisms

The most serious objection to (D. II) comes from Perry,[26] although it appears in a similar form in Nelson and Stevenson. Perry agrees with the (D)-relativist that sentences such as '$a = b$' or 'a is the same as b' cannot be judged true or false until some general noun is specified, but he denies the (D)-relativists' conclusion that the general noun *must* be packaged with the identity sign (though he admits that it may appear there).[27] If '$a = b$' is semantically incomplete, and the incompleteness does not lie in the '$=$', then it must lie in 'a' and 'b': '[W]e have accounted for the incompleteness of our examples by faulting the reference, [and] the need to fault the relation, to say there is no such thing as [absolute] identity, disappears.'[28] Perry implies that if he can show that this is the case he will have vindicated the absolute theory; while this is not quite correct he will certainly have undermined Wiggins's alternative to the absolute theory. Moreover, his theory is very close to Wiggins's,[29] and they differ mainly on how they propose to formalize their common insight.

Nelson and Stevenson use Perry's argument but give it rather less scope, using it as an *ad hominem* argument against Geach.[30] Geach holds that 'a is the same as b' is semantically

---

[26] Cf. Perry, 'Identity', pp. 17, 52, 80; 'The Same F', pp. 185, 186–8, 199; Review of Wiggins, *Identity and Spatio-Temporal Continuity*, *Journal of Symbolic Logic*, 35 (1970), 448. Dummett expresses a similar view, cf. *Frege*, pp. 570–1, 580. See also Shoemaker, 'Wiggins on Identity', p. 107, who follows Perry on this; and Quine, 'Identity, Ostension and Hypostasis' in *From a Logical Point of View*, p. 67 and *Methods of Logic*, pp. 210–11. Perry credits Quine with suggesting this positive part of his theory. ('Identity', p. 20 n.; 'The Same F', p. 182 n.)

[27] Perry, 'Identity', p. 23.

[28] Ibid., p. 17.

[29] This is recognized by Ayers, 'Individuals Without Sortals', p. 113, who rejects both theories; and Benacerraf, 'What Numbers Could Not Be', *Philosophical Review*, 74 (1965), 64–6 who considers both but prefers Perry's theory.

[30] Nelson, 'On the Alleged Incompleteness of Certain Identity Claims', pp. 109–10; Stevenson, 'Relative Identity and Leibniz's Law', pp. 156–7. Perry ('Identity', pp. 81–2) also gives the *ad hominem* version of the argument.

incomplete because it conveys no criterion of identity. But he also holds the view that every proper name conveys a nominal essence which is expressed by a general noun which conveys criteria of identity for the bearer of the name:

For every proper name there is a corresponding use of a common noun preceded by 'the same' to express what requirements as to identity the proper name conveys . . . 'Jemina'—'the same cat' . . . In all these cases we may say that the proper name conveys a *nominal essence*; thus 'cat' expresses the nominal essence of the thing we call 'Jemima', and Jemima's corpse will not be Jemima any more than it will be a cat.[31]

Nelson presses home an apparent tension between these two positions:

[I]f Geach's view of proper names is correct, then every instance of such open sentences as 'x is identical with y' which replaces 'x' and 'y' with proper names, e.g. 'Tully is identical with Cicero', will carry with it the requisite criteria of identity. In the present example, since 'Tully' and 'Cicero' both have the sense of 'man', the information conveyed is that the claim is true if and only if Tully and Cicero are the same man.[32]

Moreover, it seems that the objection can be extended to those instances of 'ζ is identical with η' which replace the place-holders with definite descriptions, for definite descriptions, in general,[33] include a general noun which could be said to express the nominal essence of the items referred to by the description. Of course, Nelson's objection will only work if we accept Geach's theory of proper names but we do not have to choose between (D) and Geach's theory of proper names. All Nelson has shown is that, at worst, (D) is made redundant by the theory of proper names, not that the two contradict each other.[34]

---

[31] *Reference and Generality*, pp. 43–4.

[32] 'On the Alleged Incompleteness of Certain Identity Claims', p. 109.

[33] There are exceptions, of course, such as 'The Napoleon of Notting Hill'. But in this case 'Napoleon' may be treated as a disguised sortal such as 'man of Napoleonic qualities'. Cf. Zeno Vendler, *Linguistics in Philosophy*, pp. 41–2, 59; but compare Chomsky, *Aspects of the Theory of Syntax*, p. 100, who claims that the 'the' in such expressions as 'The Nile', 'The Hague', and 'The U.S.S.R.' should be treated as part of the name. Chomsky's explanation seems entirely plausible for 'The Hague', less so for 'The Nile' and 'The U.S.S.R.', and not at all plausible for 'The Napoleon of Notting Hill' and 'the late Lyndon Johnson'.

[34] In fact, as I shall show in § 10.2, (R) provides Geach with a reason for holding his theory of proper names in addition to (D).

While both Nelson and Perry use this as an *ad hominem* argument against Geach, Perry also extends it as an argument against (D), without using the Geachian theory of proper names. Let us consider one of Perry's examples:[35] Suppose I point up river and then down river and ask 'Is this the same as that?'. The question cannot be answered since it might be the same river but not the same water or state. However, rephrasing the question as 'Is this the same river as that?' is not the only way to make my meaning clear, I could also ask 'Is this river the same as that river?'. Perry, however, claims not only that this second alternative is possible and plausible (both of which I grant) but also that it is the correct one[36] (of this I am more sceptical).

If Perry's strong claim is correct then it should be possible to show that in cases where the question 'Is *a* the same as *b*?' could not be answered there was some deficiency in the names '*a*' and '*b*'. Now, clearly, if we are going to use '*a*' and '*b*' referentially we need to know something about *a* and *b*, but this does not imply that we need to know everything about them before we can so use their names. Moreover, the names can be quite correctly used even when quite important features of the items they name are left undetermined. In particular the names can be correctly used even if it is not determined whether *a* and *b* are the same $\mathscr{F}$. Zemach, to whom this argument is due, considers a caterpillar named 'Mark Anthony' which turns into a butterfly named 'Cleopatra'. The question 'Is Mark Anthony the same as Cleopatra?' is unanswerable. According to Perry, this is because there is a deficiency in the names 'Mark Anthony' and 'Cleopatra' which do not make it clear whether they are the names of a caterpillar and a butterfly respectively or whether both are names of an insect. But names can be correctly used despite open-texture. If Mark Anthony had died before metamorphosis there would have been no question that I had used the name correctly all the time. Similarly, acquaintances of Dr. Jekyll and Mr. Hyde can use the names correctly without its being known that the two are the same man—how else could Stevenson's story be told? As Zemach says: '[I]t is wrong to say . . . that I am not using "Mark Anthony" referentially, . . . if I have not yet determined how

I intend to use the name in the future, when I shall have . . . a pupa, or a butterfly, instead of a caterpillar.'[37]

To support his theory Perry has two arguments, neither of which is sufficient to establish his stronger claim. In the first place he claims the advantage of matching ordinary language since 'We employ a general term next to the word 'same' in those cases in which the referring expressions do not include a general term. . . .'[38] This point about ordinary language is clearly false: we do not follow either one procedure or the other, but quite commonly use both together.

(7.9)   This river is the same river as that river.

and

(7.10)   This river is the same water as that river.

are both perfectly acceptable English sentences. Moreover, even if Perry's point were correct it does not prove that his theory is supported by ordinary usage. It merely shows that ordinary usage is indifferent between the two theories, using sometimes the one and sometimes the other to ensure the assessibility of identity claims. Perry's point may be that in (7.9) and (7.10) there is some redundancy which could be removed by the deletion of the covering concept. But this is not right either, for the result of these deletions on (7.9) and (7.10) is:

(7.11)   This river is the same as that river.

Clearly a theory which reduced both (7.9) and (7.10) to (7.11) is false.

However, Perry intends something more than a mere deletion of covering concepts. He would presumably require (7.10) to be rewritten as:

(7.12)   This water is the same as that water.

In general he would require that the substantival term in the singular terms of the identity statement should be that which covers the identity. But (7.12) doesn't even look as if it will preserve the sense of (7.10). In (7.10) the ostension was to

[37] E. M. Zemach, 'In Defence of Relative Identity', *Philosophical Studies*, 26 (1974), 214-15.
[38] 'Identity', pp. 80-1.

rivers, in (7.12) it is to expanses of water. To validate his own theory against the relativist Perry would have to show that there was something defective in the reference provided by 'this river' and 'that river' in (7.10) so that what was really intended was a reference to expanses of water. But this does not seem very plausible. There seems to be no reason why we must, in saying that '*a* is the same *ℱ* as *b*', use as covering concept the same general noun which was used (implicitly or explicitly) to make the reference to the items of which the identity is asserted. If this were the case then clearly the covering concept would be redundant. Of course, in ordinary usage this is often what happens and this gives Perry's theory its plausibility. And, equally obviously, the general term used to make the reference *could* be the one which supplies the criteria of identity, but while this is always possible there is no reason to think it is always the case.

Suppose, however, that Perry can devise some rewriting procedure for (7.9) and (7.10) so as to rid them in some plausible way of nouns in covering concept position. There is still cause for some uneasiness. It's not just that his canonical language will then become more remote from natural language but that, having come so far from natural language in reducing in-definitely many identity relations to one, why doesn't he go further and abolish identity altogether as Wittgenstein did? Of course, there are good grounds for not abolishing identity in a canonical language into which natural language can be translated,[39] but there are equally good (and very similar) reasons for not abolishing relative identity in such a language. In the range of theories, from those which have no identity relation to those which have indefinitely many, there is no good reason to think that a theory which has just one thereby achieves some special attraction.

Perry's second argument for his theory is related to Bradley's argument about the generalizability of sense-indefiniteness, except that Perry accepts the conclusion Bradley rejects and claims that as all statements in which predicates are attached to proper names have the sort of indefiniteness which (D) attributes to identity statements it can't be the identity relation that is at fault but the proper names.[40] This line of argument

---

[39] See Quine, *Methods of Logic*, p. 209.   [40] Perry, 'Identity', p. 81.

considerably underestimates the role of identity criteria in natural language. If failure to convey a criterion of identity leads to a certain sort of inadequacy among identity statements, there seems no reason to suppose that it mightn't lead to some related sort of inadequacy in referential statements, for the two are closely linked. Failure to convey a criterion of identity is, as I have stressed already, a very important omission, not merely in identity statements, but in many other statements which involve a singular term.

While I see nothing in Perry's arguments which would force his theory upon us, nothing we have so far said shows that he is wrong, and the relativist right. I think, however, that if (R) is true then we are able to dismiss Perry's theory, for if different covering concepts make a difference to the truth or falsity of an identity statement then there seems to be no sense-preserving Perryan rewrite of such a statement. We may well make ostensions to rivers (which are expanses of water) and yet intend, by an identity statement, identity of expanses of water, not rivers. Just because we intend identity of expanses of water doesn't mean that our ostensions are 'really' to expanses of water and not to rivers.

On the other hand, if (R) is false then all the covering concepts for a given identity statement must provide equivalent identity criteria so that, no matter which of the possible covering concepts is chosen, the truth-value of the resulting statement will remain unchanged. We may still hold that a substantival covering concept is required to provide criteria of identity according to which the identity statement may be judged, but it is now a matter of indifference whether this term is supplied by the singular terms of the statement or by the relation itself: the answer given by one will be the same as that given by the other. Thus it will be possible to assess the truth or falsity of an identity statement so long as some sortal under which both items fall is known.

Perry's theory is related to the Fregean analysis, in that both are devices for extracting absolute identity statements out of relative ones. One might accept one or the other for this purpose or, as Perry in fact does, employ them both. It is clear that if either is introduced into a (D)-relative identity theory then relative identity relations become no more than absolute identity relations restricted to a certain category of items. As Geach complains 'any such theory differs only in a trivial way from a theory of absolute identity'[41] and is not the true doctrine.

7.5 That (D) is False

It became clear in the last section that Wiggins's (D)-relative identity theory was a redundant complication of the theory of absolute identity. That being so the status of its main postulate (D. II) is thrown in doubt: for how can a theory which reduces to the absolute theory maintain that no thesis of the absolute theory can be assigned a truth-value? Wiggins can protect his theory against Stevenson's reduction argument by denying the Fregean analysis. And he would have good grounds for denying the Fregean analysis if only he had good grounds for accepting a strong form of (D). It is, however, not so easy to defend his theory against a collapse argument based on Perry's theory since all the arguments Wiggins adduces in favour of (D. II) can be employed by Perry to support his alternative, and thus cannot be used to block the definition on which the Perryan collapse argument is based. Only (R)-relative identity theories are protected against both forms of collapse.

Perry's natural language counter-examples to (D. II) are, I think, less worrying since it was never in dispute that in certain contexts statements of the form '$a = b$' could be assigned a truth-value. Such statements in contexts which make it clear that the sortal which appears (explicitly or implicitly) in 'a' and 'b' gives the respect in which identity is intended clearly fall within that proviso. Here again, however, the (R)-relativist is at an advantage, since for the (D)-relativist *any* sortal common to a and b will do for if a and b are identical with respect to some sortal they are identical with respect to every common sortal. Thus knowing that some sortal, '$\mathscr{F}$' say, is common to a and b is all the conceptual information we require to assign

---

[41] Geach, 'Ontological Relativity and Relative Identity', p. 282. As already remarked, Stevenson's first-order formal system for Wiggins's theory collapses into standard first-order predicate calculus with absolute identity given two definitions: one embodying the Fregean analysis for absolute identity and one, embodying Wiggins's assumptions about ultimate sortals, for unrestricted quantification. Cf. Stevenson, 'A Formal Theory of Sortal Quantification', pp. 203–4. A similar collapse follows from Perry's theory if we define:

$$(x_f = y_f) =_{df} (x =_f y).$$

a truth-value to '$a = b$'. Since Wiggins holds that a sortal under which a falls tells us what a is, it is tempting to assume that, at least in every case where '$(\exists f)(a =_f b)$' is true, we will possess the necessary conceptual knowledge to assign a truth-value to '$a = b$'. Certainly this will very often be the case. On the other hand, even if the (R)-relativist knows that '$\mathscr{F}$' and '$\mathscr{G}$' are common to a and b he still may not be able to assign a truth-value to '$a = b$' since a and b may be $\mathscr{F}$-identical yet $\mathscr{G}$-distinct. The range of exceptions to (D. II) is clearly going to be much narrower for an (R)-relativist than for a (D)-relativist.

In § 6.1 I noted three different accounts of '$a = b$' the first two of which are compatible with (R): the classical account using (LL), the ($\forall a$)-account, and the ($\exists a$)-account. It can now be shown that on each account there are occasions when '$a = b$' may be assigned a truth-value. Ironically it is on the ($\exists a$)-account, which Wiggins favours, that counter-examples are most obvious. Wiggins admits that truth-values can be assigned to statements of the form '$a =_\mathscr{F} b$'. On the ($\exists a$)-account if $\mathbf{V}(a =_\mathscr{F} b) = \mathbf{T}$ then $\mathbf{V}(a = b) = \mathbf{T}$. On the ($\forall a$)-account the reverse obviously holds: we can assign truth-values to statements of the form '$a \neq_\mathscr{F} b$'; if $\mathbf{V}(a \neq_\mathscr{F} b) = \mathbf{T}$ then $\mathbf{V}(a = b) = \mathbf{F}$. Counter-examples on the classical view are more difficult, but I have already argued in § 4.4 that so long as we can locate a and b under some sortal we may be able to judge whether or not they share all their properties. This is because once we know what a is by discovering a sortal under which it falls we know what is to count as a property of a (and similarly for b) and thus we can circumvent the Dummett–Herbst objections to the criteriality of (LL). Thus there seems to be no convincing support for the claim that we cannot assign a truth-value to '$a = b$' even on the classical account. And if all this appears too general and abstract to be convincing there is an obvious example of an absolute identity statement which is true on all three accounts, namely: '$a = a$'.[42]

It seems that (D. II) is false, even if we make appropriate allowances for context. As a result the stronger (D)-thesis (D. I) is also false, for if we are actually able to assign a truth-

[42] Since

$$\mathbf{V}((\forall \phi)[\phi(a) \equiv \phi(a)]) = \mathbf{V}((\forall a)[a(a) \supset a =_a a]) = \mathbf{V}((\exists a)(a =_a a)) = \mathbf{T}.$$

value to some statements of the form '$a = b$' such statements are not indeterminate in truth-conditions. The only support for (D. I) that we have been able to find comes from the function thesis, but no one has provided any arguments to support the function thesis and, indeed, with the possible exception of Dummett, no one actually believes it. The theory I shall be defending in what follows is like Locke's in that it includes (R) but not (D). It includes the absolute theory as a special case of the relative theory and thus has a greater range of application than the absolute theory while it loses none of the advantages (overrated though they are) of classical identity theory. The theory, however, is significantly different from Locke's—in fact, it stands Locke's theory on its head. On Locke's theory, if I have understood it correctly, items are the same or distinct absolutely. However, even though a and b are two (absolutely) distinct items they may yet be the same $\mathscr{A}$, and *a fortiori* they may be distinct $\mathscr{B}$s. Absolute identity is the fundamental type of identity on the Lockean theory. It is absolute identity which tells us how many items there are in a domain; to count them we assign 1 to an item a and to every item absolutely identical with a and to nothing else; we assign 2 to item b and to every item absolutely identical with b and to nothing else; and so on. On the theory I advocate the notion of an individual item is incoherent without reference to a set of individuative principles. It is the role of sortals in natural language to provide these principles. Accordingly, counting the number of items in a domain is impossible except by reference to some sortal. We can tell how many $\mathscr{F}$s or how many $\mathscr{G}$s there are in a domain but not how many items there are because there is no definite number of items. We count the $\mathscr{F}$s by assigning 1 to an item a and to anything which is the same $\mathscr{F}$ as a and to nothing else; and so on. (Since I shall argue that (R) is true I have no reason to expect the count of $\mathscr{G}$s to be the same as the count of $\mathscr{F}$s.) Thus on my theory relative identities are fundamental. Once $\mathscr{F}$s and $\mathscr{G}$s are individuated we can go on to inquire whether an individual $\mathscr{F}$ shares all its properties with an individual $\mathscr{G}$ and thus whether they are absolutely identical; or whether the $\mathscr{F}$ and the $\mathscr{G}$ share all their members and are thus the same set; or measure them and thus tell whether they are the same height. Thus absolute identity and all forms of relative identity (not just sortal-relative identity) can be accommodated. But until we individuate our items we have no means of knowing what their properties (or what their members) are. It seems to me that this view of identity lies behind Geach's defining being an $\mathscr{F}$ in terms of being the same $\mathscr{F}$ as something or other instead of vice versa. Wiggins was right in assigning a fundamental role to sortals in the logic of identity but wrong in trying to formulate this insight by means of (D).

8

Some General Arguments on (R)-Relative Identity

8.1 Formal Requirements of Identity

Any relation which is to count as an identity relation must satisfy the formal syntactical requirements of reflexivity, symmetry, and transitivity. A relation which failed any of these could not be an identity relation. Reflexivity for relative identity is given by:

(RR) $(\forall x)(\forall a)(a(x) \supset x =_a x).$

(The principle that $(\forall x)(\forall a)(x =_a x)$ is false, for no item falls under every general noun.) Alternatively, given the unexceptionable principle:

(8.1) $(\forall x)(\exists a)(a(x))$

we can derive an unconditionalized form of reflexivity:

(8.2) $(\forall x)(\exists a)(x =_a x).$

Relative symmetry is given by:

(RS) $(\forall x, y)(\forall a)(x =_a y \supset y =_a x)$

and relative transitivity by:

(RT) $(\forall x, y, z)(\forall a)(x =_a y \ \& \ y =_a z \supset. \ x =_a z).$

With (RS) and (RT) there is no need to adopt the conditionalized form of (RR) since if $a(x)$ or $a(y)$ fails (RS) and (RT) will still hold through failure of antecedent.

Although the consistency of (RR), (RS), and (RT) with (R) is demonstrable[1] it is worth while considering some of the arguments advanced to show that relative identities fail one or

---

[1] See Routley and Griffin, 'Towards a Logic of Relative Identity'.

more of these formal requirements. Suppose we admit the following as a well-formed, quantified version of (R):

(8.3) $\qquad (\forall x, y)(\exists a, \ell)(x =_a y \ \& \ x \neq_\ell y).$

With appropriate instantiations this becomes:

(8.4) $\qquad a =_{\mathscr{A}} a \ \& \ a \neq_{\mathscr{B}} a.$

Since, by definition of '$a \neq_{\mathscr{B}} a$', we have '$\mathscr{B}(a)$', (RR) fails on account of the second conjunct of (8.4). Given that reflexivity fails, so also will one or both of transitivity and symmetry. But all this shows is that the (R)-relativist may not permit a version of (R) with universal (or multiply-general) quantification of individual variables. It does not show that he cannot hold the more reasonable version of (R):

(8.5) $\qquad (\exists x, y)(\exists a, \ell)(x =_a y \ \& \ x \neq_\ell y).$

Perry has a non-reflexivity argument which avoids this problem, though it falls foul of another. Perry assumes[2] (with Wiggins) the principle of the indiscernibility of $\mathscr{A}$-identicals (DLL). Given:

(8.6) $\qquad a =_{\mathscr{A}} b \ \& \ a \neq_{\mathscr{B}} b$

as our case of (R), we can reconstruct his argument as follows:

[1] $(\exists a)(a =_a b) \supset (\forall \phi)(\phi(a) \equiv \phi(b))$
$\qquad\qquad\qquad\qquad$ ((DLL), U.I. $a/x, b/y$)
[2] $(\exists a)(a =_a b)$ $\qquad$ ((8.6), Simp. E.G. $a/\mathscr{A}$)
[3] $(\forall \phi)(\phi(a) \equiv \phi(b))$ $\qquad$ ([1][2], M.P.)
[4] $a \neq_{\mathscr{B}} b \supset a \neq_{\mathscr{B}} a$ $\qquad$ ([3], U.I. $a \neq_{\mathscr{B}} \zeta/\phi(\zeta)$, Simp.)
[5] $a \neq_{\mathscr{B}} a$ $\qquad$ ((8.6) Simp. [4], M.P.)

But this is not terribly damaging either, for we already know (from the proof in § 1.5) that (DLL) is incompatible with (R). In order to block Perry's proof the (R)-relativist has merely to reject (DLL) and this he has to do anyway on pain of contradiction.

I know of only two other arguments which seek to show that (R)-relative identity relations fail the formal identity requirements and both can be as easily dismissed. The first is due to

---

[2] Though he does not state it. See 'Identity', p. 27; 'The Same *F*', p. 186.

Thomason.[3] Suppose $\mathbf{V}$ is a bivalent valuation and that $\mathbf{V}(a =_{\mathscr{A}} b) = \mathbf{T}$. Then, if $\mathbf{V}(b =_{\mathscr{B}} b) = \mathbf{T}$, and $\mathbf{V}(a =_{\mathscr{A}} b \supset (b =_{\mathscr{B}} b \supset a =_{\mathscr{B}} b)) = \mathbf{T}$, it follows that $\mathbf{V}(a =_{\mathscr{B}} b) = \mathbf{T}$, and hence that (R) is false. The alternative is to reject $\mathbf{V}(b =_{\mathscr{B}} b) = \mathbf{T}$ or $\mathbf{V}(a =_{\mathscr{A}} b \supset (b =_{\mathscr{B}} b \supset a =_{\mathscr{B}} b)) = \mathbf{T}$, but $b =_{\mathscr{B}} b$ and $a =_{\mathscr{A}} b \supset (b =_{\mathscr{B}} b \supset a =_{\mathscr{B}} b)$ 'are both valid in the two-valued logic of identity'.[4] However this may be in the classical theory of identity, it is not the case in the relative theory; $b =_{\mathscr{B}} b$ is valid, even in a (D)-relative theory, only so long as $\mathscr{B}(b)$ is, so all we have is $\mathbf{V}(\mathscr{B}(b) \supset b =_{\mathscr{B}} b) = \mathbf{T}$. However, we could reconstruct Thomason's argument to allow for this. What the (R)-relativist is under no obligation to accept is the validity of

$$(8.7) \qquad a =_{\mathscr{A}} b \supset (b =_{\mathscr{B}} b \supset a =_{\mathscr{B}} b)$$

which results from the simple denial of his main thesis. (Of course, he has to accept the validity of $a =_{\mathscr{B}} b \supset (b =_{\mathscr{B}} b \supset a =_{\mathscr{B}} b)$, but the difference between the two is precisely the point in question.) In fact (8.7) follows from the relativized version of Wang's Law:

$$(8.8) \qquad \phi(a) \equiv (\exists x)(\phi(x) \ \& \ a =_{\mathscr{A}} x)$$

which gives on instantiation

$$(8.9) \qquad (\phi(b) \ \& \ a =_{\mathscr{A}} b) \equiv \phi(a)$$

and thence, substituting '$\zeta =_{\mathscr{B}} b$' for '$\phi(\zeta)$', (8.7). But the (R)-relativist would no more want to accept (8.8) than he would (DLL), for (DLL) is derivable from (8.8).[5]

The second argument is due to Quine,[6] and runs parallel to Thomason's. Suppose that '$R_1(\zeta,\eta)$' and '$R_2(\zeta,\eta)$' are two relations such that:

$$(8.10) \qquad (\forall x) R_1(x,x)$$

$$(8.11) \qquad (\forall x) R_2(x,x)$$

$$(8.12) \qquad (\forall x,y)(R_1(x,y) \ \& \ \phi(x) \supset. \ \phi(y))$$

$$(8.13) \qquad (\forall x,y)(R_2(x,y) \ \& \ \phi(x) \supset. \ \phi(y))$$

---

[3] 'A Semantic Theory of Sortal Incorrectness', p. 225. (I've paraphrased his argument slightly.)   [4] Ibid.

[5] This argument might prove awkward for Geach since he holds that any identity relation '$R(\zeta, \eta)$' must satisfy $\phi(a) \equiv (\exists x)(\phi(x) \ \& \ R(a,x))$. But see § 8.3 for discussion.

[6] 'Reply to Professor Marcus', in *The Ways of Paradox*, p. 178.

all obtain. Then it follows that '$R_1(\zeta,\eta)$' and '$R_2(\zeta,\eta)$' are coextensive, since by (8.12) we have $(\forall x)(\forall y)(R_1(x,y)$ & $R_2(x,x)$ $\supset R_2(x,y))$. From here Quine's argument duplicates Thomason's. He derives $(\forall x,y)(R_1(x,y) \supset R_2(x,y))$, by means of (8.11), and its converse by a parallel argument using (8.13) instead of (8.12), thus establishing coextensivity. The argument fails, of course, because with (R)-relative identity relations for '$R_1(\zeta,\eta)$' and '$R_2(\zeta,\eta)$' (8.12) and (8.13) do not hold. The common feature in these four attempts to prove the formal inadequacy of (R)-relative identity theories is that they each insist on attributing to the (R)-relativist principles of absolute identity which he is happy to deny. Nothing has so far been done to force us to reject (R).

8.2 Substitutivity Principles for Relative Identity[7]

While (R) does not run into trouble with reflexivity, symmetry, and transitivity (provided these are correctly formulated), we have so far provided no substitutivity principle for (R)-relative identity. Such inferences as the following clearly need justification by an adequate theory of identity:

(I) a is the same colour as b. a is red./ $\therefore$ b is red.
(II) a is the same car as b. a is 12 feet long./ $\therefore$ b is 12 feet long.

How such inferences are to be justified is problematic. Plainly (DLL) is not the principle, and neither is (8.8).

A number of attempts have been made to formulate correct substitutivity principles for (R)-relative identity. Wiggins proposed a version of (Ind. Id.) which, he claims, 'is unquestionable on any view':[8]

$$(8.14) \quad a =_\mathscr{A} b \supset (\forall\phi)[(\forall x)(x =_\mathscr{A} a \supset \phi(x))$$
$$\equiv (\forall y)(y =_\mathscr{A} b \supset \phi(y))].$$

Wiggins's objection to (8.14) is that it does not, on its own,

---

[7] My usage of 'substitutivity principle' is somewhat sloppy, since I propose to ignore the distinction in absolute identity theory between (LL) and the principle of the substitutivity of identicals for the sake of a concise terminology. (On the distinction see, e.g., Richard Cartwright, 'Identity and Substitutivity', in M. K. Munitz (ed.), *Identity and Individuation*, pp. 119-33.)

[8] *Identity and Spatio-Temporal Continuity*, p. 21.

license the inferences we want licensed. Given '$a =_{\mathscr{A}} b$' and '$\phi(a)$' then, as Wiggins rightly says, we can get as far as

$$(8.15) \qquad (\forall x)(x =_{\mathscr{A}} a \supset \phi(x)) \equiv (\forall y)(y =_{\mathscr{A}} b \supset \phi(y))$$

by universal instantiation and *modus ponens* but we cannot get to '$\phi(b)$' without the additional assumption:

$$(8.16) \qquad\qquad (\forall x)(x =_{\mathscr{A}} a \supset \phi(x)).$$

Moreover, if we admit (8.16) we rule out (R)—substitute '$\zeta =_{\mathscr{B}} a$' for '$\phi(\zeta)$'—and thus we lose the very principle we sought to preserve.

Wiggins's objection to (8.14) holds against a similar formula proposed by Odegard in which the quantifiers are placed in such a way as to prevent the instantiations which would rule out (R):[9]

$$(8.17) \quad a =_{\mathscr{A}} b \supset (\forall \phi)[(\phi(a) \supset (\exists x)(\phi(x) \& x =_{\mathscr{A}} b)) \\ \& (\phi(b) \supset (\exists x)(\phi(x) \& x =_{\mathscr{A}} a))].$$

There is nothing in (8.17) which renders it incompatible with (R). Indeed, the quantifiers are, rather, over-protected for there seems to be no way to use (8.17) in validating the inferences we wish to validate. Moreover, (8.17), as L. H. Davis has pointed out,[10] does not distinguish relative identity relations from other symmetrical relations for if '$R(\zeta,\eta)$' is symmetrical then

$$(8.18) \quad R(a,b) \supset (\forall \phi)\{[\phi(a) \supset (\exists x)(\phi(x) \& R(x,b))] \\ \& [\phi(b) \supset (\exists x)(\phi(x) \& R(x,a))]\}.$$

On the other hand, Zemach's complaint that to prevent (8.17) collapsing into (LL) we have to deny '$(\exists x)(\phi(x) \& x = a) \supset \phi(a)$' 'and it is not clear how classical logic can survive this'[11] is unfair. Since Odegard accepts both the $(\exists \alpha)$-account of '$x = a$' and (R) he can't hold either half of Wang's law on pain of contradiction. Since Wang's law is equivalent to (LL) it is hard to see why Zemach should take seriously amendments to (LL) but treat Wang's law as inviolable.

[9] Odegard, 'Identity Through Time', p. 36. (I have added the covering concepts in (8.17)—not unfairly, since Odegard accepts the $(\exists \alpha)$-account of '$a = b$'.)

[10] Reported by Odegard in a personal communication to Richard Routley (dated 18th May, 1973).

[11] E. M. Zemach, 'In Defence of Relative Identity', p. 216.

Zemach's own proposal is not very satisfactory either. He suggests:

$$(8.19) \quad a =_{\mathscr{F}} b \equiv (\exists t)\, T\{\mathscr{F}(a) \,\&\, \mathscr{F}(b) \,\&\, [(\forall\phi)(\phi(a) \equiv \phi(b))],\, t\}.$$

'Read: a is the same $\mathscr{F}$ as b iff there is some theory t in which it is true that a is [an] $\mathscr{F}$, that b is [an] $\mathscr{F}$, ..., and that for every property ϕ in t, a is ϕ iff b is ϕ.'[12] I think this account, while it permits certain cases of (R), is too restrictive in that it doesn't permit (R) *within* a theory. It makes it appear as if cases of (R) only occurred when we had, in some muddled way, two different theories in mind. Suppose we have a theory T, in which '$a =_{\mathscr{F}} b$' and a theory T_1 in which '$a \neq_{\mathscr{G}} b$', could we not combine the two, to give theory T_2, in which '$a =_{\mathscr{F}} b \,\&\, a \neq_{\mathscr{G}} b$'? Moreover, (R) will be ruled out altogether by (8.19) if we take an entire language as the theory in question. In effect, (8.19) relativizes identity to theories but no more. As such, I don't think it goes far enough to meet the relativist's real claim.

As an alternative to (8.14) Wiggins suggests the following as a substitutivity rule:[13]

$$(8.20) \quad a =_{\mathscr{A}} b \supset (\phi(a) \text{ as an } \mathscr{A} \equiv \phi(b) \text{ as an } \mathscr{A}).$$

I am not at all sure what to make of this bizarre formula. How, for instance, are predications for which the 'as an $\mathscr{A}$' qualification is inappropriate to be taken? If a and b are the same number does it follow that a is prime as a number iff b is prime as a number? This is surely absurd and results, like many philosophical absurdities, from pursuing an analogy too hard: in this case the analogy between (R)-relative identity and what Wiggins (rather idiosyncratically) terms 'attributive adjectives'[14] such as 'big', 'small', 'tall', and 'short' where it does make sense to say that someone is tall as a man but short as a basketball player. But in any case the proposal seems of doubtful value since it does not entitle us to infer '$\phi(b)$' from '$a =_{\mathscr{A}} b$' and '$\phi(a)$', but only to infer '$\phi(b)$ as an $\mathscr{A}$' from '$a =_{\mathscr{A}} b$' and '$\phi(a)$ as an $\mathscr{A}$'. Wiggins can't just delete the 'as

---

[12] Ibid., p. 217. I've altered his formulation slightly to accord with my own notation and to remove parts of his account which become redundant in the notation I use.

[13] *Identity and Spatio-Temporal Continuity*, p. 23.

[14] Ibid. Geach uses the term somewhat similarly (cf. 'Good and Evil', p. 33) but does at least qualify them as 'logically attributive adjectives'. The linguists' use of the expression is different.

an $\mathscr{A}$' at the end of an inference as a sort of final step because, presumably, his idea is that when we have '$a =_{\mathscr{A}} b$' and '$a \neq_{\mathscr{B}} b$' and '$\phi(a)$ as an $\mathscr{A}$' we can infer '$\phi(b)$ as an $\mathscr{A}$' even though '$\sim (\phi(b)$ as a $\mathscr{B})$'. If 'as an $\mathscr{A}$' were merely deletable he would have no more than an open formula corresponding to (DLL). However, Max Cresswell has persuaded me that this proposal might be viable if we treated all predicates as having built-in (and possibly disguised) general nouns (or, in particular, sortals). Identity relations could then be treated as two-place predicates on a par with all others in carrying general nouns. If this were true, though I am not persuaded (and neither, I think, is Cresswell) that it is, it would remove the two objections just made to (8.20). The trouble now is that instead of needing only (8.20) as an axiom for identity we need an entire new axiomatics for second-order predicate calculus. How this is to be achieved in a natural way is not at all clear. The suggestions which come to mind seem hopelessly contrived and *ad hoc*.

Wiggins, of course, is not too anxious to devise adequate substitutivity principles for (R)-relative identity, but he does suggest a version which, I think, gets us close to part of what we want:[15]

(8.21) $\quad (\forall a)[(a(a) \vee a(b)) \supset a =_a b]$
$$\supset [a =_{\mathscr{B}} b \supset (\forall \phi)(\phi(a) \equiv \phi(b))].$$

Firstly, I'm not sure what '$a =_{\mathscr{B}} b$' is doing in (8.21), for if a is identical to b with respect to every general noun under which either falls, there seems little reason to add the requirement that there is some general noun under which they are identical since every item falls under some noun. Since whenever one or other of '$\mathscr{A}(a)$' or '$\mathscr{A}(b)$' is false '$a =_{\mathscr{A}} b$' will be false, it seems natural to replace Wiggins's disjunction by a conjunction. Given these two amendments we have:

(8.22) $\quad (\forall a)[(a(a) \& a(b)) \supset a =_a b] \supset (\forall \phi)(\phi(a) \equiv \phi(b))$.

With the $(\forall a)$-account of absolute identity, we have:

(8.23) $\qquad a = b \supset (\forall \phi)(\phi(a) \equiv \phi(b))$

which is classical indiscernibility of identicals.

[15] *Identity and Spatio-Temporal Continuity*, p. 20.

Wiggins's objection to (8.21) is 'how on earth does one ever establish that $(\forall a)[(a(a) \vee a(b)) \supset a =_a b]$?'[16] But, if this is to be an objection, how could we ever establish that $(\forall \phi)(\phi(a) \equiv \phi(b))$? It seems to me (see above, § 4.4) that, in certain circumstances, both can be established and that Wiggins's crisis is overdrawn. In particular, to establish $(\forall a)[a(a) \vee a(b) \supset . a =_a b]$ we need to exclude intensional general nouns (e.g. 'red object thought of by Napoleon'), however, Wiggins is prepared to admit only sortals as covering concepts and in this case it is quite easy to see that $(\forall f)[(f(a) \vee f(b)) \supset a =_f b]$ can be established in a number of cases, at least given some initial identity statement, $a =_g b$. For example, if a and b are the same number it seems highly likely that they are identical with respect to every sortal under which either falls.

The fact that (8.23) is the indiscernibility of identicals does not mean that (R) is ruled out, for (R) cuts out on just those occasions when '$a = b$' is glossed by (8.23). If a and b are identical with respect to every general noun under which they fall, they are not distinct with respect to any such general noun, so no case of (R) of the '$a =_{\mathscr{A}} b$ & $a \neq_{\mathscr{B}} b$' variety can occur. Thus there is nothing in (R)-relative identity to cause us to reject (8.22). But (8.22)'s use is limited. We can use it to validate (I) but only when a and b are not only the same colour but the same with respect to every general noun under which they fall. What of the case in which a and b are the same colour but, for example, distinct cars? (I) is still a valid inference, but we have no principle which validates it. On the other hand, the principle we propose mustn't be so strong as to licence:

(III) a is the same colour as b. a is a car./ $\therefore$ b is a car.

The formal solution is simple, what it amounts to is more difficult. For each general noun '$\mathscr{A}$' there is a class $\Delta_{\mathscr{A}}$ of predicates such that $\mathscr{A}$-identity implies indiscernibility with respect to the predicates in $\Delta_{\mathscr{A}}$, or $\Delta_{\mathscr{A}}$-indiscernibility. Formally, the principle is:

(RLL) $x =_a y \equiv (\forall \phi \in \Delta_a)(a(x) \ \& \ a(y) \ \& \ \phi(x) \equiv \phi(y))$.

Although it is difficult to know exactly for each '$\mathscr{A}$' what goes into $\Delta_{\mathscr{A}}$ and what stays out, we can say quite a bit about it. We can give at least a partial account of its member predicates since $\Delta_{\mathscr{A}}$ is closed under negation, conjunction, and material implication:

(i) $\mathscr{A}(\zeta) \in \Delta_{\mathscr{A}}$.

(ii) If $\phi(\zeta) \in \Delta_{\mathscr{A}}$ then $\sim \phi(\zeta) \in \Delta_{\mathscr{A}}$.

(iii) If $\phi(\zeta) \in \Delta_{\mathscr{A}}$ and $\psi(\zeta) \in \Delta_{\mathscr{A}}$ then $\phi(\zeta)$ & $\psi(\zeta) \in \Delta_{\mathscr{A}}$; and conversely (provided $\sim [\phi(\zeta) \equiv \sim \psi(\zeta)]$).

(iv) If $\phi(\zeta) \in \Delta_{\mathscr{A}}$ and $(\forall x)(\phi(x) \supset \psi(x))$ then $\psi(\zeta) \in \Delta_{\mathscr{A}}$.

(v) If $\phi(\zeta) \in \Delta_{\mathscr{A}}$ and $\psi(\zeta)$ results from $\phi(\zeta)$ by the replacement of every occurrence of one or more variables in $\phi(\zeta)$ then $\psi(\zeta) \in \Delta_{\mathscr{A}}$.

Finally, to ensure that $\Delta_{\mathscr{A}}$-indiscernibility is sufficient for $\mathscr{A}$-identity we add the identity criteria conveyed by '$\mathscr{A}$'. However, the complex predicate '$C_{\mathscr{A}}(\zeta, \eta)$' which expresses the identity criteria conveyed by '$\mathscr{A}$' is two-place whereas $\Delta_{\mathscr{A}}$ is a set of one-place predicates. But $C_{\mathscr{A}}(\zeta, \eta)$ can be converted to a one-place predicate by closing off one argument place with an arbitrary constant.

(vi) $$C_{\mathscr{A}}(\zeta, c) \in \Delta_{\mathscr{A}}.$$

One might be tempted to add the principle:

(iv)* If $\phi(\zeta) \in \Delta_{\mathscr{A}}$ and $(\forall x)(\psi(x) \supset \phi(x))$ then $\psi(\zeta) \in \Delta_{\mathscr{A}}$.

But in fact (iv)* is false: if we have 'ζ is the same token word as a' for $\psi(\zeta)$ and 'ζ is a type word' for $\phi(\zeta)$ then, since $(\forall x)[(x$ is the same token word as $a) \supset (x$ is a type word)] and since 'ζ is a type word' is a member of $\Delta_{\text{type word}}$, we could use (iv)* to validate

(IV) a is the same type word as b. a is the same token word as a./ $\therefore$ b is the same token word as a.

(IV) is clearly invalid. Moreover, there seems to be no further restriction that we can place on (iv)* in order to avoid such difficulties. This characterization of $\Delta_{\mathscr{A}}$ is somewhat clumsy but simplifications are not easy to find. Attempts to link $\Delta_{\mathscr{A}}$ with the significance range of '$\mathscr{A}$', for example, have so far failed.

That (RLL) is compatible with (R) is easily shown. Suppose that we have some general noun '$\mathscr{A}$' such that $\mathscr{A}(a)$ & $\mathscr{A}(b)$ and $(\forall \phi \in \Delta_{\mathscr{A}})(\phi(a) \equiv \phi(b))$, thus $a =_{\mathscr{A}} b$ by (RLL). Suppose also that there is a general noun '$\mathscr{B}$' such that $(\exists \phi \in \Delta_{\mathscr{B}})(\phi(a)$ & $\sim \phi(b))$, though $\mathscr{B}(a)$ & $\mathscr{B}(b)$, then $a \neq_{\mathscr{B}} b$. Moreover, it can be shown that (RLL), if added to a classical second-order logic, is sufficient for a complete and consistent theory of relative identity. In particular (RR), (RS), and (RT) are derivable. Thus (RLL) gives us a single axiom theory of relative identity.[17] Formally, therefore, relative identity theory shapes up every bit as well as the absolute theory.

8.3 Geach's Argument from Ontology

General arguments in favour of relative identity (like general arguments in favour of absolute identity) are rather scarce. This is not unduly surprising since when a notion as fundamental as identity is in dispute there are few principles left untouched by the dispute which may be non-question-beggingly appealed to. I know only two general arguments for (R): Zemach's argument from open-texture which, as I shall argue in § 8.4, shows that the price of rejecting certain cases of (R) is the rejection of the open-texture of general nouns; and Geach's argument from ontology which, as I argue in this section, is a lengthy failure.

Geach talks about I-predicates,[18] rather than about *the* identity relation. An I-predicate he defines as a two-place predicate '$I(\zeta, \eta)$' that satisfies Wang's schema for the constructible expressions of a theory T:

$$(8.24) \qquad \phi(a) \equiv (\exists x)(\phi(x) \ \& \ I(x, a)).$$

He takes it as unexceptionable that a two-place predicate should be an I-predicate only in relation to a given theory or language T. This is not the thesis of the relativity of identity but only notes the fact that 'what an expression signifies is

---

[17] See Routley and Griffin, 'Towards a Logic of Relative Identity' for details. For technical reasons we there adopt (RLL) as a definition rather than an axiom since this makes the completeness proof a trivial extension of the Henkin proof for second-order logic.

[18] I ignore, except in quotation, his distinction between predicates and predicables. Cf. *Reference and Generality*, pp. 24–5.

relative to the language we are using'.[19] Nor does this conflict
with his account of what an I-predicate is: different I-predicates
can be defined for different theories, for the allowable substitutions for '$\phi(\zeta)$' in (8.24) will be different. (For the predicates
which form the descriptive resources of the theory and which,
therefore, can be substituted for '$\phi(\zeta)$' Geach borrows Quine's
term 'ideology'.) According to Geach there is nothing in this
which shows that an I-predicate in a theory T must express
absolute identity for it may express only indiscernibility relative
to the ideology of T.[20]

Now what this amounts to as far as the theory of relative
identity is concerned is not at all clear. From (8.24) we can
derive:

$$(8.25) \qquad\qquad \phi(a) \ \& \ I(a, b) \supset \phi(b).$$

Suppose we have two I-predicates '$I(\zeta, \eta)$' and '$I^*(\zeta, \eta)$', both
of which satisfy (8.24)—and therefore (8.25)—and reflexivity.
Then we can, by means of Quine's argument of § 8.1, prove
that they are coextensive. But if they are coextensive they
cannot be used to generate a case of (R). Thus in the sense of
'absolute identity' which contrasts with Geach's use of 'relative
identity' we must interpret I-predicates as expressing absolute
identity. In return, by limiting substitutions to the ideology of
a given theory, we have achieved a form of relativism which
even Quine could accept. The whole notion of an I-predicate
as defined by Geach seems to have contributed nothing to the
defence of (R). On the one hand, within a theory T all I-
predicates will be coextensive, while on the other the claim that
two I-predicates in different theories are not necessarily co-
extensive is uncontroversial. But let us leave this on one side
for a while and consider the remainder of Geach's argument.

According to Geach we cannot take satisfaction of (8.24)
as a necessary and sufficient condition for an I-predicate's
expressing absolute identity. An I-predicate which satisfies
(8.24) relative to the ideological resources of some theory may

[19] Geach, 'Identity', p. 240; also 'A Reply', p. 249. This position on identity is
generally accepted by absolutists. Cf. for example, J. N. Crossley et al., What is
Mathematical Logic? (Oxford: Oxford University Press, 1972), p. 21; Quine, Set
Theory and its Logic, p. 15; Nelson, 'Relative Identity', pp. 244–5. It seems to
conflict with some of the other things Geach says, as we'll see later.

[20] 'Identity', p. 240.

either express theory-relative relative identity, or theory-relative absolute identity (if we may allow ourselves these ill-begotten expressions for the present section only). On the other hand, it does appear that Geach holds that if we don't relativize *I*-predicates to the ideological resources of a given theory we have to interpret them as absolute identity relations (theory-independent absolute identity). Geach doesn't state such a principle but his next move is incomprehensible without it, for he proceeds to sketch an argument to show that we *have* to relativize *I*-predicates to a given theory.[21] If we do not so relativize the *I*-predicates then we can say that whatever is true of something identical to *a* is true of *a*, and this unqualified talk of 'whatever is true of' leads to the semantic paradoxes.[22] On pain of paradox we have to relativize the *I*-predicates to the ideology of a given theory. If all this is correct then Geach has shown that the relative identity interpretation of the *I*-predicates is permissible, he has not shown that it is obligatory.

This last stage of the argument, however, is only valid if relativizing substitutions to the ideology of a theory is the only way of avoiding the semantic paradoxes.[23] As an alternative we may deny that all sentences are either true or false and claim, in particular, that those which give rise to the paradoxes are neither. We then get no paradox from the claim that whatever is *true* of something identical with *a* is *true* of *a*.[24] On the other hand, there might be independent grounds for relativizing substitutions to the ideology of a given theory, so that this course is unavoidable whether or not the semantic paradoxes argument is valid.

Be this as it may we have still to decide whether Geach is correct in claiming that an *I*-predicate need not express

---

[21] Ibid. Clearly, given the concerns of the present argument, there would be no point in showing that we had to relativize *I*-predicates to a theory if the question was totally irrelevant to the interpretation of *I*-predicates as expressing either relative or absolute identity.

[22] 'Identity', p. 240.

[23] The connection between the paradoxes and the classical account of identity is problematic. See Feldman, 'Geach and Relative Identity', *Review of Metaphysics*, 22 (1968/9), pp. 549–50; Geach, 'A Reply', ibid., p. 557 (deleted in *Logic Matters*).

[24] This suggestion comes from Carl Calvert, 'Relative Identity', pp. 18–19. For a more general account of such suggestions see R. L. Martin (ed.), *The Paradox of the Liar* (New Haven: Yale University Press, 1970). In my entire discussion of this argument I am indebted to Calvert's long and careful discussion.

absolute identity when it is relativized to a given theory. Geach argues for this claim in the following way. Suppose we have two theories T and $T+$ such that T's ideology is a proper subset of the ideology of $T+$ and that the predicate '$I(\zeta, \eta)$' is common to both. Suppose further that '$I(\zeta, \eta)$' is an I-predicate in T but not in $T+$. It follows, since satisfaction of (8.24) is a necessary condition for '$I(\zeta, \eta)$' expressing absolute identity, that '$I(\zeta, \eta)$' does not express absolute identity in $T+$. But '$I(\zeta, \eta)$' in T is synonymous with '$I(\zeta, \eta)$' in $T+$ and since it does not express absolute identity in $T+$ it does not in T either. Thus satisfaction of (8.24), though a necessary condition for '$I(\zeta, \eta)$' expressing absolute identity, is not a sufficient condition. Thus there is no need to assume that an I-predicate expresses absolute identity.[25] Geach will also, presumably, argue that there is nothing to stop us adding predicates to our present natural language, L, in such a way that things previously identical (because indiscernible) in L become discernible (and thus non-identical) in $L+$. If this occurs then the I-predicates in L will be found not to express absolute identity, and as we do not wish to impede the development of the ideology of our language we had best not assume that any predicate in L expresses absolute identity. Now if all this is correct Geach has gone further than his original argument for the *permissibility* of a relative identity interpretation of I-predicates, and has given us a positive reason for not accepting the absolute identity interpretation. Whether it is correct I shall consider later.

According to Geach,[26] Quine's view of this matter would be that if we find an I-predicate in T we must[27] construe the range of the quantifiers of T as the class of objects for which the I-predicate expresses absolute identity and construe the other predicates of T accordingly. In the wider system $T+$ the range of the quantifiers may be different and, although each complete sentence of T is unchanged in $T+$ and has the same

[25] Geach, 'Identity', p. 240.

[26] Ibid., pp. 241–2. For evidence that this is indeed Quine's view see *Set Theory and its Logic*, p. 15.

[27] 'Must' is in dispute here. Quine's *Set Theory and its Logic* suggests 'may', but if we use 'may' there is no conflict with Geach's permissive conclusion. See Perry, 'Identity', p. 38 and Calvert, 'Relative Identity', p. 25 for a discussion of the issues.

truth-conditions, the parts of each sentence will need reconstruing. Suppose, to use Geach's example, we let the quantifiers of T range over the words and letters in a book, and furthermore suppose that the ideology of T is so impoverished that it cannot discriminate between different tokens of the same type. Let '$I(\zeta, \eta)$' be an I-predicate in T. Now, on the considerations of the preceding argument we have two possible interpretations: (i) We can treat the quantifiers of T as ranging over token words and token letters and read '$I(a, b)$' as 'a is a token equiform with b'; or (ii) we can treat the quantifiers as ranging over type words and type letters and read '$I(a, b)$' as 'a is absolutely identical with b'. Quine, says Geach, would have us choose the second alternative.

We can construe the difference between the two interpretations in terms of set theory: in the first the quantifiers range over individuals and in the second over sets of individuals. With this in mind we can get a better idea of the concept of absolute identity which Geach is here using to contrast with relative identity and thus resolve some of the puzzlement with which this section opened. A *partition* π of a set A is a set of mutually exclusive, non-empty subsets of A whose union equals A. Partition π_1 *is finer than* partition π_2 iff they are not the same and every set of π_1 is included in some set of π_2. The *finest partition* of a set is a partition finer than any other partition of the set.[28] Every I-predicate determines a partition of the domain over which range the quantifiers of the theory with respect to which the I-predicate was defined. An I-predicate which expresses absolute identity determines the finest partition of the domain. According to Quine, therefore, we should always interpret the quantifiers of a theory in such a way that the I-predicate of the theory determines the finest partition of the domain of the quantifiers. According to Geach we need not do this. Now, as Calvert points out,[29] we can always reinterpret a theory whose I-predicate does not determine the finest partition in such a way that it does. Let π_D be the partition of the domain $\mathbf{D}$ determined by the I-predicate, '$I(\zeta, \eta)$', of the theory T. Now either π_D is the finest partition of $\mathbf{D}$, or it is not. If

[28] Cf. Patrick Suppes, *Axiomatic Set Theory* (Princeton: van Nostrand, 1960), pp. 80–5.
[29] 'Relative Identity', pp. 28–9.

it is then the equivalence class of '$I(\zeta, \eta)$' is a unit class. If it is not then we can reinterpret the quantifiers of T in such a way as to range over π_D, the set of equivalence classes of '$I(\zeta, \eta)$', instead of over **D**. Thus an absolute identity interpretation of '$I(\zeta, \eta)$' is always possible. Alternatively, if '$I(\zeta, \eta)$' doesn't determine the finest partition of **D** we can delete from each class of π_D all but one member; or again, we can increase the ideology of T until '$I(\zeta, \eta)$' does produce the finest partition. In dealing with cases of (R) all three methods are sometimes used by absolutists.

Geach then goes on, in the third part of his argument, to give a reason for rejecting Quine's interpretation. Suppose we have a range of theories, T_1, T_2, T_3, etc. each of which is a sub-theory of a richer theory T, from which they might be formed by, say, the omission of certain predicates. We can then suppose a range of two-place predicates, '$I_1(\zeta, \eta)$', '$I_2(\zeta, \eta)$', '$I_3(\zeta, \eta)$', etc. each of which was an I-predicate in one of the sub-theories: '$I_1(\zeta, \eta)$' in T_1, etc. Now, according to Quine, '$I_1(\zeta, \eta)$' would have to express (or should be thought of as expressing) absolute identity in T_1, '$I_2(\zeta, \eta)$' in T_2, etc. As a consequence of Quine's view the quantifiers in T_1 would have to be construed as having a different range from those in T_2, and similarly for all the sub-theories. But, claims Geach, this offends against 'a highly intuitive methodological program'[30] adumbrated by Quine himself, namely that we should allow our ideology to expand fairly easily but that our ontology, though always revisable, should be kept relatively definite and not allowed to expand without good reason. For if we construe '$I_1(\zeta, \eta)$', '$I_2(\zeta, \eta)$', etc. as absolute identity predicates in T_1, T_2, etc., respectively, then our ontology is going to change as we move from one theory to the next.[31] Geach concludes: 'We wanted to keep our ontology comparatively fixed while allowing changes in our ideology, but now some quite trivial changes in our ideology—the mere omission of some predicates from a theory—will result in quite large additions to our ontology, to the realm our quantifiers are supposed to range over.'[32]

[30] 'Identity', p. 243.
[31] Quite how it will change is left unclear. Geach implies that ontology will expand as ideology does (ibid., p. 243) but gives an example in which ontology expands as ideology contracts (ibid., p. 245).
[32] Ibid., p. 244.

Now Quine, because he insists that I-predicates should always be interpreted as expressing absolute identity, is presumably prepared to accept some changes in ontology, so what Geach is called on to show is that the changes in ontology are undesirable ones from Quine's point of view. The example which Geach uses to support this claim is one of the most misunderstood parts of his paper. Suppose we have a theory, T, the ideology of which cannot discriminate between men with the same surname. Let '$I(\zeta, \eta)$' (read: 'ζ is the same surman as η') be the only I-predicate in T, where 'ζ is the same surman as η' means 'ζ and η are both men and have the same single surname'.[33] According to Geach, interpreting '$I(\zeta, \eta)$' as expressing absolute identity calls into being, as values of the quantifiers of T, a universe of androids (viz. surmen) who differ from men only in that different surmen cannot have the same surname. Such ontological expansion is undesirable for 'Leeds does not contain androids as well as men.'[34] One absolutist response to this is to claim that if '$I(\zeta, \eta)$' is to be interpreted as an absolute identity relation then it holds between classes of men and not between men. Nothing ontologically undesirable follows from this because Leeds does contain classes of men as well as men.[35] But, as Geach replies,[36] this is simply to rewrite his account of '$I(\zeta, \eta)$'. He did not intend it to hold between classes of men but between men, and, since he invented the notion, he can define it as he will. Until the absolutist can show that there is something incoherent in the notion as Geach defined it he will have to stick with Geach's account. As Geach defined it, however, Perry can't give any absolute identity interpretation at all, for, he claims, '$I(\zeta, \eta)$' is simply equivalent to 'ζ has the same surname as η', where the names of men fill the place-holders and that 'is clearly not an identity predicate'.[37] Well, it is clearly not an absolute identity predicate but there is nothing, on present showing, which prevents it from being a relative identity predicate and, since it is the only I-predicate of T, it looks as though the upholders of T will have no option but to reject the absolute interpretation of their I-predicate

---

[33] For this definition see 'Ontological Relativity and Relative Identity', p. 294. (For an equivalent, though more cumbersome, one see 'Identity', p. 245.)

[34] 'Identity', p. 245.   [35] Perry, 'Identity', p. 55.

[36] 'Ontological Relativity and Relative Identity', p. 295.

[37] 'Identity', p. 55.

and this concession was no more than Geach wanted to force them to.

A second possible reply to Geach's argument is that it depends as much on an ontological interpretation of the quantifiers as on absolute identity. Geach himself combines ontological quantification within restricted domains with unrestricted substitutional quantification.[38] In the cases in question here he takes it that the quantifiers occur within a theory applying to a restricted domain and are therefore to be objectually interpreted. On the other hand there is nothing to force us to accept the ontological interpretation of the quantifiers, and the most Geach's argument shows is that we cannot have both the ontological interpretation and absolute identity (as Quine does).

The third absolutist reply is that given by Feldman.[39] Feldman supposes that he used to speak a certain simple language[40] T and then came, by and by, to adopt a more complex one $T+$. He claims that in this case he would be able to drop the existential commitments of T in favour of those of $T+$. For example, suppose that in T he could not discriminate between a and b, he would be committed to the existence of only one entity which was named by both 'a' and 'b'. Later, as his language expands to $T+$, he is able to discriminate between a and b and is therefore committed to the existence of two entities, one named by 'a' and another named by 'b'. But he is not committed to a third object, named by both 'a' and 'b', which is a hangover from the earlier language T. In other words, although our ontology may expand it will not expand indecently.

Geach replies[41] that the relation he envisaged between T

---

[38] Cf. *Reference and Generality*, pp. 144–67. For further details on the substitutional interpretation see, *inter alia*, Ruth Barcan Marcus, 'Interpreting Quantification', *Inquiry*, 5 (1962), 252–9. For some of the difficulties with the substitutional interpretation see J. M. Dunn and N. D. Belnap, 'The Substitution Interpretation of the Quantifiers', *Nous*, 2 (1968), 177–85; and for a similar theory which avoids these problems see R. Routley, 'Domainless Semantics for Free, Quantification and Significance Logics', *Logique et Analyse*, 14 (1971), 603–26.

[39] 'Geach and Relative Identity', pp. 553–4.

[40] Although Feldman speaks of 'languages' his argument will go through, *mutatis mutandis*, if 'theories' is substituted. The difference is potentially an important one in view of Geach's use of objectual quantification within theories. See 'Ontological Relativity and Relative Identity', p. 298.

[41] 'A Reply', p. 248. (Geach here follows Feldman in speaking of 'languages' rather than 'theories'.) See also 'Ontological Relativity and Relative Identity', p. 299.

and $T+$ is not historical but set-theoretic. T is a sub-language of $T+$ and as such users of $T+$ will be committed to all the existential commitments of T which is a mere part of $T+$: these commitments cannot be repudiated by anyone who still continues to speak $T+$. To go back to Feldman's example: when we can't distinguish between a and b we are committed to one object named by both 'a' and 'b', when we can distinguish them we have to admit two objects. But, here, Geach's argument becomes obscure. He seems to be claiming that the identity of a and b in T, if it is construed as absolute identity, cannot then be repudiated—hence the hangover of the third object when $T+$ is formed. Whereas, on the relative identity thesis, such claims could be repudiated and the hangover doesn't occur. But he has already distinguished[42] between the relative identity thesis and the view that a predicate is an I-predicate only relative to a given theory (a view which is uncontroversial). Now if the relation between a and b expressed in T is only *relative to* T, although *absolute in* T, is there really any reason why we cannot repudiate our existential commitments in T when we go on to develop $T+$? Admittedly, the situation envisaged by Feldman is simpler: for there T is repudiated and, with it, its existential claims. In the situation envisaged by Geach T is not repudiated but only incorporated into a wider theory $T+$. But a statement '$I(a, b)$' in T is construed as an (absolute in T) identity statement relative to T-*on-its-own*. This last clause is essential, for it is admitted by the absolutist that in the wider system, $T+$, '$I(a, b)$' might not be construed as an identity statement. Now the existential commitments of T which follow from '$I(a, b)$' being an identity statement are commitments of T-*on-its-own*. When this last clause is violated, however, (by the addition to T of predicates to form $T+$) there seems no reason to retain the existential commitments of T-*on-its-own*. In other words, when we repudiate a theory we repudiate its existential commitments. But when the existential commitments of a theory depend essentially on the theory's not being added to in certain ways, then when we add to the theory in just those ways we are surely justified in repudiating those existential commitments even though we don't actually repudiate any of the theses of the original theory.

42 'Identity', pp. 239–40.

Thus, even with both absolute identity and the ontological interpretation of the quantifiers, we do not get an indecently bloated ontology. Neither are we prevented from expanding our ideology. Perry[43] supposes a language T in which no distinction could be made between different tokens of the same type word. In this language the predicate '$I(\zeta, \eta)$' is construed as an I-predicate. We then suppose the development of a richer language $T+$ by adding to T the predicate '$K(\zeta, \eta)$'. '$K(a, b)$' is true iff token a is more legible than token b. Thus in $T+$ '$I(\zeta, \eta)$' is not an I-predicate. Now Perry argues that even though we interpret '$I(\zeta, \eta)$' as expressing absolute identity, this wouldn't stop us from adding the predicate '$K(\zeta, \eta)$' to T, although to make this addition useful we would have to add names for token words as well. This language, i.e. T plus '$K(\zeta, \eta)$' plus names for tokens, he calls $T++$. By interpreting '$I(\zeta, \eta)$' as an I-predicate in T we do not prevent the development of $T++$. Of course '$I(\zeta, \eta)$' is no longer an I-predicate in $T++$, but this amounts to no more than the claim that Geach admits to be uncontroversial that the sense of '$I(\zeta, \eta)$' is relative to the language in which it is expressed. If all this is right then the absolutist can maintain the twin advantages of expanding his ideology whilst keeping his ontology in check without even having to give up the ontological interpretation of the quantifiers.

In his later article, however, Geach suggests a different version of his argument, in which the trouble is not caused by surmen, or better by reduplicating surmen *and* men, but by a third type of item: absolute surmen. Absolute surmen are entities for which 'ζ is the same surman as η' expresses a criterion of absolute identity.[44] At this the argument becomes even more obscure. For a paper and a half Geach has led us to believe that what worries him is that Leeds might, on the absolutist view, turn out to be populated by both men and surmen, but now the trouble seems to be that it might contain absolute surmen as well. Clearly a demographer's nightmare. But the trouble in Leeds is not just overcrowding, but that absolute surmen are logically incoherent and it is this that Geach now attempts to demonstrate:[45]

[43] 'Identity', pp. 43–5; 'The Same F', pp. 194–5.

[44] 'Ontological Relativity and Relative Identity', p. 299.

[45] The expression 'criterion of absolute identity' is a little puzzling since Geach holds that there is no such thing. In fact, all we need here is that for absolute surmen 'ζ is the same surman as η' expresses absolute identity.

[W]hatever is a surman is by definition a man. Then suppose . . . that absolute surmen are in fact men. Then since . . . the count of surmen comes out smaller than the count of men, absolute surmen will be just some among men. There will, for example, be just one surman with the surname 'Jones'; but if this is an absolute surman, who *is* a certain man, then *which* of the Jones boys is he?[46]

If the single surman with the surname 'Jones' is an absolute surman, then, since the surman with the surname 'Jones' is a man, the absolute surman will be a man and all is well— Leeds can easily cope with such men under different sortals. It is surely only if the surman with the surname 'Jones' is a family of men (as Perry has been suggesting all along) that we can't hold both that the surman with the surname 'Jones' is an absolute surman and a man.

While Geach's exposition is dreadfully confusing, Calvert has restated the argument in a way which gives it considerable force.[47] We have in theory T and its extension, $T+$, the I-predicate '$I(\zeta, \eta)$'—'ζ is the same surman as η'—which we are invited to construe as expressing absolute identity. The ideology of T cannot distinguish between different men with the same surname, the ideology of $T+$ can. The quantifiers of T thus range over a domain of surmen, those of $T+$ over a domain of men. Suppose we have two men both with the surname 'Jones', since we are construing '$I(\zeta, \eta)$' as expressing absolute identity, these two men are absolutely identical: not merely the same surman but distinct men (for that is mere relative identity), but the same absolutely. But in that case they will be the same man, for they are men and they are identical.[48] This argument will work so long as the notion of a surman is well made-out, as I believe it is. What goes wrong is the attempt to make the relation 'ζ is the same surman as η' carry more weight than it can bear—namely, that of expressing the notion of absolute identity. But then the same is true of every $\mathscr{A}$-identity relation, because for each '$\mathscr{A}$' we might extend our conceptual resources in such a way as to make $\mathscr{A}$s distinguish-

[46] 'Ontological Relativity and Relative Identity', p. 300.

[47] 'Relative Identity', pp. 43–4; fn. 41 (p. 111). Geach in his unpublished comments on Calvert's thesis raises no objection to Calvert's interpretation—which gives good reason to think that Calvert has got it right.

[48] There is no difficulty about having the predicate 'ζ is a man' even in T. Indeed, the definition of '$I(\zeta, \eta)$' requires it.

able with respect to some other general noun. This version of the argument has a lot more plausibility than any of its predecessors.

Yet Geach's conclusion is still not demonstrated. Let me list some of its doubtful assumptions. Firstly, it requires that the quantifiers of T and $T+$ be interpreted ontologically. This is not only an unnecessary assumption for the absolutist but there are good reasons for thinking it undesirable. Secondly, to avoid the embarrassment of having distinct men made identical, it is merely necessary to relativize the I-predicate to a theory. The paradox is generated by establishing results in T and then transferring them over to $T+$. If '$I(\zeta, \eta)$' conveyed absolute identity only in T the paradox could be avoided for in T the two men called 'Jones' cannot be distinguished and are therefore identical. It is only in $T+$ that we can distinguish them and generate the paradoxical result that two distinct men are one and the same man (in T we cannot even speak of 'two distinct men'). Clearly the absolutist could hold that '$I(\zeta, \eta)$' expresses absolute identity in T, while '$I^*(\zeta, \eta)$'—'ζ is the same man as η'—expresses absolute identity in $T+$.

Against this Geach has only the argument that if T is a proper part of $T+$ then the predicates which are common to both have the same sense in each. Let us now examine this assumption. In the move from T to $T+$ we have added predicates which permit different men with the same surname to be distinguished and we have changed our ontology from one of surmen to one of men. As Nelson has remarked on this argument:

[I]f the move from T to $[T+]$ does bring with it a change of ontologies it is also reasonable to think that at least some of the predicables of T, which all occur in $[T+]$, will have different senses, different dictionary readings, in $[T+]$. And if this is so it seems neither surprising nor obviously objectionable that a predicable should express [absolute] identity in T but not in $[T+]$.[49]

Moreover, Geach's conclusion that '$I(\zeta, \eta)$' has the same sense in T as in $T+$ jars with his earlier claim that 'what an expression signifies is relative to the language we are using.'[50] If Geach believes this, he should not be unduly surprised if

49 'Relative Identity', p. 248.   50 'Identity', p. 240.

'$I(\zeta, \eta)$' expresses absolute identity in T but not in $T+$. He might want to qualify his claim so that an expression signifies the same in T and $T+$ when T is a part of $T+$ but for this qualification he gives no argument. There seems to me no reason why all predicates should retain the same sense when ideologies *and* ontologies change.

Of course, Geach might well imagine that the ontology of T contains men as well as surmen, even though the ideology of T could not distinguish between different men with the same surname. Then the move to $T+$ does not alter the ontology. But such a situation is not, as Nelson points out,[51] one which the (Quinean) absolutist would accept because the ontology of T would contain distinct elements which were indiscernible in T, and appropriate Quinean measures would be taken to cut back the ontology so that only discernible distinct elements were left (effectively this would mean removing men from the ontology of T).

Thirdly, even if we insist that '$I(\zeta, \eta)$' has the same sense in $T+$ as in T we still do not have to follow Geach. As Calvert points out,[52] we could delete all but one man from the equivalence class specified by '$I(\zeta, \eta)$' in T. Alternatively, we could, following Perry[53] and Nelson,[54] adopt an ontology of classes of men in T, though '$I(\zeta, \eta)$' would not then be the relation 'ζ is the same surman as η'. This move, however, ought to be ruled out on the grounds that it is the relation 'ζ is the same surman as η' that is under discussion.

Fourthly, the notion of an absolute surman was coherent in T but incoherent in $T+$. We are only justified in rejecting the notion *in toto* if we can show that it is necessarily carried over from T to $T+$. This takes us back to the earlier question as to whether the ontological commitments of T must carry over in $T+$. I see no reason to think that they should. Despite a great deal of ingenuity it seems that Geach has not produced an argument which forces one to interpret I-predicates as expressing relative identity.

8.4 Zemach's Argument from Open-texture

Zemach rejects Geach's argument from ontology but claims

51 'Relative Identity', p. 249. 52 'Relative Identity', p. 45.
53 'The Same F', p. 196. 54 'Relative Identity', p. 253.

that while 'absolute identity does not result in *ontological* slums, it does create *ideological* jungles.'[55] In fact, Zemach has two arguments from open-texture: the first is the argument from the open-texture of singular terms which I used in § 7.4; the second is from the open-texture of general nouns. As a preliminary he slightly revises (R) to:

(R′) If '$\mathcal{A}$', '$\mathcal{B}$', and '$\mathcal{C}$' are such that $\mathcal{A} \subseteq \mathcal{C}$ and $\mathcal{B} \subseteq \mathcal{C}$ then $\mathcal{C}(a)$ & $\mathcal{C}(b)$ & $a =_{\mathcal{A}} b$ & $a \neq_{\mathcal{B}} b$ can be true.[56]

His argument is then stated concisely:

[W]e can place [general nouns] on a scale of determination, such that if a term $\mathcal{C}$ is just like a term $\mathcal{A}$ except that $\mathcal{C}$ is closed with respect to a certain concept (e.g. 'identical to a') and $\mathcal{A}$ is opened with respect to it, $\mathcal{C}$ has a degree of determination higher than that of $\mathcal{A}$. Thus, for every term $\mathcal{C}$, of degree of determination n, there may be some other terms, $\mathcal{A}$ and $\mathcal{B}$, such that $\mathcal{A} \subseteq \mathcal{C}$ and $\mathcal{B} \subseteq \mathcal{C}$ and such that their degree of determination is m, and $m > n$, and $\mathcal{C}(a)$ & $\mathcal{C}(b)$ & $a =_{\mathcal{A}} b$ & $a \neq_{\mathcal{B}} b$. This is (R′).[57]

In the example he has in mind '$\mathcal{C}$' is the sortal 'word' and '$\mathcal{A}$' and '$\mathcal{B}$' are 'type word' and 'token word' respectively. 'Type word' and 'token word' have a higher degree of determination than 'word' since if a is a word we cannot answer the question 'Is a the same word as b?' (i.e. 'word' is open with respect to 'ζ is the same as b') though we can answer the questions 'Is a the same token word (type word) as b?' (i.e. 'type word' and 'token word' are closed with respect to 'ζ is the same as b').

Zemach's argument is, I think, valid. Suppose we have singular terms 'a' and 'b' such that $\mathcal{A}(a)$ & $\mathcal{A}(b)$ & $\mathcal{B}(a)$ & $\mathcal{B}(b)$ then, since $\mathcal{A} \subseteq \mathcal{C}$ and $\mathcal{B} \subseteq \mathcal{C}$, it follows that $\mathcal{C}(a)$ & $\mathcal{C}(b)$. Since '$\mathcal{C}$' is open with respect to 'ζ is the same as b' we cannot assign a truth-value to '$a =_{\mathcal{C}} b$'; since '$\mathcal{A}$' and '$\mathcal{B}$' are both closed with respect to this concept we can assign truth-values to '$a =_{\mathcal{A}} b$' and '$a =_{\mathcal{B}} b$'. Now Zemach, I think, holds that the openness of '$\mathcal{C}$' with respect to 'ζ is the same as b' can only be understood if different *restrictions* of '$\mathcal{C}$' give different answers to 'Is a the same as b?' (for if every restriction of '$\mathcal{C}$' gave the same answer we could assign a truth-value to 'a is

[55] 'In Defence of Relative Identity', p. 211.
[56] Ibid., pp. 207, 215. (I have altered his formulation to fit my own notation.)
[57] Ibid., p. 215.

the same $\mathscr{C}$ as b'). Very well, let '$\mathscr{A}$' and '$\mathscr{B}$' be two such restrictions, it follows that '$a =_{\mathscr{A}} b$' and '$a =_{\mathscr{B}} b$' cannot both be true. Any doubts about the validity of Zemach's argument must rest on his (implied) claim that the openness of '$\mathscr{C}$' with respect to 'ζ is the same as b' depends upon there being different *restrictions* of '$\mathscr{C}$' which give different answers to the question 'Is a the same as b?'. Indeed, I think this requirement is unnecessarily strong, for surely it is sufficient if the general terms in question intersect in an appropriate way (viz., so that $\mathscr{A}(a)$ & $\mathscr{A}(b)$ & $\mathscr{B}(a)$ & $\mathscr{B}(b)$ & $\mathscr{C}(a)$ & $\mathscr{C}(b)$ holds). But if we drop the requirement that $\mathscr{A} \subseteq \mathscr{C}$ and $\mathscr{B} \subseteq \mathscr{C}$ then we get (R) rather than (R'). Certainly I think it clear that for any term open with respect to a certain concept two terms are constructible which are closed with respect to that concept for one of which the concept applies while it fails for the other. The best absolutist defence against this argument is to claim that even the intersection requirement is unfulfilled on the grounds that what is an $\mathscr{A}$ cannot be a $\mathscr{B}$—the claim that Zemach's use of the singular terms 'a' and 'b' is referentially ambiguous. Replies of this type will be considered in § 10.2.

8.5 Quantification and Semantics

In the classical semantics of the lower predicate calculus (LPC) an interpretation is defined as an ordered pair $\langle \mathbf{D}, \mathbf{I} \rangle$, where $\mathbf{D}$ is a non-empty set (the domain) and $\mathbf{I}$ is a function which assigns to each individual term of LPC an element of $\mathbf{D}$; and to each n-ary predicate letter of LPC an n-place relation on $\mathbf{D}$.[58] According to Dummett:

[I]n the explanation of what it is for a formula (of first-order predicate calculus *without* identity) to come out true under a given interpretation, no appeal is made to our capacity to determine whether or not two assignments of elements of the domain assign the *same* element to any one given free variable; all that is necessary is that we should be able to tell when we have made such an assignment, and, in some way, to survey the totality of such assignments.[59]

Be this as it may, it does not avoid the need to specify

[58] For a standard presentation see Elliott Mendelson, *Introduction to Mathematical Logic* (New York: van Nostrand, 1964), pp. 49–56.

[59] *Frege*, p. 562.

identities between elements of **D** even in the interpretation of LPC (without identity). If we are to interpret classically:

(8.26) $(\exists x)(x$ is a carnivore & x is timid)

we have to be sure that not more than one element of the domain is assigned to each individual term.[60] And in standard formulations of the semantics of LPC it is usually stipulated that **I** assigns to each individual term a unique element of **D**.[61] Thus, even if we grant Dummett's point that we do not need to know whether two assignments assign the same element of **D** to one individual term, we need to be sure that one assignment does not assign more than one element to any one individual term— and that requires some theses as to the identity of elements of **D**.

Clearly such theses are even more obviously required in the classical semantics of LPC with identity (LPC=). There we have a bivalent function, **V**, such that:

(8.27) $\mathbf{V}(a = b) = \mathbf{T}$ iff $\mathbf{I}(a) = \mathbf{I}(b)$.

But clearly if we are to give a semantics to LPC= by assigning elements of a domain to individual terms we naturally pre-suppose absolute identity relations among these elements since LPC= includes absolute identity theory.

Quine objects to relative identity on the grounds that it 'is antithetical to the very notion of quantification . . . [which] depends on there being values of variables, same or different absolutely'.[62] And Geach accordingly amends the theory of the quantifiers.[63] However, Quine underestimates both the flexibility of quantification theory and the flexibility of relative identity. After a long discussion Dummett rightly concludes that 'there is no formal entailment between Geach's rejection of absolute identity and his opposition to the classical treatment of the quantifiers'.[64] Relative identity does not depend upon the rejection of the orthodox interpretation of the quantifiers;[65] and neither does quantification theory depend on there being

---

[60] Dummett considers this ibid., pp. 554–5. He puts it forward hypothetically as a view Geach might want to adopt but gives no reason for rejecting it.

[61] For example, Mendelson, op. cit., p. 49 talks of 'some fixed element of **D**'.

[62] Review of *Reference and Generality*, p. 101.

[63] Cf. *Reference and Generality*, pp. 149–65.   [64] *Frege*, p. 562.

[65] Cf. Routley and Griffin, 'Towards a Logic of Relative Identity' where classical semantics could be provided for a number of relative identity theories; although the ontological interpretation is rejected on independent grounds.

values of variables, same or different absolutely as Quine supposes. There are both classical semantics for relative identity and non-classical (substitutional or domainless) semantics for the quantifiers which do not rely on absolute identity.

None the less, a doubt remains as to whether the classical semantics for LPC can really capture what the relativist has in mind: in particular the relation between sortals and individuation. Dummett expresses it thus: '[T]he *picture* we have of what constitutes a domain of objects which serve as the range of the individual variables is such that it is impossible to see how there could be any objection to supposing an absolute relation of identity to be defined on it: the elements of the domain are thought of as being, in Quine's words, the same or different absolutely.'[66] And this, of course, is exactly what can be done in those relative identity logics for which classical semantics can be provided.[67] One way of bringing in the connection between sortals and individuation is to group the elements in the domain into sorts, as Leslie Stevenson does.[68] For each sort an identity relation is defined, but since Stevenson rejects (R) he can treat each such relation as an absolute identity relation restricted in its field to items of the sort in question. By means of appropriate, but in my opinion unreasonable, conditions on the structure of sorts he is able to field a consistent theory of relative identity but one which collapses to the classical theory if we add a suitable definition for absolute identity.[69] As Dummett noted, if we choose a classical semantics for relative identity there is nothing to stop us defining an absolute identity relation on our domain and our theory collapses to the classical theory or not depending upon the absence or presence of (R).

However, my main objection to using the classical semantic notion of a domain for relative identity arises not from the fact that an absolute identity relation could then be defined on it—for, as I've argued, there is less harm in absolute identity than most relativists have thought—but rather that it gets the semantics upside down. It is hard to see how any sense can be made of the notion of an individual item without individuation, and it is hard to see how sense can be made of

---

[66] *Frege*, p. 562.   [67] Again, see Routley and Griffin, op. cit.
[68] See 'A Formal Theory of Sortal Quantification', pp. 196–7.
[69] See ibid., pp. 190–1 (for consistency); pp. 203–4 (for collapse).

individuation without sortals which supply the principles which make individuation possible. In view of this, it seems to me that, while all types of identity statements are admissible, sortal-relative identity statements have the most fundamental role to play, for without them we cannot make sense of the notion of an individual item. Once we have individuated some items by means of a sortal and found, say, that the item named by 'a' and that named by 'b' are the same $\mathscr{F}$, we can go on to ask if they share all their properties and are thus the same absolutely. The classical semantics suggests things proceed in exactly the opposite manner. Absolute identity, even if other forms of identity are admitted at all, plays the most fundamental role since each item in the domain is distinct absolutely from all the others. If 'a' and 'b' are the names of two such distinct items we can go on to ask whether none the less there is some general noun with respect to which they are identical. The difficulty with this approach, it seems to me, is in trying to make sense of the notion of individual items on which it is based. What are these items? and how much of the world does each take up? These are unanswerable questions until we specify that our quantifiers range over, say, a domain of numbers or persons. While it is quite clear how a sortal-relative identity relation can be used to answer these questions, it remains obscure how an absolute identity relation could do so. For what possible sense can there be in claiming that item a has all its properties in common with item b unless we have some independent means of individuating a and b?

If classical semantics gets the cart before the horse what alternative is there? It seems as though all set theoretic semantics will suffer from the same problem since set theory is based on absolute identity: set members being the same or different absolutely. The loss of set theory, of course, makes things much more difficult but the development of category theory for foundational work in mathematics at least provides an alternative of comparable (and possibly greater) power. We are not entitled to assume that if a semantics cannot be done in set theory it cannot be done at all. An adequate formal semantics for relative identity is still a long way off and will probably arise from the development of a more adequate formal semantics for general nouns than has hitherto been possible within set theory. None the less, we can give some clue as to what sort of picture would satisfy the relativist. I think only Dummett, among non-relativists, has got this far in understanding the relativist position. He writes: '[I]t seems that Geach means us to picture that over which the variables range as an amorphous lump of reality, in itself not articulated into distinct objects. Such an articulation may be accomplished in any one of many different ways: we slice up reality into distinct individual objects by selecting a particular criterion of identity.'[70] Dummett's objection to this is that once we have carved off an item a in a certain way we can say whether or not a is the same item as an item b sliced off in possibly the same or possibly a different way—the answer will, in general, be quite determinate.[71] This is indeed a problem for the relativist who holds (D) as Geach does, but it presents no problem for the theory proposed here.

It may seem that such a view of relative identity gives a lot of trouble for little return. After all (R) can be established and even (D) not encroached on within classical semantics for quantification theory. However, while such 'minimal' relativist theories have great advantages, as I shall show in Chapter 10, it seems to me that relative identity secures a further important advantage from the position Dummett has sketched. Suppose we have two sortal-relative identity relations 'ζ is the same $\mathscr{F}$ as η' and 'ζ is the same $\mathscr{G}$ as η' such that (R) holds for them. Suppose an absolutist, who commits himself to a reference theory via the standard semantics, takes 'ζ is the same $\mathscr{F}$ as η' to be a genuine identity relation (i.e. a relation construable by (LL), a disguised absolute identity relation). Since it is an equivalence relation it determines a partition of his domain and he treats each equivalence class thus determined as a unit class containing just one element of the domain. If 'ζ is the same $\mathscr{G}$ as η' is a different equivalence relation with the same field then the absolutist is forced to do two things: at the syntactic level, he has to give a non-identity account of the new relation (i.e. an alternative account to that given by (LL)); and, semantically,

---

[70] *Frege*, p. 563. Dummett's reference to 'reality' is unfortunate in that it limits the individuating resources of natural language to actual items. Basing the semantics on an unarticulated logical space instead of 'an amorphous lump of reality' would permit the individuation of possibilia and impossibilia.

[71] Ibid.

he has to treat the equivalence classes it determines as being at a different level to those determined by 'ζ is the same $\mathscr{F}$ as η' (typically, as sets the members of which are the items assigned to unit classes in the partition generated by 'ζ is the same $\mathscr{F}$ as η'). It is clear that the absolutist has to confer a differential status on $\mathscr{F}$s and $\mathscr{G}$s: $\mathscr{F}$s are more basic than $\mathscr{G}$s, since a $\mathscr{G}$ is analysed as a set of $\mathscr{F}$s. Thus in the familiar type word/ token word example, type words are treated as sets of token words which are basic. Syntactically, 'ζ is the same token word as η' is treated as an (absolute) identity statement; 'ζ is the same type word as η' is treated as an equivalence relation falling short of identity.

The relativist, on the other hand, is not forced to adopt such prejudices. He has to reject the talk of partition since that presupposes a domain of already individuated items. However, he can adopt Dummett's 'articulation' idiom: 'ζ is the same $\mathscr{F}$ as η' and 'ζ is the same $\mathscr{G}$ as η' impose different articulations on the logical space; they represent different ways of slicing the logical space up into individual items. His great advantage is that on the syntactic level he is not forced to accord different treatment to the two relations (he treats each as an identity relation) and semantically he is not forced to give a privileged position to $\mathscr{F}$s or $\mathscr{G}$s. He can treat type words and token words even-handedly. 'Token word' and 'type word' both provide equally good ways of articulating the logical space. Counting token words and counting type words are equally good ways of counting items; whereas counting token words as if they were primary indicates an unreasonable prejudice against type words; and counting items without reference to any general noun is impossible. If the relativist wishes to accord different status to certain types of item he can, of course, do so by adopting appropriate metaphysical theories. What is surely desirable is that identity should precede, rather than presuppose, our metaphysics.

9

The Constitutive 'is'

9.1 Constitutive uses of 'is'

Since the relativist can make out a coherent theory which is not subject to irrefutable *a priori* objections, the rest of his task looks easy. He simply needs a case of (R) to establish his theory. In the course of our discussion we have already given several examples of such statements, and thus it looks as if our problems are over. However, those who have objected to (R)-relative identity are well aware of most of the examples we have cited and in each case have sought to evade their force. One way of doing this is to deny that one or both conjuncts of a case of (R) is an identity statement and thence to claim that such examples constitute no problem for the theory of absolute identity which is a theory restricted to identity statements strictly construed. In this chapter and the next I want to examine these attempts to cope with examples of (R) within an absolute identity theory. In the next chapter I shall deal with the issues rather more generally, while in this chapter I want to consider a particular class of cases—namely those cases which are said to involve the constitutive 'is' rather than the 'is' of identity.

Examples of (R) which are said to involve the constitutive 'is' include the following:

(9.1) Heraclitus jumped into the same river twice, but not into the same water.

(9.2) Two Meccano models may be the same collection of Meccano pieces but distinct models.

According to Wiggins, to whom this view is due,[1] in (9.1) the second conjunct and in (9.2) the first, involves the constitutive

---

[1] Wiggins, *Identity and Spatio-Temporal Continuity*, p. 10.

'is' and not the 'is' of identity because they are paraphraseable as:

(9.3)   The river into which Heraclitus jumped the first time was not constituted by the same water as the river into which he jumped the second time.

(9.4)   This model is composed of the same collection of Meccano pieces as that model.

This, of course, is plausible enough, and Wiggins doesn't simply claim that the possibility of such a paraphrase alone suffices to show that we do not have identities in (9.1) and (9.2):[2] 'I am saying [he writes] that the independent plausibility of this paraphrase, *plus* the plausibility of Leibniz's Law which would otherwise have to be amended or abandoned, *plus* the difficulty of amending Leibniz's Law, force us to postulate this distinct sense of "is".'[3] By 'Leibniz's Law' Wiggins means (DLL) which permits indiscernibility inferences from relative identities. Of course, (DLL) is incompatible with (R). To do anything to validate (DLL) Wiggins must refute all cases of (R), and yet, in doing this, he constantly makes appeals to (DLL)—although he sometimes does it (as in the passage quoted above) by an apparently more innocuous appeal to the 'plausibility' of (DLL) which suggests that (DLL) is independently plausible. This, of course, does not imply that there are no better arguments for the independence of the constitutive 'is' and such arguments will be considered below.

However, before we do this we need to know which group of statements we are talking about, which statements actually employ the 'is' of constitution whether they express identity or no. If we consider the following statements certain features become clear:

(9.5)   The desk is the same wood as the bookshelf used to be.

(9.6)   The desk is the same plank of wood as the bookshelf used to be.

(9.7)   The desk is the same piece of furniture as the bookshelf.

---

[2] In other cases Wiggins does seem to think that the possibility of a paraphrase is sufficient to rule out the example as an identity statement. Wiggins's general procedure for using paraphrases to get rid of examples of (R) will be considered in § 10.3.

[3] *Identity and Spatio-Temporal Continuity*, fn. 19 (p. 67).

(9.8)   The desk was the same plank of wood as that plank of wood.

(9.9)   This plank of wood is the same plank of wood as that plank of wood.

The covering concept in (9.5) is a mass term, while in (9.6)–(9.9) it is a sortalized mass term. Of the five statements (9.7) and (9.9) plainly do not involve the constitutive 'is'. Whether a statement involves the constitutive 'is' has nothing to do with the nature of the covering concept. The important feature seems to be whether we can obtain a paraphrase along the lines of (9.3) and (9.4). With all but (9.7) and (9.9) we can, with these two alone the paraphrase fails. We have to construe the paraphrase fairly widely to ensure that we get an idiomatic sentence. For example, 'The desk is made of the same wood as the bookshelf used to be' is a more idiomatic paraphrase of (9.5) than 'The desk is constituted of the same wood as the bookshelf used to be' and with further examples more glaring anomalies may occur unless we permit some latitude in our paraphrase.[4]

   None the less, it is difficult to accept that the possibility of this paraphrase is necessary for the constitutive 'is'. Consider (9.8), we clearly have the paraphrase:

(9.10)   The desk was made of the same plank of wood as that plank of wood.

But if we turn (9.8) round to form:

(9.11)   That plank of wood was the same plank of wood as the desk.

the paraphrase fails:

(9.12)   *That plank of wood was made of the same plank of wood as the desk.

But we might have expected that (9.11) would involve the constitutive 'is' if (9.8) did. The reason is, of course, that 'ζ is constituted by η' is not symmetrical, unlike 'ζ is identical with η'. A further reason for rejecting this paraphrase as a necessary

---

4 Cf. Sheehan, 'The Relativity of Identity', pp. 42–50.

condition is that it completely ignores the constitutive use of 'is' in the following statements:

(9.13)   The desk is wood.

(9.14)   The desk is a plank of wood.

For (9.13) and (9.14) we can use the paraphrase and give the following criterion:

(I)   A statement of the form (α) 'a is (det) $\mathscr{A}$' involves the 'is' of *constitution* iff (α) can be paraphrased:

$$\text{'}a\text{ is} \begin{cases} \text{constituted} \\ \text{composed} \\ \text{made up} \\ \text{made} \end{cases} \text{of } (det)\ \mathscr{A}\text{'}.$$

It is not statements which satisfy (I), however, which can be used to form cases of (R). Given (I) we can now give a criterion for constitutive uses of 'is' in statements, like (9.6), which can be used to form examples of (R):

(II)   A statement of the form (α) 'a is the same $\mathscr{A}$ as b' involves the *constitutive* 'is' iff either 'a is (det) $\mathscr{A}$' or 'b is (det) $\mathscr{A}$' satisfies criterion (I).[5]

(II) preserves the intuition that the constitutive 'is' appears in both (9.8) and (9.11). It excludes (9.7) and (9.9) which is what we want. It also makes the constitutive 'is' indifferent as to covering concept. (II) seems to fit all the cases which Wiggins would want to include as constitutive 'is' cases and should therefore be acceptable to both sides.

It will be convenient to have an expression for those terms which appear in covering concept position in statements satisfying (II). I propose to call them *compositional nouns*, or rather compositional *uses* of nouns for it will not be possible to rule out any noun from playing a compositional role (for example, 'men' in 'The team is composed of men'). I shall say that the noun '$\mathscr{A}$' has a use as a compositional noun iff there is a statement of the form (α) 'a is (det) $\mathscr{A}$' such that (α) satisfies (I).

We can now define the circumstances in which a statement

---

[5] (I) and (II) do not give an exhaustive specification of the constitutive 'is' since they ignore compositional uses of adjectives as in 'The table is wooden'.

of the form '*a* is the same $\mathscr{A}$ as *b*' involves the constitutive 'is'. This, of course, does not prove the independence of the constitutive 'is' from the 'is' of identity: it could be that constitutive 'is' statements were just an identifiable sub-class of identity statements.

9.2 The Nature of Constitutivity

The criteria (I) and (II) of §9.1 enable us to define the scope of our problem. One further preliminary will be useful and that is a list of the various ways in which constitutivity might be construed. Stephen Voss[6] lists a number of ways in which such a relation could be taken and I shall deal with each in turn. The proposals are the following: constitutivity is a variably polyadic relation; a relation between an individual and the Lesniewskian sum of its constituents; a relation between an individual and the set of its constituents; a relation between an individual and the physical object its parts compose; and a relation between an individual and the kind of stuff of which it is composed. I'll use the example of a train, *a*, composed of an engine, *b*, and carriages *c*, *d*, etc. The type of stuff of which *a* is composed is rolling stock.

Suppose that constitutivity is variably polyadic. In the case where *a* is made up of an engine and one carriage 'ζ is composed of η' is a triadic relation holding between *a*, *b*, and *c*. But in a case where *a* is made up of an engine and two carriages, it is tetradic. 'To put the point summarily, the relation is regarded as being $n+1$-adic, where *n* is the number of listed constituents.'[7] There is some doubt as to whether such a theory even gets off the ground, since it is a fairly common presumption that relations cannot be of variable adicity. This view is less commonly explicitly stated, although Patrick Suppes does so.[8] However, the arguments aren't overwhelmingly convincing and other logicians see no objection to such relations and it will not do to rule out the possibility of such relations. Clearly if we adopt such a theory the relation between an individual and its constituents cannot be identity. But then if this is our theory of

6 'The Indiscernibility of Non-Identicals' (Unpublished, n.d.), pp. 2–6.

7 Chandler, 'Constitutivity and Identity', *Nous*, 5 (1971), 313.

8 Suppes, *Introduction to Logic* (Princeton: van Nostrand, 1957), pp. 210–12. Butchvarov also holds this view, cf. *Resemblance and Identity*, pp. 109–10.

constitutivity the examples which gave rise to the puzzles with
which we started are generally unlikely to arise. If the relation
of the team to the n men who compose it is an $n+1$-place
relation of constitutivity we are hardly likely to confuse this with
identity, and we certainly can form no case of (R) with it.
There will remain cases where constitutivity is a relation with
two places for individual terms: as in 'Cleopatra's Needle is
composed of a block of stone' or 'The team is composed of
a group of men.' Indeed such cases could always be constructed
from cases of variable polyadicity.

This is what Chandler does in what he terms 'the reductive
theory of constitutivity'[9] in which the variably polyadic relations
are analysed away in favour of relations of definite adicity.
Chandler considers a reduction of 'a is composed of b and c'
in terms of the dyadic relation 'ζ is part of η' and gives an
English reading. It is clear that a reductive theory can best be
expressed in terms of Lesniewski's mereology or Goodman's
calculus of individuals.[10] Such a statement as 'a is composed of
b and c' could be analysed by two formulae of Goodman's
calculus:

$$(9.15) \qquad (\forall x)(x \circ a \supset x \circ (b+c))$$

$$(9.16) \qquad (\forall x)(x \circ (b+c) \supset x \circ a)$$

where 'o' is the overlapping relation, and '$b+c$' denotes the
Lesniewskian fusion of b and c. Putting (9.15) and (9.16)
together gives:

$$(9.17) \qquad (\forall x)(x \circ a \equiv x \circ (b+c)).$$

But identity in Goodman's system is given 'in the usual Leibnizian way'[11] by:

$$(9.18) \qquad x = y =_{df} (\forall z)(z \circ x \equiv z \circ y).$$

Hence in Goodman's calculus an individual is identical with

[9] 'Constitutivity and Identity', p. 314.

[10] See Alfred Tarski, 'Foundations of the Geometry of Solids', in Logic, Semantics,
and Metamathematics (Oxford: Oxford University Press, 1956), pp. 24–9, especially
p. 25; E. C. Luschei, The Logical Systems of Lesniewski (Amsterdam: North-Holland,
1962); and Goodman, The Structure of Appearance, pp. 46–56. As elsewhere I have
used Goodman's notation in preference to the alternatives.

[11] Goodman, The Structure of Appearance, p. 49. Voss has a slightly different form
of this argument. ('The Indiscernibility of Non-Identicals', pp. 5–6.)

the Lesniewskian fusion of its parts. To fit this account out for relative identity we need some covering concept:

(9.19)   The train is the same collection of items of rolling stock as the Lesniewskian fusion of the engine and carriage.

The view that constitutivity is the relation between the train, a, and the object which is composed of b and c trivially makes the relation identity, for we have:

(9.20)   The train a is the same train as the train composed of b and c.

What is more, in this case the 'ζ is composed of η' paraphrase fails for we do not have:

(9.21)   *The train a is composed of the train composed of b and c.

Thus no case of the constitutive 'is' as we've defined it occurs here.

The last two theories—that constitutivity is a relation between an object and the set of parts which compose it or the kind of stuff which makes it up—each give us a case of the constitutive 'is'. Whether they also give us a case of the 'is' of relative identity we shall inquire in the next section.

9.3 The Alleged Independence of the Constitutive 'is'

It must be conceded to Wiggins that not all statements involving the constitutive 'is' are identity statements. For example, statements of the form

(9.22) a is $\mathcal{M}$

are not identity statements since they fail symmetry. This is scarcely an important concession since statements like (9.22) don't even have the right form to be relative identity statements. However, for each statement of the form (9.22) there is a corresponding statement of the form:

(9.23) a is the same $\mathcal{M}$ as b.

For example, to the statement

(9.24)   This earring is gold.

there corresponds the statement:[12]

(9.25)   This earring is the same gold as some gold.

The quantification of 'some gold' is rather tricky,[13] but an obvious alternative to (9.25) is:

(9.26)   This earring is the same piece of gold as some piece of gold.

At least (9.25) and (9.26) have the right form for relative identity statements; whether they are identity statements remains to be seen. Ayers[14] makes much of the failure of symmetry just mentioned, but only sustains his case by considering the paraphrase of statements such as (9.24). It is scarcely of great concern to the relativist if statements which are not relative identity statements are proved not to be identity statements. For Wiggins to establish his claim that the constitutive 'is' is not a form of identity he has to show that *no* constitutive 'is' statement can be an identity statement.

The most popular argument to show that (9.26) is not an identity statement is that if the earring and the piece of gold were identical they would both come into and pass out of existence at the same time.[15] Clearly the earring might be beaten out in which case the earring would cease to exist though the piece of gold would be preserved and, of course, the piece of gold must antedate the earring which was made out of it. This argument invokes what Wiggins calls 'The Life Histories Principle', namely that if *a* and *b* are identical they must have the same life history.[16] However, I prefer not to

[12] This proposal comes from Tyler Burge. Cf. his 'Truth and Mass Terms', p. 278.

[13] Difficult, but not impossible. F. J. Pelletier introduces a non-partitive quantifier '*sm*', read 'some' (with weak stress), which operates with mass terms (and plural sortals) in much the same way as the partitive quantifier 'some' in English (pronounced with primary stress) operates with +count nouns (and mass terms where a 'kind of' sortalization is understood). See F. J. Pelletier, 'On Some Proposals for the Semantics of Mass Nouns', *Journal of Philosophical Logic*, 3 (1974), 95. The two uses of 'some' are noted, for example, by H. A. Gleason, *An Introduction to Descriptive Linguistics* (New York: Holt, 1955), p. 145.

[14] 'Individuals without Sortals', p. 121.

[15] Cf., for example, Wiggins, *Identity and Spatio-Temporal Continuity*, pp. 10–13; Burge, 'Truth and Mass Terms', p. 278; Herbst, 'Names and Identities and Beginnings and Ends', pp. 44–5.

[16] *Identity and Spatio-Temporal Continuity*, p. 31. As in formulating Leibniz's Law, we need to take due care to exclude opaque contexts.

use the Life Histories Principle in discussing matters that have
a bearing on (R) since it is a special case of (DLL) and thus
presupposes the falsity of (R). It does not follow from the fact
that a and b are $\mathscr{A}$-identical that they have the same life
histories when they may be $\mathscr{B}$-distinct. Apart from the Life
Histories Principle other arguments based on (DLL) can be
used to prove that a whole cannot be identical with its constituents. For example, we register a car but not its parts, hence,
by (DLL), the two are distinct.

However, the Life Histories Principle (properly formulated)
may have independent plausibility and, moreover, there may
be principles weaker than the Life Histories Principle, which
would also rule statements satisfying (II) out of the class of
identity statements. The weakest principle sufficient for this
seems to be:

(LHP) x cannot be outlasted by anything with which it is
identical.

If (LHP) is true then the constitutive 'is' is not the 'is' of
identity. What we cast round for is a relativist argument for
(LHP).

The best place to look is in (RLL). Consider:

(9.27) The jug is the same collection of bits as the collection
of bits on the table.

Suppose that at time t_2 ($t_1 < t_2 < t_3$) the jug is smashed and
becomes the collection of bits on the table. We may then
advance the following argument. Given the premiss:

(9.28) $(\forall a)(\forall x)(\forall t)[a(x,t) \supset \text{exists}(x,t)]$

we get, on substituting 'collection of bits' for 'a':

(9.29) If the collection of bits on the table is a collection of bits
at t_3, then the collection of bits on the table exists at t_3.

It is accepted by the relativist that the jug is a collection of bits.
Thus, if (9.27) is an identity statement, from (9.29) by (RLL)
and clauses (i) and (iv) of the specification of $\Delta_{\mathscr{A}}$, we get:

(9.30) The jug exists at t_3.

But the jug ceased at t_2 and therefore did not exist afterwards.
Thus we get the contradiction that the jug both existed and

did not exist at t_3. Therefore, it is claimed, (9.27) isn't an identity statement.

The trouble with this argument, of course, is the premiss (9.28). Orthodox logicians will object that 'ζ exists' is not a predicate and hence may not be substituted for '$\phi(\zeta)$' in (RLL). On the other hand, unorthodox logicians, who accept that 'ζ exists' is a predicate, will argue that the material implication in (9.28) doesn't hold and that, in general, '$\mathscr{A}(a)$' does not imply that 'a exists' (since, e.g., 'a is a unicorn' does not imply 'a exists'). So the argument fails.

We may, however, seek to use (RLL) in another way. This argument capitalizes on a remark of Stephen Voss's in dealing with the view that constitutivity is a relation between an object and the set of its parts. He writes: 'But surely we are under no obligation to suppose that such an abstract object as a set is located just where its members are.'[17] Voss may be making one of two claims here: he could be claiming either that sets are not located where their members are because they are located somewhere else; or he could be claiming that they are not located where their members are because they are not located anywhere. If we have:

(9.31) The jug is the same set of bits as the set of bits on the table.

then, on the second interpretation, if being a set implies having no location it follows from (RLL) that the jug has no location either. Plainly this is false. On the other interpretation, however, both the jug and the set of pottery pieces will have a location—but not the same location. However, clause (v) of the specification of $\Delta_{\mathscr{A}}$ requires that if both are located they should have the same location. Either way, it may be argued, the jug cannot be the same set of pieces as a set of pieces.

But what does this argument show? Simply that we cannot combine a relative identity account of constitutivity with an account in terms of the relation between an object and the set of its constituents (together with some assumptions about sets). There are several ways out for the relativist: he could deny the (so far unargued) assumptions about sets—but to take up that issue would carry us far from our goal. Alternatively he

---

[17] 'The Indiscernibility of Non-Identicals', p. 2.

could simply drop the term 'set' in favour of 'collection' where collections behave exactly like sets except that they are located where their members are. This is surely an entirely reasonable move since something is certainly there (their Lesniewskian sum, for example). It is well to remind ourselves of our over-all enterprise here. It is the absolutist who has to force the relativist to give up treating constitutivity as a relative identity relation, and he cannot do this if his arguments appeal to principles to which the relativist is not committed—any more than he can do so if he appeals to principles to the *denial* of which the relativist *is* committed. The absolutist can rule out such cases of (R) as (9.1) and (9.2) only if he can show that on any interpretation of constitutivity it is *not* an identity (i.e. by showing that there is no coherent identity account of constitutivity for the relativist to mount). This he has not done so far.

If (RLL) is too weak a principle to permit the sort of derivation the absolutist wanted, it seems he can do better with the other formal properties of identity: reflexivity, symmetry, and transitivity. Consider (9.27), if the jug is the same collection of pottery pieces as that collection of pottery pieces then that collection of pottery pieces is certainly the same collection of pottery pieces as the jug. So symmetry seems to be preserved. Of course, symmetry is not preserved by the 'ζ is composed of η' paraphrase of (9.27) which is thus not an identity statement. But from this it doesn't follow that (9.27) is not an identity statement, and we are interested in (9.27) not paraphrases of it which cannot be used to form examples of (R). Reflexivity is clearly satisfied by (9.27) and its paraphrase: the jug both is, and is composed of, the same collection of pottery pieces as itself.

A combination of symmetry and transitivity:

$$(\text{RST}) \qquad (\forall x, y, z)(\forall a)(y =_a x \ \& \ y =_a z \supset \cdot \ x =_a z)$$

gets us further. Consider Cleopatra's Needle which gets corroded by air pollution and is replaced at time t_2 by another block of stone of similar dimensions.[18] Let us call the block of stone of which it was composed at time t_1 ($t_1 < t_2$) 'block of stone X';

---

[18] The example, but not the argument, was first suggested by Linsky in his Critical Notice of *Reference and Generality*, *Mind*, 73 (1964), 579 and was developed by Wiggins (as devil's advocate) in *Identity and Spatio-Temporal Continuity*, p. 8.

and the block of stone which replaced the original, 'block of stone Y'. Then we have at time t_3 $(t_3 > t_2)$:

(9.32) Cleopatra's Needle was the same block of stone as block of stone X.

(9.33) Cleopatra's Needle is the same block of stone as block of stone Y.

But:

(9.34) Block of stone X is not the same block of stone as block of stone Y.

Assume that all three statements are relative identity statements (we here use 'identity statement' as a generic term to include relative distinctness statements), we can then symbolize them:

(9.32a) $b =_{\mathscr{A}} a$

(9.33a) $b =_{\mathscr{A}} c$

(9.34a) $a \neq_{\mathscr{A}} c.$

Given (RST) we can derive a contradiction, since (9.32a) and (9.33a) then give us

(9.35) $a =_{\mathscr{A}} c.$

The easiest way to avoid the contradiction is to claim that at least one of (9.32)–(9.34) is not a relative identity statement, and thus that at least one of these statements is incorrectly formalized by (9.32a)–(9.34a). Now we can exempt (9.34) from blame for it is clearly a distinctness statement and is clearly correctly formalized by (9.34a). Hence either (9.32) or (9.33) is not an identity statement. There is no ground for preferring one to the other and therefore neither are identity statements, though both involve the constitutive 'is'. Hence the constitutive 'is' is not a form of identity relation.

However, tenses cause a difficulty for this argument. (9.32) is past tense while (9.33) is present, in view of the fact that the whole argument hinges on just this difference we cannot simply gloss over it. In particular, if (9.33a) is the correct symbolization of (9.33)—i.e. a correct symbolization of a present tense identity statement—it then appears that (9.32a) is not the correct symbolization of (9.32) which is past tensed.[19]

---

[19] I owe this point to Richard Routley.

We may symbolize (9.32), roughly but adequately for present purposes, in a way which marks the tense difference thus:

(9.32b) $b \simeq_{\mathscr{A}} a.$

But (9.32b) and (9.33a) do not give us the antecedent of (RST), and thus the derivation of the contradiction fails.

The point is of wider significance than the issue of the constitutive 'is' for if we ignore the tense of identity statements in stating transitivity from the fact that Nixon was President and Ford is President we could prove that Nixon is Ford—the truth of which would cause more than logical consternation. Absolutists are inclined to say that temporally restricted identity statements are not really identity statements or do not express absolute identity.[20] This, of course, depends upon what you mean by 'real identity' or 'absolute identity', but if the absolutist doesn't want to include them then he is obliged to offer us an alternative account, and this he rarely does. It is surely to the relativist's credit that his theory covers more ground than the classical theory.

The problem about marking tenses in the identity statement can be removed by rewriting the statement in Priorese. This involves keeping the identity relation present tensed by putting it within the scope of a tense operator (alternatively: within the scope of the realization operator 'R_t'). In Priorese (9.32) becomes:

(9.32c)   It *was* the case that: $(b =_{\mathscr{A}} a)$.

But now the 'It was the case that' in (9.32c) is effectively an intensional operator and substitutivity will not be permitted within its scope.[21]

The absolutist, however, can mount another argument similar to the one just given which doesn't give rise to any troubles about tenses. The argument is due to Prior who uses it for rather different purposes. It deals with the splitting of

[20] For example, Ayers, 'Individuals without Sortals', p. 135; Gabbay and Moravcsik, 'Sameness and Individuation', p. 514 n.; Dummett, *Frege*, p. 571. (Dummett offers a particularly bizarre alternative; namely that the President was 'realized' by Nixon. The notion of 'realization' is completely unexplicated and is certainly not the ordinary one. It is, I claim, one of the most important advantages of (R)-relative identity that it obviates the need for an immense range of such doubtful *ad hoc* expedients.)

[21] Cf. A. N. Prior, *Time and Modality* (Oxford: Clarendon Press, 1957), pp. 18–28.

unicellular animals and 'easily imaginable' cases of 'conscious organisms which divide in two and retain after division a clear memory of their undivided state'.[22] The conscious organisms I shall ignore as they raise extraneous problems[23] and I shall concentrate on the amoebas. Let a be such an amoeba which splits at t into two, b and c, each of which is identical with a but not with each other. Prior's argument in its original form runs:[24]

$$[1] \quad a = b \supset (\phi(a) \supset \phi(b)) \qquad \text{(premiss, from (LL))}$$
$$[2] \quad a = b \supset (a = c \supset b = c) \qquad ([1], \zeta = c/\phi(\zeta))$$
$$[3] \quad a = b \qquad \text{(premiss)}$$
$$[4] \quad a = c \qquad \text{(premiss)}$$
$$[5] \quad b \neq c \qquad \text{(premiss)}$$
$$[6] \quad b = c \qquad ([2]\,[3]\,[4], \text{M.P.})$$

On the strength of this Prior urges the rejection of Leibniz's Law. However, the same result can be obtained assuming only (ST), the absolutist version of (RST):

$$[1] \quad (a = b \,\&\, a = c) \supset b = c \qquad \text{(ST)}$$
$$[2] \quad a = b \qquad \text{(premiss)}$$
$$[3] \quad a = c \qquad \text{(premiss)}$$
$$[4] \quad b \neq c \qquad \text{(premiss)}$$
$$[5] \quad b = c \qquad ([1]\,[2]\,[3], \text{M.P.})$$

In seeking a way out of this paradox we are subject to two constraints: we cannot reject (ST) and we cannot deny that two *distinct* amoebas are produced from the fission of the original. What we have to deny, then, is at least one of the identity relations asserted in [2] and [3]: in other words, we have to deny that the original amoeba is identical with both of its progeny. But we have no grounds for preferring one progeny to the other as the heir of its parent's identity; thus

---

[22] Prior, 'Time, Existence and Identity', in *Papers on Time and Tense* (Oxford: Clarendon Press, 1968), p. 81.

[23] See, however, Bernard Williams, *Problems of the Self* (Cambridge: Cambridge University Press, 1973), Chapters I–III, for the more complex problem of person splitting. Williams's problems can be resolved in the same way as the ship of Theseus problem. See below.

[24] Prior, op. cit., pp. 81–2.

we should reject the identification of either with its parent. Hence we deny lines [2] and [3] of the argument. Moreover, we have good grounds for denying them because what we have in each case is the 'is' of constitution: amoebas b and c share with a the protoplasm of which they are composed and on this hangs the (mistaken) identity claim.[25]

But this last claim moves too far too fast and loopholes are left in the argument. I grant that at least one of lines [2] and [3] must be false,[26] and that if one of them is false there is every reason to suppose that the other is as well. But the grounds for asserting [2] and [3] amount to much more than the sameness of protoplasm of a and b and of a and c: both b and c are spatio-temporally continuous (in a weak sense) with a and, what's more, we could use 'amoeba' as a covering concept throughout the argument instead of 'piece of protoplasm'. The fact that all the identity statements in the argument could be covered by the sortal 'amoeba' (which does not in these cases have a compositional use) indicates that more is in question here than just the constitutive 'is'. Moreover, the constitutive 'is' is not, in fact, involved in [2] and [3] for it is surely false that:

(9.36) a is the same piece of protoplasm as b

and

(9.37) a is the same piece of protoplasm as c

for b consists of only half the piece of protoplasm of which a consists and similarly for c. In other words, a is not the same amoeba as b or as c, but neither does it consist of the same protoplasm as either. The relation between a and b cannot, then, be represented by identity, but neither can it by the 'is' of constitution. The reconstruction of Prior's argument thus fails to touch the question at issue here. What is shows is that (weak) spatio-temporal continuity and intersection of protoplasm are not jointly sufficient for amoeba-identity, but neither are they for human-identity (*vide* Siamese twins).

None the less we can construct an argument in which the

[25] This position has been argued by Jack Nelson, 'Prior on Leibniz's Law', *Analysis*, 30 (1969/70), 92–4.

[26] This is provable within Woodger's axiomatization of biology. Cf. J. H. Woodger, *The Axiomatic Method in Biology* (Cambridge: Cambridge University Press, 1937), p. 61—but his system embodies the classical identity theory.

situation is less clouded by other issues. The vexed question of the ship of Theseus provides us with such an argument. Suppose we have a ship, call it *Theseus I*, which undergoes a plank-by-plank replacement. Let us call the ship which results *Theseus II*. Suppose further that someone keeps the old planks and fashions them into a ship which I'll call *Theseus III*.[27] The following seem to be unassailable:

(9.38)   *Theseus I* is spatio-temporally continuous with *Theseus II*.

(9.39)   *Theseus I* is the same collection of planks as *Theseus III*.

(9.40)   *Theseus II* is not the same ship as *Theseus III*.

At least one of these is not an identity statement nor provides grounds for an identity statement. (9.40) clearly is a distinctness statement and can't be rejected in this way. That leaves (9.38) and (9.39). The trouble now is that each of these involves different principles and the question of which to reject might not be clear cut. If the constitutive 'is' is independent of the 'is' of identity then, of course, we have good reason for rejecting (9.39). It might be argued that we have good reason for rejecting (9.39), even without the constitutive 'is', because *Theseus I* and *Theseus III* cannot be spatio-temporally traced under covering concept 'ship' and found to coincide. But this appeal is defective on two grounds: Firstly, it begs the question, for *Theseus I* and *Theseus III* can be spatio-temporally traced under the covering concept 'collection of planks' and found to coincide. Secondly, spatio-temporal continuity under a non-compositional sortal covering is not, for artefacts, a necessary condition for the ascription of identity: watches may be taken to bits and the same watch reconstructed from the parts. On the other hand, if spatio-temporal continuity was a sufficient condition for the ascription of identity we would be able to accept (9.38) as grounds for an identity statement and hence be forced to reject (9.39)—but, though I can't give entirely

27 This form of the problem seems to have received its first statement from Hobbes who, however, attributed it to 'the Ancients'. See *De Corpore*, Part II, Ch. 11, § 7; in W. Molesworth (ed.), *The English Works of Thomas Hobbes* (London: John Bohn, 1839), vol. i, pp. 136–7. The ancient source is Plutarch's *Lives* ('Theseus', 23). Hobbes, however, gives it an important new twist. That the problem is still taken seriously is made clear by Brian Smart's witty restatement in 'How to Reidentify the Ship of Theseus', *Analysis*, 32 (1972), pp. 145–8 and F. W. Dauer's reply, 'How not to Reidentify the Parthenon', *Analysis*, 33 (1972), pp. 63–4.

convincing counter-examples, I'm not sure that this principle of the sufficiency of spatio-temporal continuity is correct. Moreover, unless we have the independence of the 'is' of constitution already, I can't see why we are entitled to give preference in formulating this principle to non-compositional sortals. At any rate it seems to me that the argument for the independence of the constitutive 'is' will not be conclusive until we find a case in which we *have* to reject, as an identity statement, a statement involving the constitutive 'is'. And this, I submit, the present example doesn't give us.

Even though the problem of the ship of Theseus doesn't do what we introduced it to do, it is none the less instructive. The (R)-relativist can provide a simple and appealing solution to the problem since he can hold both:

(9.41)   *Theseus I* is the same collection of planks as *Theseus III*.

and

(9.42)   *Theseus I* is not the same ship as *Theseus III*.

Moreover, neither (9.38) nor (9.39) provides the basis for an argument via (RST) to the conclusion that *Theseus II* is the same anything as *Theseus III*. Thus relativized symmetry and transitivity are protected.

Christopher Kirwan and Michael Ayers, so far as I know, are alone in having considered this solution to Hobbes's problem.[28] However, Kirwan rejects the solution in favour of Wiggins's unargued constitutive 'is' as a result of two invalid arguments. He holds that the relativist is committed to 'two absurdities: that [*Theseus I*] and [*Theseus III*] are the same and both of them ships, yet not the same ship; and that [*Theseus I*] and [*Theseus II*] are the same, and [*Theseus I*] and [*Theseus III*] the same, yet [*Theseus II*] and [*Theseus III*] are not the same (not the same anything).'[29] In fact, neither claimed 'absurdity' is really absurd. The first, which appears to rely on some variant of the Fregean analysis, amounts to a dogmatic denial of even the weakest versions of (R) and, far from being absurd, is a fairly obvious truth: for two things might both be ships

[28] Kirwan, 'How Strong are the Objections to Essence?' *Proceedings of the Aristotelian Society*, 71 (1970/1), pp. 57–8; Ayers, 'Individuals without Sortals', pp. 133–5.

[29] 'How Strong are the Objections to Essence?', p. 58.

and not the same ship but the same colour. The second is merely a failure to use relative identities in stating transitivity. The root cause of Kirwan's mistakes is a tendency to lapse into absolutist principles while discussing a relativist solution: not surprisingly, relative identities do not satisfy absolute identity principles.

Ayers is content to dismiss the relativist's solution as 'extravagant'.[30] He does, however, essay an absolutist solution by denying that *Theseus I* is identical with either *Theseus II* or *Theseus III*. The trouble with this response is the difficulty Ayers discovers in distinguishing the ship of Theseus case from other cases in which we would unhesitatingly agree that an item survives dismantling and reconstruction or a piece-by-piece replacement of parts. Ayers admits that dismantling and reconstructing a chair doesn't result in the creation of a new chair,[31] but seems prepared to countenance the possibility that this doesn't hold for ships. Yet we can construct a chair of Theseus problem exactly analogous to the problem of the ship. Similarly, he is also prepared to admit that biological items may survive piece-by-piece replacement, whilst wanting to claim that ships cannot. The difference appears to be that in the case of ships 'replacement is at a grosser level, the parts remain clearly defined and are in themselves unchanged by incorporation in the whole, and the agency is external.'[32] This is scarcely satisfactory since the second and third criteria are met by biological items; while in the first it is not clear how gross the level of replacement may be before replacement results in the destruction of the item in question; and in the fourth there remains unconsidered the possibility of self-replacing automata. A general danger in Ayers's account is that he will end up relativizing identity by admitting different identity criteria for different types of item—a view which, though plausible enough even on absolutist principles, he is not prepared to accept. At any rate it is clear that Ayers's absolutist solution requires a great number of *ad hoc* principles if it is to work. It plainly lacks the simplicity and appeal of the relativist solution.

We have still to consider the possibility that the constitutive

[30] 'Individuals without Sortals', p. 133.
[31] Ibid., p. 134.   [32] Ibid., p. 133.

'is' leads to a violation of (RST). If it does the relativist's solution of the ship of Theseus problem collapses since, in that case (9.41), though true, would not be an identity statement. For this we require an example which gives rise to a set of statements which entail the failure of (RST) and such that all statements in the set are unexceptionable except those that involve the constitutive 'is'. Chandler[33] suggests a plausible looking candidate. I will introduce his argument on the back of the ship of Theseus example. Suppose that we can identify *Theseus I* with the set of planks which make it up—this will be necessary if (9.41) is a true identity statement. We then have as an identity statement:

(9.43)   *Theseus I* is the same set of planks as the set of planks which composes *Theseus I*.

But on another level of analysis we could talk not of a set of planks but of a set of cellulose molecules and claim as a true identity statement:

(9.44)   *Theseus I* is the same set of cellulose molecules as the set of cellulose molecules which composes *Theseus I*.

Then, with (RST), we should have:

(9.45)   The set of planks which composes *Theseus I* is the same set as the set of cellulose molecules which composes *Theseus I*.

But (9.45) is certainly false because for sets to be identical they have to have the same members. Therefore, at least one of (9.43) and (9.44) must be rejected as an identity statement. But why should we prefer one level of analysis to the other? It seems that we have no grounds for choosing to reject one or the other and should reject them both. In fact, however, the case is not proven, for (RST) gives no warrant for inferring (9.45) from (9.43) and (9.44) since the covering concept is different in all three statements. What we get from (9.43) and (9.44) is not the antecedent of (RST) but '$a =_{\mathcal{A}} b$ & $a =_{\mathcal{B}} c$' and this does not entitle us to infer '$a =_{\mathcal{A}} c$' or '$a =_{\mathcal{B}} c$', let alone '$a =_{\mathcal{C}} c$' which corresponds to (9.45).

A similar argument to Chandler's has been suggested to me

by Peter Röper. Consider a circle, C, which can be divided up one way into two areas, A and B, and in another way into D and E, each different from A and B. We have, therefore:

(9.46) C is composed of A and B

(9.47) C is composed of D and E.

If constitutivity is an identity relation, given (RST) we can deduce a contradiction. If (9.46) and (9.47) are identities we have:

(9.46a) $C = (A \text{ and } B)$

(9.47a) $C = (D \text{ and } E)$

but we also have, it is claimed,

(9.48) $(A \text{ and } B) \neq (D \text{ and } E)$.

But from (9.46a) and (9.47a) with (RST) we have:

(9.49) $(A \text{ and } B) = (D \text{ and } E)$.

Hence to avoid the contradiction we have to deny that (9.46) and (9.47) license (9.46a) and (9.47a) respectively: i.e. deny that constitutivity is a form of identity.

This way of setting up the problem masks an important ambiguity in (9.46) and (9.47). If this ambiguity is brought into the open we get two parallel arguments for the independence of the constitutive 'is' neither of which is valid. On the one hand, we might be talking about unions of areas and on the other about sets of areas. The relativist demand for covering concepts for (9.46a), (9.47a), (9.48), and (9.49) makes this clear. Suppose, first, that we are talking about unions of areas, so that (9.46) amounts to 'The area, C, is composed of the area $A \cup B$.' In this case (9.46) and (9.47) become, respectively:

(9.46b) $C =_{\text{area}} (A \cup B)$

(9.47b) $C =_{\text{area}} (D \cup E)$.

But then we don't get our contradiction, for clearly

(9.50) $(A \cup B) =_{\text{area}} (D \cup E)$

is true.

To give (9.48) any plausibility, however, we have to be talking about sets of areas: and clearly the set of areas $\{A, B\}$ is a different set from the set $\{D, E\}$. But then we have to use the same covering concept throughout the argument in order to form the antecedent of (RST). In this version the argument runs:

(9.46c) $\qquad C =_{set} \{A, B\}$

(9.47c) $\qquad C =_{set} \{D, E\}.$

By (RST) therefore

(9.51) $\qquad \{A, B\} =_{set} \{D, E\},$

which is false. But this argument is unsound because (9.46c) and (9.47c) are not true. It is not the case that the circle, C, is the same set as either $\{A, B\}$ or $\{D, E\}$. Either C is a set or it is not. If it is, it cannot be the same set as $\{A, B\}$ or $\{D, E\}$, for $\{A, B\}$ and $\{D, E\}$ have two members and $\{C\}$ has only one. On the other hand, if C is not a set, then C is not the same set as any set, and neither (9.46c) and (9.47c) can be true.

We begin to see now why there cannot be any conclusive argument along these lines against treating the constitutive 'is' as a form of identity. None of the formal properties of relative identity are violated by including constitutivity as a form of relative identity. The relativist thus has to his credit not only a perfectly general and completely intuitive account of constitutivity but simple solutions to two antique puzzles: the ship of Theseus and the bath-water of Heraclitus. Moreover, the techniques used to solve these problems can easily be applied to resolve difficulties in the notion of person-splitting which do not involve constitutivity. I shall argue in Chapter 10 that the theory also solves a number of equally puzzling but less time-honoured problems.

In dealing with arguments of this kind even authors who accept the indiscernibility of identicals seem driven towards (R)—without quite realizing it. An example is the following argument from Chandler.[34] Consider two regions r_1 and r_2, four times $t_1,..., t_4$, and six particles $p^1,..., p^6$ distributed as follows:

	t_1	t_2	t_3	t_4
r_1	(p^1, p^2, p^3)	(p^1, p^2, p^4)	(p^1, p^5, p^4)	(p^6, p^5, p^4)
r_2	(p^4, p^5, p^6)	(p^3, p^5, p^6)	(p^3, p^2, p^6)	(p^3, p^2, p^1)

[34] 'Constitutivity and Identity', pp. 316–17. Elsewhere Chandler appears sympathetic to (R), cf. his 'Wiggins on Identity', *Analysis*, 29 (1968/9), pp. 173–4.

An 'alphe' is a physical object composed of three particles and can be identified by the spatial region they occupy: i.e. if a group of three particles moves from one region to another the original alphe is destroyed and a new one created—there are two alphes, not one. On the other hand, if the constituent particles are replaced the alphe remains the same—so long as there are three particles. An alphe may thus be defined as a group of any three particles occupying a given region of space. An aggregate of particles, however, remains the same only so long as its constituent members do. Thus, in the situation supposed, we have two alphes and six aggregates of particles. Chandler's argument runs (where 'the aggregate of p^4 plus p^5 plus p^6' is written '$Agg(p^4, p^5, p^6)$'):

(9.52) The alphe in r_1 at t_4 was in r_1 at t_1.

(9.53) $Agg(p^4, p^5, p^6)$ was not in r_1 at t_1.

(9.54) Hence, by the indiscernibility of identicals, the alphe in r_1 at t_4 cannot be one and the same as $Agg(p^4, p^5, p^6)$.

The argument, as it stands, is a non-starter for the relativist because of its appeal to the indiscernibility of identicals. But it can be reformulated to avoid this:

(9.52a) The alphe in r_1 at t_4 is the same aggregate of particles as $Agg(p^6, p^5, p^4)$.

(9.53a) The alphe in r_1 at t_4 was the same aggregate of particles as $Agg(p^1, p^2, p^3)$.

(9.54a) $Agg(p^6, p^5, p^4)$ is not the same aggregate of particles as $Agg(p^1, p^2, p^3)$.

Given (RST) not all of these can be true hence we reject constitutivity as an identity relation. Of course, this argument fails for the same reason as the argument about Cleopatra's Needle fails: it does not take account of tenses. But Chandler proposes a different rewriting as he is anxious to preserve the indiscernibility of identicals and this takes him close to (R) although he backs away at the last moment. He claims that what (9.52) and (9.53) amount to are:

(9.55) The alphe in r_1 at t_4 has the property of being something which, if traced according to the rules for identifying alphes, is traceable to the alphe in r_1 at t_1.

(9.56) $Agg(p^4, p^5, p^6)$ does not have the property of being something which, if traced according to the rules for identifying alphes, is traceable to the alphe in r_1 at t_1.

But now (9.56) is false for $Agg(p^4, p^5, p^6)$, if traced according to the rules for tracing alphes, *does* lead back to r_1 at t_1—for alphes don't move. On the other hand, if we traced $Agg(p^4, p^5, p^6)$ back according to the rules for identifying *aggregates* we get:

(9.57) $Agg(p^4, p^5, p^6)$ does not have the property of being something which, if traced according to the rules for identifying aggregates, is traceable to the alphe in r_1 at t_1.

(9.57) is true but there is no conflict between it, (9.55), and the indiscernibility of identicals. '[W]hy', Chandler asks, 'can't one and the same thing be traceable to one region, if traced according to one set of rules, and traceable to another region, if traced according to a different set?'[35]

This, of course, looks very similar to (R) but Chandler does not go the whole way because he is not prepared to accept (9.55), (9.56), and (9.57) as the basis for identity statements. But this is surely implausible for according to the identity criteria which Chandler explicitly defines for alphes and aggregates (9.55) simply states necessary and sufficient conditions for the alphe-identity statement:

(9.58)   The alphe in r_1 at t_4 is the same alphe as the alphe in r_1 at t_1.

Likewise, (9.56) states necessary and sufficient conditions for:

(9.59) $Agg(p^4, p^5, p^6)$ is not the same alphe as the alphe in r_1 at t_1.

and (9.57) for:

(9.60) $Agg(p^4, p^5, p^6)$ is not the same aggregate as the alphe in r_1 at t_1.

which are distinctness statements for alphes and aggregates respectively. That (9.59) is false and the others true simply indicates that we have here another example of (R).

In considering cases like this the usefulness of a relative

---

[35] Ibid., p. 317.

identity theory can be demonstrated. It provides a relatively simple and entirely plausible account of issues which otherwise appear intolerably murky and confused. In the next chapter I shall show that it has similar advantages in areas which have nothing to do with constitutivity.

On Some Examples of (R)

10.1 The Five Ways of David Wiggins

Not all cases of (R) involve the constitutive 'is'; examples occur in different circumstances throughout natural language. I've already argued that the absolutist's attempts to prove the relative identity theory incoherent are failures. If relative identity is not incoherent, the absolutist has, at least, to provide a convincing alternative account for every example of (R) that the relativist puts up. If even this proves impossible then there will be no option but to reject absolute identity as an adequate account of identity relations in natural language. On the other hand, if the absolutist can provide an alternative to (R), he could further show that his account was preferable to (R) in that it preserved independently plausible principles which the relativist would be committed to denying in order to keep his example in play. (Conversely, of course, the relativist could argue that his account was preferable because the principles which the absolutist appealed to in his alternative were independently implausible.) At this level I think the relativist has a good case. The absolutist is, I think, compelled either to restrict the applicability of absolute identity until it covers only a small number of the cases normally thought of as involving identity or else to introduce a large number of *ad hoc* expedients to maintain the scope of absolute identity. Zemach's argument from open-texture, considered in § 8.4, illustrates the alternatives to which the absolutist may be forced. In the face of the open-texture argument the absolutist might concede open-texture in a number of what would normally be thought of as identity relations yet maintain that 'genuine' identity relations had no such open-texture—thus restricting the applicability of 'genuine' or absolute identity, while giving some non-identity account of the open-textured relations. Alternatively, he may accept all the relations as identity relations but reject the claim that any of them are open-textured in order to avoid a case of (R). This keeps a widely applicable identity relation at the cost of adding extraneous and implausible postulates about open-texture. I think some of the examples considered in §§ 10.2 and 10.3 force a similarly invidious choice upon the absolutist. It seems to me that the best the absolutist can do is to provide an alternative account of each example of (R). The techniques he uses in doing so will be considered in the remainder of this chapter.

As a preliminary to dealing with the examples, Wiggins[1] lists five ways in which '$a =_{\mathscr{B}} b$' might be false. The first way (actually Wiggins's second)[2] occurs when a is not just not the same $\mathscr{B}$ as b but not the same anything as b. Here we have a case where

$$(10.1) \qquad (\forall a) \sim (a =_a b).$$

In fact, there are two subcases: one in which '$\mathscr{B}(a)$' and '$\mathscr{B}(b)$' are true and one in which they are not. In neither instance, however, can we have a case of (R).

The second case is one we have already considered and put in abeyance in § 1.4. It is the case in which we have '$a =_{\mathscr{A}} b$ & $\sim (a =_{\mathscr{B}} b)$' because $\sim \mathscr{B}(a)$ & $\sim \mathscr{B}(b)$. Our earlier example illustrates such a case:

(1.9)   W. S. Porter is the same man as O. Henry but they are not the same number.

It is worth briefly reconsidering this example because we can now see precisely why the relativist does not have a good case here. The absolutist uses the Fregean analysis to translate statements of the form 'a is the same $\mathscr{A}$ as b' into his canonical notation. In the case of the first conjunct of (1.9) we get:

(10.2)   W. S. Porter = O. Henry & man(W. S. Porter) & man(O. Henry).

And the truth of the second conjunct of (1.9) is guaranteed by the Fregean analysis:

(10.3)   W. S. Porter = O. Henry & $\sim$ number(W. S. Porter) & $\sim$ number(O. Henry).

[1] *Identity and Spatio-Temporal Continuity*, pp. 5–7.   [2] Ibid., p. 6.

Unlike cases of (R) in which '$\mathscr{B}(a)$' and '$\mathscr{B}(b)$' are both true no contradiction results from this simple application of the Fregean analysis. The relativist and absolutist accounts seem equally plausible here and there is thus no point in pursuing this sort of case further.

The third case can also be illustrated by an earlier example:

(1.10)   W. S. Porter is the same man as O. Henry but they are not the same boy.

In such cases we have '$a =_{\mathscr{A}} b$ & $\sim (a =_{\mathscr{B}} b)$' because either '$\sim \mathscr{B}(a)$ & $\mathscr{B}(b)$' or '$\mathscr{B}(a)$ & $\sim \mathscr{B}(b)$'. Here again the Fregean analysis provides an account (though one prone to difficulties) for we have (10.2) for the first conjunct and

(10.4)   W. S. Porter = O. Henry & boy(W. S. Porter) & $\sim$ boy(O. Henry)

which guarantees the truth of the second conjunct. But Wiggins doesn't make this point. Instead he makes two claims the force of which is rather obscure. He claims, firstly, that the example shows 'the necessity for care about tenses, both in the interpretation . . . of $\sim (a =_{\mathscr{B}} b)$ and in the interpretation of Leibniz' Law'; if we take tenses into account 'it follows that "$\sim (a =_{\mathscr{B}} b)$", properly read, is not true.'[3] This suggests that

(10.5)   O. Henry is the same boy as W. S. Porter.

is true[4] *because* it is true that:

(10.6)   O. Henry *was* the same boy as W. S. Porter.

But from the fact that (10.6) is true[5] it doesn't follow that (10.5) is true. From the fact that *a* and *b* were the same boy, it doesn't follow that they are the same boy after they have ceased to be boys. Of course, the conjunction of (10.6) with the first conjunct of (1.10) will not give us a case of (R) but this is irrelevant since it is (1.10) which is up for discussion. It is precisely by taking

---

[3] Ibid., pp. 6–7.

[4] Wiggins does not state that he is using a more than two-valued logic, but compare his second argument on (1.10).

[5] In fact, there is some doubt as to whether (10.6) is true for, in a certain sense, O. Henry never was a boy since W. S. Porter only adopted his pseudonym when adult. But let us grant this point.

tenses into account that one can tell the difference. Now it may be that (10.5) should be timelessly interpreted:

(10.7) $(\exists t)[R_t(\text{O. Henry is (tenselessly) the same boy as W. S. Porter})]$.

And let us grant Wiggins that (10.7) is true. But why suppose that we had (10.7) in mind when we set up (1.10)? Why not interpret the second conjunct of (1.10) as straight-forwardly present tensed and straight-forwardly false? What Wiggins needs here is the point about the use of tenses in the interpretation of Leibniz's Law, for unless we use tensed Leibniz's Law (10.4) will be contrary to the indiscernibility of identicals. But I see no need for his other points.

Wiggins's second comment is equally obscure. He uses the example to draw a distinction between phase sortals (e.g. 'boy') and 'substance-concepts'[6] (e.g. 'man'). Though we made such a distinction in § 3.4 it is not quite clear what it amounts to. None the less, in the case under discussion the difference between the two covering concepts seems clear enough. While Wiggins initially claims that 'boy' is a sortal 'and . . . make[s a] perfectly good covering concept. One can count and identify such things, and so on',[7] he later seems to renege on this claim by denying that 'boy' is a substance-concept because phase sortals do not give 'the privileged and (unless context makes it otherwise) the most fundamental kind of answer to the question "what is x?" '.[8] The point he wants to make seems to be that since 'boy' is not a substance-concept it cannot act as a completing concept and thus identity statements in which it is the covering concept are incomplete. He writes: '[T]hat for all x and all y, every concept which adequately individuates x for any stretch of its existence yields the same answer, *where it does yield any answer at all*, as every other genuinely individuating concept for x and y to the question whether x coincides with y or not.'[9] This suggests that on occasion 'boy' does not yield an answer at all and therefore cannot be a proper completing concept. Hence any identity statement which it covers lacks clear sense and hence cannot be said to be true or false. This salvages Wiggins's earlier point about (10.5) which would, under this interpretation, be neither true nor false,

⁶ Ibid., p. 7.   ⁷ Ibid., p. 6.   ⁸ Ibid., p. 7.   ⁹ Ibid.

but wrecks his point about (10.6) which is neither true nor false either. As a result (1.10) lacks a truth-value and the relativist loses his case of (R).

But surely 'boy' does yield an answer in the case in point: for if a is not a boy then a is not the same boy as anything. And two further points: firstly, from the fact that '$\mathscr{F}$' does not give the most fundamental kind of answer to the question 'what is x?' it does not follow that '$\mathscr{F}$' never supplies an answer of any kind to the question 'is x the same $\mathscr{F}$ as y?' The connection between substance-concepts (as Wiggins defines them) and the role which Wiggins ascribes to them as covering concepts has not been made out despite the efforts we have devoted to the task in Chapters 4 and 7. Secondly, if Wiggins's distinction between the two types of covering concept is going to sustain his point, I think that it needs to be made a lot more sharply than he makes it.[10] We need to know in some detail what is wrong with phase sortals.

Wiggins's response to these cases, however, seems to be needlessly complex, for the Fregean analysis together with tensed Leibniz's Law provides a consistent absolutist account, thus (where $t' < t$):

$$(10.8) \quad R_t(\mathrm{man}(a)) \,\&\, R_t(\mathrm{man}(b)) \,\&\, R_t(a = b) \,\&\, \sim R_t(\mathrm{boy}(a))$$
$$\&\, \sim R_t(\mathrm{boy}(b)) \,\&\, R_{t'}(\mathrm{boy}(a)) \,\&\, R_{t'}(\mathrm{boy}(b)).$$

In fact there is no need to place '$a = b$' in (10.8) within the scope of a realization operator since both $R_t(a = b)$ and $R_{t'}(a = b)$.

I'm not sure that Wiggins adequately differentiates his fourth type of case. Wiggins characterizes them as cases where '$a =_{\mathscr{A}} b \,\&\, \sim (a =_{\mathscr{B}} b) \,\&\, (\mathscr{B}(a) \vee \mathscr{B}(b)) \,\&\, (\mathscr{B}(a) \,\&\, \sim \mathscr{B}(b))$'[11] but his type-(3) cases satisfy this requirement. I suspect that he intends type-(4) cases to be distinct from type-(3) cases in that they are not resolved by consideration of tenses and phase sortals. Wiggins gives a number of examples[12] and an

---

[10] Later he recognizes that there are cases in which it is hard to know whether we have a substance-concept or a phase sortal. (Ibid., pp. 59–60; see also Tobias Chapman, 'Identity and Reference', *Mind*, 82 (1973), 550 for further examples and Gerald Vision, 'Essentialism and the Senses of Proper Names', *American Philosophical Quarterly*, 7 (1970), 321–30 for discussion.) Wiggins's reference to context in the passage quoted above indicates that he cannot make an absolute distinction.

[11] Ibid., p. 7. [12] Ibid., pp. 8–9.

extended discussion of them,[13] but the examples all (except for one which seems properly to belong to his fifth type)[14] involve tenses as Wiggins himself notes.[15] In fact, it is rather difficult to find examples of the fourth type which do not involve identity through change and therefore collapse into the third type. However, I think the following will serve. Let us define the term 'pair' in such a way that it is indifferent between 'ordered pair' and 'pair class' or 'unordered pair'. To be the same pair is to be a pair and to have the same members. From what has just been said it follows that the ordered pair $\langle 1, 2 \rangle$ and the pair class $\{2, 1\}$ are both pairs, and moreover:

(10.9) $\langle 1, 2 \rangle$ is the same pair as $\{2, 1\}$ but they are not the same ordered pair (though $\langle 1, 2 \rangle$ and $\{2, 1\}$ are both pairs and $\langle 1, 2 \rangle$—though not $\{2, 1\}$—is an ordered pair).

We can apply the Fregean analysis, which in this case gives us:

(10.10) $\langle 1, 2 \rangle = \{2, 1\}$ & pair($\langle 1, 2 \rangle$) & pair($\{2, 1\}$) & ordered pair($\langle 1, 2 \rangle$) & $\sim$ ordered pair($\{2, 1\}$).

But (10.10) runs into trouble with (LL) which it violates. No manipulation of tenses will reconcile a consistent Fregean analysis with (LL) unless we replace the first conjunct of (10.10) by '$\langle 1, 2 \rangle \neq \{2, 1\}$' which scarcely represents (10.9).

The treatment of examples of the fourth type which Wiggins offers admits, rather than resolves, the problems which (10.9) poses for the absolutist. Wiggins denies that fourth type examples are possible, but his reasons are obscure:

In fact it begins to appear why there simply *cannot* be cases of type-(4). Where $(\exists a)(a =_a b)$ and allegedly $(\exists \ell) \sim (a =_\ell b)$ and $\ell(a) \vee \ell(b)$[16] either ℓ is a substantial sortal or it is not. If it is not substantial then it will always need to be proved that we have more than a type-(3) case or a case of the constitutive 'is'.[17] If it is a

---

[13] Ibid., pp. 10–16.

[14] Wiggins's (β) on p. 8, ibid.

[15] Ibid., p. 16.

[16] This must be the exclusive 'or'.

[17] Presumably Wiggins holds that compositional nouns are not substantial concepts, though he does not say so explicitly. Indeed, he implies that there is no 'hard and fast or canonically correct answer to the question "what is Cleopatra's Needle?"' (ibid., p. 15). So much is undeniable—*unless* we can find some reason for denying that compositional uses of nouns are substantival terms. After the last

substantial sortal then either a or b has to be a ℓ without the other being a ℓ. But this violates Leibniz' Law.[18]

But the distinction here between substantial and non-substantial covering concepts is spurious, for the case will violate Wiggins's (DLL) whichever the covering concept is. Nor is the appeal to (DLL) any sort of defence at all. The absolutist can hardly claim that no such cases arise because, if they did, his theory would be violated. Rather, it is an admission that the absolutist has to give some alternative account.

In Wiggins's fifth type of case we have:

$$(10.11) \quad a =_{\mathscr{A}} b \ \& \ a \neq_{\mathscr{B}} b \ \& \ \mathscr{A}(a) \ \& \ \mathscr{A}(b) \ \& \ \mathscr{B}(a) \ \& \ \mathscr{B}(b).$$

As an example of the fifth type consider the list:

(I)　a　Dog
　　　b　Dog

We have:

(10.12)　a is the same type word as b but they are not the same token word (though both are token words and both are type words).

The Fregean analysis runs into trouble here:

(10.13)　$a = b$ & $a \neq b$ & token word(a) & token word(b) & type word(a) & type word(b).

We gain the same sort of contradiction from using the Fregean analysis on an example similar to (10.9), for we have:

(10.14)　$\langle 1, 2 \rangle$ is the same pair as $\langle 2, 1 \rangle$ but they are not the same ordered pair though both are pairs and both are ordered pairs.

Of Wiggins's five ways, the first gives rise to no examples of (R) and hence poses no difficulty; the second is easily dealt with by the absolutist by means of the Fregean analysis; the absolutist can also deal with the third type fairly easily by combining the Fregean analysis with tensed Leibniz's Law. The fourth and fifth, however, are more troublesome for the

chapter it is hardly necessary to add that Wiggins's appeal to the constitutive 'is' is not very convincing.

[18] Ibid., pp. 15–16.

absolutist, who is forced to find some alternative analysis for them. In general, attempts have fallen into two main classes. Firstly, there is the attempt to show that there is some equivocation in the use of singular terms in formulating the example of (R) and secondly an attempt to show that the relations involved in stating the particular examples of (R) are not identity relations.[19] In Chapter 9 we have already examined, and found wanting, one major absolutist attempt along the second line to show that the relativist uses other than identity relations in formulating (R). I shall consider such moves further in § 10.3, but in the next section I want to examine the absolutist's first type of argument: namely that the relativist trades on an equivocation in the use of singular terms in formulating cases of (R).

10.2 The Relativist's Alleged Referential Equivocation

It is easiest to approach this absolutist argument by considering how it could be used to dismantle the relativist's examples of (R). The absolutist urges, in the case of (10.12), for example, that if both conjuncts of (10.12) are identity statements then the first asserts identity between type words while the second asserts it between token words. Moreover, 'if "a" is the name of a word-token, then "a" cannot be the name of a word-type.'[20] If we accept this, then our example of (R) perforce collapses. Let us introduce the name 'c' as the name of the word-type of which 'a' and 'b' are both the names of word-tokens. Then instead of (10.12) we have:

(10.15) c is the same word-type as c & a is not the same word-token as b.

The case of (R) entirely disappears. Consider Geach's man/surman example: 'if "Tom Jones" names a man, then it cannot name a surman.'[21] Again the example of (R) collapses since in such a case Tom Jones is not the same surman as anything for he is not a surman. A similar response deals with (10.14): if '$\langle 1, 2 \rangle$' is the name of an ordered pair it is not the name of

---

[19] See, for example, Perry, 'Identity', pp. 52–3, for an explicit statement of this two-pronged attack on (R).

[20] Stevenson, 'Relative Identity and Leibniz's Law', p. 157; see also Perry, 'Identity', p. 54; 'The Same F', p. 188.

[21] Stevenson, ibid.

a pair, or, if it is the name of a pair, then it is not the name of an ordered pair. Every example of (R), the absolutist hopes, will collapse in this way.

What the absolutist has now to do in order to show that this model works for (10.12) is to show us that his claim that if '*a*' names a word-token it does not name a word-type is true. According to Stevenson '*a*' cannot be the name of a word-type as well as the name of a word-token 'since the noun "word-token" supplies a different criterion of identity from the noun "word-type" '.[22] This, of course, guarantees that his point will work against any case of (R) whatsoever since there can be no case of (R) unless the two covering concepts provide different criteria of identity. But it also guarantees that his argument is circular since he simply appeals to a principle which he can only demonstrate if (R) is rejected: namely, that an item may not fall under two terms conveying conflicting criteria of identity. But can't the absolutist reply that since identity criteria tell us what constitutes identity, if an allegedly single item turns out to have two distinct sets of identity criteria, then surely that is as good a proof as we'll ever have that it is not a single item after all but two distinct items? What can we hope to use identity criteria to show if not to show that?

Arguments of this type are employed fairly generally against (R). Wiggins[23] and Stevenson[24] both make appeal to Geach's theory of proper names, according to which 'for every proper name there is a corresponding use of a common noun preceded by "the same" to express what requirements as to identity the proper name conveys.'[25] If this is so, how, the absolutist asks, can it be proper to use the same name when two conflicting sets of identity criteria are intended? Wiggins uses the point to dispose of Linsky's[26] Cleopatra's Needle example. If Cleopatra's Needle wears away and is replaced by a similarly shaped obelisk, we have:

(10.16)   Cleopatra's Needle at t_0 is the same landmark as Cleopatra's Needle at t_1 but they are not the same block of stone.

[22] Ibid.   [23] *Identity and Spatio-Temporal Continuity*, p. 14.
[24] 'Relative Identity and Leibniz's Law', pp. 156-7.
[25] *Reference and Generality*, p. 43.
[26] L. Linsky, Critical Notice of *Reference and Generality*, p. 579.

(where Cleopatra's Needle wears away at t and $t_0 < t < t_1$).
Wiggins writes:

> It seems to follow [from Geach's theory of proper names] that if
> 'Cleopatra's Needle' had two equally good but different 'nominal
> essences'[27] then it ought to be ambiguous, in which case [(10.16)]
> should not surprise or impress us any more than any startling
> paradox arrived at by equivocation . . . The example may owe a
> specious plausibility precisely to the fact that 'Cleopatra's Needle'
> can sustain itself indefinitely long ambiguously poised between these
> [viz. the sense given by 'block of stone' and that given by 'landmark']
> and perhaps yet other incompatible senses.[28]

Nelson generalizes this conclusion to make it fit all cases of (R):
'Identity is, then, not relative. It is not relative because if it
were there would have to be individuals which are in themselves
of no particular kind, but hover ambiguously between many
kinds. There neither are, nor could there be, such individuals.'[29]
Wiggins doesn't generalize his argument, although he does use
it elsewhere.[30]

Let us deal first with the *ad hominem* argument about Geach's
theory of proper names, for it is not clear that Geach has
involved himself in contradiction. On the Geachian theory
proper names have sense and the sense is given by a general
term with which the proper name is associated. Now quite
obviously most proper names will be associated with several
different terms of different sense (the name 'Jemima' will be
associated with 'pet' as well as 'cat', and 'pet' and 'cat' have
clearly different senses). Geach does go on to claim that 'the
sense of the proper name "Jemima" need not include the sense
of any predicables like "female" and "tabby" that apply to
Jemima but not to all cats.'[31] But this still leaves in both 'cat'
and 'animal' which have different senses. If it were the case
that Geach was claiming that the sense of a proper name is
completely given by a general term with which the name is

---

[27] In fact Geach (*Reference and Generality*, pp. 43–4) says that the general term
which conveys the identity criteria associated with a proper name also conveys
the nominal essence of the *thing* which the name names—not, as Wiggins says,
of the proper name itself.

[28] *Identity and Spatio-Temporal Continuity*, pp. 14–15.

[29] 'Relative Identity', p. 257.

[30] Cf., for example, *Identity and Spatio-Temporal Continuity*, pp. 16–18.

[31] *Reference and Generality*, p. 44.

associated (subject to the proviso just quoted) then it would follow that just about every proper name was ambiguous in sense. Instead Geach is claiming that part of the sense of the proper name is given by the identity criteria which the general terms it is associated with convey. Now despite the multiplicity of general terms there might turn out to be only one set of identity criteria since all the general terms convey equivalent identity criteria. This, however, does not so far touch the point at issue for we are concerned with cases in which there are conflicting identity criteria so that the name will remain ambiguous after all this has been taken into account.

However we can interpret Geach's theory of proper names in a way suggested by Tobias Chapman:

Most objects of reference are such that no guarantee can be given that the general concepts by means of which they can be referred to each 'contain' a principle of identity which will individuate in exactly the same way (either at one time or over time) *and further, we cannot restrict the sense of the proper name to just those concepts which do individuate in the same way* . . . Geach says, for instance, 'different proper names of different material objects convey different requirements as to identity' ([*Reference and Generality*] p. 43). To this he might have added that the same proper name may convey different requirements as to identity because the thing named falls under different concepts, *and that this is precisely what makes (R) true.*[32]

Of course, Wiggins can still claim that 'Cleopatra's Needle' is ambiguous for precisely that reason: it conveys different sets of identity criteria. Against this Chapman raises two objections.[33] Firstly, it imposes a certain sort of conceptual conservatism for we could never discover that the bearer of a non-ambiguous proper name (in the sense the absolutist requires) fell under some substantival term which conveys identity criteria which conflicted with those conveyed by the substantival terms under which we already knew that it fell. This, indeed, is a form of conceptual conservatism against which Wiggins himself objects,[34] and is clearly related to Zemach's argument from the open-texture of singular terms. Secondly, Chapman claims that such an argument leads to 'a specious form of Platonism'.[35]

[32] 'Identity and Reference', p. 546.   [33] Ibid.
[34] *Identity and Spatio-Temporal Continuity*, pp. 59–60; fn. 37 (p. 69).
[35] 'Identity and Reference', p. 546.

I'm not quite sure what this objection amounts to, but it seems to be the claim that Wiggins would require that we had not merely the material Cleopatra's Needle in London (i.e. Cleopatra's Needle *qua* block of stone) but various other Cleopatra's Needles, abstracted from their physical instantiation, in Plato's heaven (e.g. Cleopatra's Needle *qua* landmark). This objection, if I have understood it aright, is rather like the slick objections to Meinong's theory of objects and I'm not willing to place too much weight on it.

There is a convincing absolutist reply to Chapman's charge of Platonism, however, although it turns out to be rather a double edged weapon. The absolutist can reply that from the fact that 'Cleopatra's Needle' is ambiguous in sense it does not follow that there are two or more Cleopatra's Needles—either on earth or in heaven. But this shows, also, that even if the absolutist is right in claiming that, on a Geachian view of proper names, proper names are ambiguous in sense he is still unable to dismantle the examples of (R). If Wiggins is going to dismantle (10.16) as a case of (R) he needs to claim more than that 'Cleopatra's Needle' is ambiguous in sense—he needs to make the further claim that it is also ambiguous in reference or designation. Nothing would have been done to avoid a case of (R) if the proper names used in both conjuncts, though used in a different sense in each, none the less designated the same item in both. This is brought out clearly in Stevenson's original statement of the case (that if '*a*' is the name of a type word it is not the name of a token word) rather than in Wiggins's exposition. In this case, therefore, the appeal to Geach's theory of proper names is irrelevant unless it can be shown that the sense-ambiguity of proper names leads to a referential ambiguity (and this has not been argued).

If we are to see whether there is a referential ambiguity in the use of 'Cleopatra's Needle' we need to look at what exactly it is the name of. Let us introduce some neutral names for the items we want to refer to. According to Wiggins we use 'Cleopatra's Needle' ambiguously between 'Cleopatra's Needle *qua* landmark' and 'Cleopatra's Needle *qua* block of stone', and (he must further claim) the reference of each term is different. Let '$a_{\mathscr{L}}$' be read 'Cleopatra's Needle *qua* landmark' and let '$a_{\mathscr{G}}$' be 'Cleopatra's Needle *qua* block of

stone'.[36] We also need to take time into account in our nomen-
clature, so let '$a_{\mathscr{F}}$' be read 'Cleopatra's Needle *qua* landmark
at t_0' and let '$b_{\mathscr{F}}$' be read 'Cleopatra's Needle *qua* landmark at
t_1', and similarly for '$a_{\mathscr{G}}$' and '$b_{\mathscr{G}}$'. We can now rewrite (10.16)
somewhat more neutrally:

$$(10.17) \qquad\qquad a_{\mathscr{F}} =_{\mathscr{F}} b_{\mathscr{F}} \ \& \ a_{\mathscr{G}} \neq_{\mathscr{G}} b_{\mathscr{G}}.$$

The question now is: what is the relation between $a_{\mathscr{F}}$ and $a_{\mathscr{G}}$
and between $b_{\mathscr{F}}$ and $b_{\mathscr{G}}$? The absolutist claims that it is not
identity in either case. And clearly it is not absolute identity,
for the indiscernibility of identicals is violated. The relativist,
on the other hand, is not claiming that they are absolutely
identical, but that they are identical relative to the sortal
'$\mathscr{G}$'. And this is surely the case, for Cleopatra's Needle *qua* landmark at t_0 is the same block of stone as Cleopatra's Needle *qua*
block of stone at t_0, and Cleopatra's Needle *qua* landmark at t_1
is the same block of stone as Cleopatra's Needle *qua* block of
stone at t_1. To deny this might well lead one into a specious
form of Platonism with entities multiplied *praeter necessitatem*, for
Cleopatra's Needle clearly exists at t_0 (and at t_1) both *qua* landmark and *qua* block of stone. It would be bizarre not to prune
one's ontology by a few simple relative identities.

It is important to see why settling for relative identities
between $a_{\mathscr{F}}$ and $a_{\mathscr{G}}$ and $b_{\mathscr{F}}$ and $b_{\mathscr{G}}$ involves neither a referential equivocation nor putting up with an unsatisfactory situa-
tion in order to save the theory. In view of our account of the
individuative role of sortals, the notion of an individuated item
makes no sense unless the item is individuated with respect to
some sortal. Thus there is no way of significantly assigning
a name to an item except by reference to a sortal, for, without
the sortal, we have no means of knowing what we have so
named. Let us suppose we individuate some item by means of
the sortal '$\mathscr{F}$' and assign the name 'a' to it; suppose also we
individuate another item by means of the sortal '$\mathscr{G}$' and call it
'b'. Now if we discover that $a =_{\mathscr{F}} b$ (or that $a =_{\mathscr{G}} b$) we have,
not merely a reason, but the best reason there could be for
assigning the same name to both individuated items—notwith-
standing the fact that a and b may be distinct with respect to

---

[36] The notation is familiar from our account of what it is for a singular term
to refer under a sortal. Cf. § 3.4 above.

a sortal '$\mathcal{H}$'. Of course, it may turn out that a and b share all their predicates and are thus absolutely identical; this, of course, confirms our right to use the same name of both, but if our account of individuation is correct it is strictly unnecessary for the business of assigning names. Thus the relativist has as good a reason as he could ever have for writing:

$$(10.18) \qquad\qquad a =_{\mathcal{F}} b \ \& \ a \neq_{\mathcal{G}} b$$

for (10.17). (It should be noted that only identity with respect to some *sortal* is adequate for ensuring that the same name may be assigned to two independently individuated items.)

Nelson's claim that the relativist requires items to hover ambiguously between sorts takes the obvious truth that items may fall under many different sortal terms too far, but doesn't take far enough the idea of a sorted domain. It is not the case that Cleopatra's Needle must be either a landmark or a lump of stone, or that, in (I), a must be either a type word or a token word. It is not incoherent to claim that Cleopatra's Needle is both a landmark and a lump of stone and many other things besides. As Geach says: 'It is . . . the question "But which is it *really*?" that is incoherent.'[37] This has long been recognized in philosophical psychology in connection with levels of description of action: in hailing a taxi one raises one's arm. It is ridiculous to ask 'Which did you *really* do?' But the idea that we must individuate our items in only one way at a time dies hard in philosophical logic. The idea that this simple fact somehow requires that such items are neither one thing nor the other, completely fails to appreciate the role sortals play in sorting the domain.[38]

While the claim that a landmark is not identical with the stone of which it is composed is only marginally counter-intuitive (largely, I suspect, because of the way in which the prevailing absolute theory has coloured our intuitions, appeals

[37] 'Ontological Relativity and Relative Identity', p. 294. It is for this reason that Wiggins's talk about the 'privileged' and 'most fundamental' answer to the question 'what is x?' (*Identity and Spatio-Temporal Continuity*, p. 7) is so perplexing.

[38] It is fair to point out here that Nelson was attacking Geach's relative identity theory rather than the theory presented here. However, this does not help him to sustain his attack since Geach rejects absolute identity and can reply that Nelson's unsorted items arise from imposing relative identities on a domain the members of which are differentiated from one another by absolute identity— a situation Geach rejects.

to the Life Histories Principle, and the like, are likely to prove effective) there are other examples of (R) where the absolutist treatment leads to definitely counter-intuitive results. Consider:

(10.19)   1/2 is the same rational number as 2/4 but they are not the same fraction.

The absolutist has to claim that if '1/2' is the name of a fraction then it is not the name of a rational number. But this is false since every fraction is a rational number. The same is true of (10.9), it is simply false for the absolutist to claim that if '⟨1, 2⟩' is the name of an ordered pair it cannot be the name of a pair, for an ordered pair is just a pair with structure. It is precisely the presence or absence of structure which gives pairs and ordered pairs different identity criteria. To claim that they must be distinct for that reason is mere absolutist dogma.

Equally the absolutist is in a difficult situation with the man/ surman example. Since Geach decided to define 'ζ is the same surman as η' as 'ζ and η are both men and have the same surname' it is scarcely open to the absolutist to claim that if 'Tom Jones' and 'Jack Jones' are both the names of men then they cannot be the names of a surman. It seems that Stevenson is here relying on Perry's assumption that surmen are sets (or families) of men. The same assumption seems to underlie his treatment of the type/token case. If type words are really sets of token words, then it would be wrong to claim that the token word a is (even relatively) identical to a set of which it is a member. But the relativist is not forced to agree with this account of what type words are. He could analyse 'ζ is the same type word as η' as 'ζ and η are token words and ζ is equiform with η'. He then gets an example exactly analogous to the surman/man example. Moreover, this analysis of 'ζ is the same type word as η' has distinct advantages over the alternative. It meshes much better with the way we talk about type words. If type words are really classes of token words we could, for example, never say ' "Dog" is a type word' for in each case it would be the token word we were referring to. Instead we would have to say something like '$\{x : x$ is equiform with "dog"$\}$ is a type word', which is manifestly not what we do say. But it is not my business here to defend particular theories about type words and nor do I have to, for we can give the absolutist his

account of what a type word is[39] and introduce the notion of
(say) 'an equitoken word' such that 'ζ is the same equitoken
word as η' is given the relativist analysis suggested above. There
seems to be nothing wrong with such a concept, I can think of
no way in which it might be thought incoherent, yet it gives
cases of (R), for a may be the same equitoken word as b though
they are distinct token words, against which the absolutist
argument is, by definition, unavailing.

It may be objected that the relativist has, in these examples,
simply defined his position into existence by defining special
sortals ('pair', 'surman', 'equitoken word') from which examples
of (R) can be constructed. I don't think that this is a very
powerful objection, for there seems no reason to take conceptual
conservatism to such an extreme as to prohibit the introduction
of new sortals into a language—and every reason not to. Moreover, in some cases it seems desirable to define new terms to
capture senses which seem to be present in terms already in the
language (as when we defined 'official*' to capture explicitly
one sense of 'official').[40] Additionally, we may point to cases in
which the natural language terms seem fairly clear-cut as far as
identity criteria are concerned. Consider a discussion about
whether two people who speak different dialects speak the same
language. It seems natural to say that they speak the same
language but different dialects. But this does not suppose that
what they speak must be either a language or a dialect; nor does
it imply (as Nelson seems to think) that they speak something
which is neither a language nor a dialect. In truth, they speak
both—but this does not mean they are bilingual. Nor can we
claim that a language is a set of dialects, for then to speak
a language would require speaking many dialects. The facts
are simple and natural language makes them plain: that which
they speak is both a language and a dialect and, since the

[39] None the less it is surely a poor theory of identity which requires buttressing
so frequently by these special conceptual manœuvres.

[40] A range of similar examples are considered, from an absolutist point of view,
by Roderick M. Chisholm, 'Problems of Identity', in M. K. Munitz (ed.), *Identity
and Individuation*, pp. 3–30. For obvious reasons I concentrate here on identity
puzzles related to (R). It does seem to me however that relative identity does offer
the hope of principled solutions to such identity puzzles as those considered by
Berent Enç, 'Numerical Identity and Objecthood', *Mind*, 84 (1975), 10–26 which
are not connected with (R) but are none the less difficult from the absolutist point
of view.

identity criteria associated with each term are different, we
have, between the two of them, one language spoken but two
dialects.

   This last example goes beyond Zemach's appeal to the open-
texture of general nouns for it seems that 'language' and
'dialect' are not open-textured in any way relevant to the
present problem. Linguistics furnishes another such example:
'-ise' and '-ize' are two distinct allomorphs yet are both the
same morpheme. (Similar examples clearly arise with allo-
phones and phonemes but are obviously more difficult to write
down.) This fact doesn't seem to be due to open-texture since
neither term is open-textured in the relevant way. Moreover,
it is clearly counter-intuitive to claim that if '-ise' is an allomorph it is not a morpheme and makes the morpheme useless
for its original purpose as the minimal unit of syntactic analysis.
The examples also enable us to see how the theory of absolute
identity forces one to adopt some one level of analysis as more
fundamental than any other. Since a single morpheme may
be two (or more) allomorphs the absolutist adopts the allomorph as his minimal unit and treats 'ζ is the same morpheme
as η' as a mere equivalence relation over allomorphs. Of course,
he can concede that 'for certain purposes' the morpheme could
be 'treated as' basic. What he cannot do is operate with morphemes and allomorphs simultaneously without having an
ontological prejudice in favour of allomorphs. There has been
a resultant tendency for linguists to treat morphemes as
theoretical constructions out of allomorphs. But however
defensible this may be, it is plainly not possible to treat languages as theoretical constructions out of dialects. And it
would also appear reasonable to take the morpheme as given
and construe its associated allomorphs as variants of it. What
does seem unreasonable is to be forced into one position or the
other by a theory of identity. Neither position is incompatible
with (R)-relative identity; and neither is a third in which 'ζ is
the same allomorph as η' and 'ζ is the same morpheme as η'
simply provide different methods of individuating items, such
that two distinct allomorphs are yet the same morpheme as some
one morpheme.

   The relativist's case, so far, is as follows: Firstly, the absolutist's argument from referential equivocation is circular and

therefore ineffective. It presupposes that the relativist is committed to absolutist principles of individuation which he explicitly rejects. Secondly, we have argued that in certain cases (particularly in the rational number/fraction and language/dialect examples) the absolutist is committed to denying principles which we intuitively accept: viz. that fractions are rational numbers and that dialects are languages. Thirdly, we have argued that in the case of certain defined terms (e.g. 'surman', 'equitoken', 'pair') the absolutist if he is to carry his argument forward is committed to denying principles which are by definition true. Fourthly, Chapman has argued that if the absolutist takes his claim about the ambiguity of proper names seriously he will fall into a species of conceptual conservatism which it is desirable to avoid.

There are two further points I want to raise: Fifthly, so long as the absolutist cannot prove relative identity theory incoherent we may urge that all the examples of (R) considered are true conjunctions of sentences of English (or of coherent extensions of English). Thus, even if we grant the efficacy of the absolutist treatment as a coherent alternative to the relativist account, we can still claim that the relativist account fits better with ordinary English. In fact, it seems fairly clear that the conceptual system underlying natural language is not so neat and tidy as the absolutist's account suggests. It has been a constant assumption running through the absolutist account that the concepts we employ are to an astonishing extent well-ordered. It was claimed that no individual falls under more than one ultimate sortal, that any two intersecting sortals both restrict some third sortal, and now that no item falls under two substantival terms which convey conflicting criteria of identity. (Various absolutist positions might be proposed which did without one or more of these simplifying assumptions but none of those so far proposed have managed to do without any of them.) The third simplifying assumption, we now see, leads to results which conflict with our intuitions about the way in which terms are used in natural language. What the absolutist is trying to do is not so much describe the actual conceptual system we use as to reconstruct it so that it fits his preconceptions.

The sixth argument I want to consider is whether the

absolutist's alternative is really adequate at all. I think I have shown that on occasions it conflicts with some of our intuitions, but the absolutist may simply claim that these intuitions need reorganizing just as much as the original examples of (R). However, if his account is to be adequate he has to show us, since he rejects (for example) that Cleopatra's Needle *qua* landmark at t_0 is identical with Cleopatra's Needle *qua* lump of stone at t_0, just what the relation between Cleopatra's Needle *qua* landmark and Cleopatra's Needle *qua* lump of stone is. It is not surprising that Wiggins claims that it can be represented by the 'is' of composition, but whether this is an identity statement or not hangs, as we saw in Chapter 9, on whether one accepts or rejects (R). With other examples, the absolutist is forced to other expedients. On the absolutist account of 'type word' and his (mistaken) account of 'surman', the word-token 'dog' is a member of the appropriate type word and Tom Jones is a member of the appropriate surman. However, what the relation might be, on an absolutist account, between a token word and an equitoken word or between a man and a surman (on Geach's actual interpretation) is surprisingly obscure. Yet the absolutist must provide such a relation if his theory is to be adequate and, moreover, he must demonstrate that it is not a relative identity relation if his argument is to be conclusive. So far, he has not even satisfied the first requirement in the 'equitoken' and 'surman' cases; and has not yet satisfied the second in the case of Cleopatra's Needle.

10.3 Are Relative Identity Statements Really Identity Statements?

The second common absolutist ploy against examples of (R) is to deny that identity or distinctness is expressed in both conjuncts. It is denied, for example, that

(10.20) ζ is the same surman as η

expresses identity. This argument is usually run in conjunction with the referential equivocation argument just considered. For if we fill in the place-holders of (10.20) with the names of surmen it is hard to deny that the result is an identity statement, yet to get an example of (R) we need to fill in the place-holders with the same names as we used to fill the place-holders of 'ζ is the same man as η'. The total argument is thus a dilemma: in any case of (R) either the singular terms refer to the same items in each conjunct or they do not. If they do not, then there is a referential equivocation and no case of (R); if they do, then either the first conjunct is not an identity statement or the second is not a distinctness statement.[41]

The case is, perhaps, most easily exemplified with 'ζ is the same colour as η'. The absolutist denies that

(10.21)   Bill's car is the same colour as Tom's

is an identity statement.[42] But he would probably accept that

(10.22)   The colour of Bill's car is the same colour as the colour of Tom's

is an identity statement. Yet we can only get a case of (R) if we use the same singular term in both conjuncts, namely:

(10.23)   Bill's car is the same colour as Tom's but Bill's car is not the same car as Tom's.

Clearly 'Bill's car' and 'Tom's car' are used without referential ambiguity in (10.23), but the absolutist denies that we have a genuine case of (R) because the first conjunct of (10.23) is not an identity statement. We can thus see how the two absolutist arguments complement each other. If 'a is the same $\mathscr{A}$ as b' is a (true) identity statement then 'a' and 'b' are both the names of an $\mathscr{A}$. If 'a is not the same $\mathscr{B}$ as b' is the (true) denial of an identity statement then either (i) neither 'a' nor 'b' is the name of a $\mathscr{B}$; or (ii) both 'a' and 'b' are the names of $\mathscr{B}$s; or (iii) one of 'a' and 'b' is the name of a $\mathscr{B}$ but not the other. If (i) holds then the absolutist can apply the Fregean analysis, for we have one of Wiggins's type-(2) examples. If either (ii) or (iii) holds then either 'a' or 'b' or both are used with referential ambiguity, since what is the name of an $\mathscr{A}$ cannot be the name of a $\mathscr{B}$ since '$\mathscr{A}$' and '$\mathscr{B}$' convey conflicting requirements as to identity.

I have already challenged the last part of this argument, but now I want to challenge the first part: the claim that if 'a is the

---

[41] The second horn of this dilemma, like the first, is often stated in a way that begs the question against the relativist by using absolute identity. See Perry, 'The Same F', p. 188; 'Identity', p. 53, for a statement of the argument and Calvert, 'Relative Identity', p. 81, for this objection to it.

[42] Perry, 'Identity', pp. 51, 53.

same $\mathscr{A}$ as b' is a true identity statement 'a' and 'b' must both be names of an $\mathscr{A}$. Now, it is obviously true that both a and b must fall under '$\mathscr{A}$', but that is not to say that they are both $\mathscr{A}$s. If (10.21) is true then it follows that both Bill's car and Tom's car fall under 'colour' but not, of course, that they are both colours. The absolutist is plainly making a stronger claim here. If statements like (10.21) are identity statements they are not absolute identity statements, for sharing a common property does not, in general, imply indiscernibility. But, of course, the relativist is not claiming that they are absolute identity statements. There seems to be far less wrong with the claim that they are relative identity statements: they satisfy reflexivity, symmetry, transitivity, and (RLL). To argue that they are not identity statements because they are not absolute identity statements just begs the whole question against the relativist. If the absolutist claims that the relativist is blurring a distinction between common-property statements and identity statements it is open to the relativist to demand some precise account of what this distinction is.

Let us consider a few attempts to distinguish between identity relations and common-property relations.[43] Only absolute identity relations, it will be claimed, satisfy (LL) which is the defining law for identity statements. Even this claim must be taken with qualification in view of the modal paradoxes, and in any case (LL) isn't of the correct form to enable us to decide whether '$a =_{\mathscr{A}} b$' is an identity statement or not. (DLL) is of the right form but it begs the question against the relativist because (DLL) is incompatible with (R).

A second, related, attempt is the following: the absolutist may claim that only if '$a =_{\mathscr{A}} b$' is an identity statement can we license inferences from '$\phi(a)$' to '$\phi(b)$'. But this does not give him the distinction he wants. (10.21) licenses the inference from 'Bill's car is red' to 'Tom's car is red'. The difference seems to be one of degree only. Even (LL), because of the modal paradoxes, does not license such inferences for all '$\phi(\zeta)$'. I will not attribute to the absolutist the absurdity of claiming that if '$a =_{\mathscr{A}} b$' licenses n such inferences it is an identity statement,

---

[43] I don't know of any absolutist work to make this distinction plain. It is usually assumed to be intuitively obvious. The suggestions considered in what follows are therefore my own.

but if it only licenses $n-1$ of them it is merely a common-property statement.

A third attempt at the distinction might be to try and find some difference between the covering concepts of identity statements and those of common-property statements. For example, it might be urged that compositional uses of nouns can cover only common-property statements. This does nothing to help with (10.21) but perhaps there is some other similar distinction which we can use to show that (10.21) is only a common-property statement. But which? None of the distinctions we have so far made among general nouns will serve this purpose. We need to make some further distinction between completing terms, but what such a distinction might be I have no idea, and no absolutist seems to have suggested one. There is, however, a related possibility of making the distinction the absolutist wants. He might claim that '$a =_{\mathscr{A}} b$' is an identity statement iff 'a' and 'b' are the names of $\mathscr{A}$s (names of the same $\mathscr{A}$ if '$a =_{\mathscr{A}} b$' is true, names of different $\mathscr{A}$s if it is false). Now this argument can disarm all examples of (R) only if the absolutist can maintain his referential equivocation argument —which we have just argued he cannot. However, the relativist is so far under no obligation to accept the absolutist's legislation about when '$a =_{\mathscr{A}} b$' is an identity statement, since it always satisfies the formal requirements of relative identity theory. Moreover, it clearly widens the scope of relative identity theory, without so far as I can see incurring any disadvantages, to reject this account of identity statements—for example, quantitative identity statements could then be included as relative identity statements.

There is, however, an argument which the absolutist might use to get rid of cases of (R). The approach is to take an alleged example of (R) and to provide a paraphrase of one or other conjunct such that the paraphrase is neither an identity nor a distinctness statement, and then to claim, on the strength of that, that the original conjunct was not an identity statement either. I shall call this Wiggins's paraphrase procedure. Although only Wiggins makes this last claim explicitly (hence my attribution of the procedure to him—apart from the claims of historical priority) it is clear that Perry, also, needs to make the claim if his strategy is to be successful. A couple of examples

will serve to make clear how the technique is applied. Wiggins[44]
deals with:

(10.24) a is the same official* as b but they are not the same
          man.

We can paraphrase:

(10.25) a is the same official* as b

as

(10.26) a holds the same office as b.

Wiggins concludes that (10.26) '*predicates* something of a and b
in common, holding a certain office'.[45] But to claim that as
a result (10.25) is not an identity statement begs the question
against the relativist again.

Perry[46] deals with:

(10.27) a is the same surman as b but they are not the same
          man

claiming that:

(10.28) a is the same surman as b

is paraphraseable as

(10.29) a is a member of the same surname class as b.[47]

(10.29) is not an identity statement and thus (though Perry
doesn't explicitly make this claim) neither is (10.28).

Let us grant Wiggins and Perry their claim that the result of
applying the paraphrase procedure is not an identity statement.[48] We can see straight-away that their argument that the

---

[44] *Identity and Spatio-Temporal Continuity*, p. 18.

[45] Ibid. Likewise we could say that 'a is identical to b' predicates something of
a and b in common, sharing all their properties.

[46] 'Identity', p. 55.

[47] The terminology of 'surname classes' is my own. Perry uses 'family' while
pointing out that the sense in which it is used is different from the usual. a and b
are members of the same surname class iff a has the same surname as b. We could,
of course, have used 'a has the same surname as b' as our paraphrase but that
would not have brought out the point about classes which Perry wants to make.
Cf. 'Identity', p. 55.

[48] In fact Geach is prepared to claim that 'any equivalence relation . . . can be
used to specify a criterion of relative identity' ('A Reply', p. 249). But this is
contentious since we would expect other conditions (e.g. that it had the form
'$\zeta =_{\mathscr{A}} \eta$') to be satisfied as well. It looks as if Geach might be applying the paraphrase procedure in reverse. In 'Ontological Relativity and Relative Identity'

originals are therefore not identity statements is not valid unless we have some additional premiss. Wiggins is not explicit about the premiss he uses and as Perry is not even explicit about the need to make the inference we get no help from him. I want now to consider various principles which might be thought to validate the inference and to show why they fail.

It is clear that not every property of a statement can be transferred across paraphrases in the way that Wiggins and Perry need the property of not being an identity statement to. For example, many statements in the active voice can be paraphrased in the passive, which does not imply that the original was not really in the active voice at all. Clearly we want a much more restrictive principle of transference which applies to identity statements and not, I suspect, to very much else. This alone should make us suspicious, for why should identity statements be singled out for special treatment? When we consider some of the principles which would do the job Wiggins wants, I think we shall find our suspicions justified.

The broadest plausible candidate appears to be the following:

(P1)   For any statement, S, if S is equivalent to a statement S^* such that S^* is not an identity statement, then S is not an identity statement.

But (P1) is too strong.

(10.30) a's office is the same office as b's office

and

(10.31) a's surname is the same surname as b's surname

are both identity statements even for the absolutist. To deny that they are identity statements is tantamount to denying that we can have identity statements between offices and surnames—for if (10.30) and (10.31) are not such statements what could be? Yet (10.30) is paraphraseable as (10.26) and (10.31) as (10.29). Thus if (P1) is correct either (10.30) and (10.31) are not identity statements or (10.26) and (10.29) are: neither result seems to be acceptable to Wiggins and Perry and so (P1) fails.

The difficulties with (P1) are even more radical. Although

(p. 292), however, he claims that only certain equivalence relations express relative identity.

Wiggins only explicitly commits himself to accepting the indiscernibility of identicals, as expressed in (DLL),[49] he must also be committed to the reflexivity of '$\zeta =_{\mathscr{A}} \eta$', and given these two we can derive the identity of indiscernibles. But if he has both the identity of indiscernibles and the indiscernibility of identicals then it will follow that for each statement of the form '$a =_{\mathscr{A}} b$' there is an equivalent statement of the form:

$$(10.32) \qquad\qquad (\forall\phi)(\phi(a) \equiv \phi(b)).$$

But (10.32) is not an identity statement and, therefore, by (P1), no statement of the form '$a =_{\mathscr{A}} b$' is an identity statement. I cannot think that Wiggins believes there are no identity statements.

Thus we need some weaker principle than (P1) such that (10.30) and (10.31) are identity statements while (10.26) and (10.29) and (10.25) and (10.28) are not. If we compare (10.25) and (10.26) on the one hand, with (10.30) on the other, we see that while the relation in (10.25) holds between the same items as the relation in (10.26) the relation in (10.30) holds between different items. Similarly, with (10.28) and (10.29) in contrast to (10.31). This suggests the following alternative to (P1):

(P2)   For any relational statement, S, if S is equivalent to a relational statement S^* such that the relation in S^* holds between the same items as the relation in S, then if S^* is not an identity statement S is not an identity statement.

This licenses the inference Wiggins and Perry want from the fact that neither (10.26) nor (10.29) are identity statements to the conclusion that neither are (10.25) nor (10.28)—without jeopardizing the status of (10.30) and (10.31). But (P2) is subject to our second objection to (P1). Given (DLL) any identity statement '$a =_{\mathscr{A}} b$' will be paraphraseable as:

(10.33) a shares all its predicates with b

which is not an identity statement. Again, with (P2) there can be no identity statements.

Moreover, I can see no way in which we can formulate a principle which licenses all the inferences Wiggins and Perry want to license and still preserve the sort of paraphrase of

[49] *Identity and Spatio-Temporal Continuity*, pp. 2–3.

identity statements which the relativized identity of indiscernibles principle provides. It looks as though the entire theory of absolute identity will collapse in the face of Wiggins's efforts to preserve it against some examples of (R). We could, of course, exclude (DLL)-type paraphrases by stipulation but that is scarcely a decent policy, though it is hardly more *ad hoc* than the other principles we've considered. Moreover, even if the (DLL) paraphrases were excluded any successful paraphrase procedure would undermine the whole notion of identity criteria which Wiggins and Perry share with the relativist, for it would be possible to paraphrase any identity statement away in favour of criteria for the statement. There seems little independent reason to think that any adequate principle of the kind we've been considering is true. We have no good reason to think that being an identity statement should always be the victim of conceptual imperialism.

But let us grant that the absolutist can make good the distinction between identity statements and common-property statements, and, moreover, can substantiate Wiggins's paraphrase procedure to complete the absolutist analysis of cases of (R). In other words, let's grant the absolutist everything that he's been arguing for in this section. Does he, even then, have a valid objection to (R)? Surely not, for all he has shown is that the relative identity theory can handle common-property statements *as well as* identity statements. Moreover, he has pointed up an inadequacy of his own theory which can treat only identity statements. He then has to propose an alternative theory (or, more likely, alternative theories) to account for common-property statements (including, for example, some form of (RLL)). And this only shows that the relative identity theory does all the work of the absolute theory and more besides, which is scarcely a disadvantage. Similarly, one can scarcely hold it against the theory of relative identity if it deals with common-property statements as well as identity statements. By the standard principles of theory selection the relativist's theory is, for this very reason, to be preferred to the absolutist's. But if, as I think, the distinction between identity and common-property statements cannot be made good then the absolutist can pursue a totally arbitrary distinction between relative identity statements, treating some as identity statements and some as mere equivalence statements, or an equally arbitrary ontological prejudice in favour of certain types of item. Alternatively, he can reject all relative identity statements, claiming them to be mere equivalence statements except where they admit of a (DLL)-type analysis. This policy does at least give him the advantage of a principle by means of which to separate the identity statements from the others. However, it also leads him to restrict identity statements to a small number of necessary identity statements in the face of the Barcan proof of § 1.2. This restriction is scarcely less surprising than the relativist's extension of the concept of identity and an absolutist with an uncommonly narrow concept of identity can scarcely criticize the relativist for having an uncommonly wide one.

Plainly we are not going to achieve a knock-down argument against the absolute theory. It is, after all, provably consistent. The absolutist can thus defend it at every turn by rejecting principles extraneous to the theory. The relativist can at best, firstly, argue *ad hominem* that the absolutist denies principles which he elsewhere avows; secondly, show that some principles thus denied are intuitively plausible; and thirdly, show that his own theory is of much greater scope and power than the absolutist's. I claim that in what has gone before I have done all three.

APPENDIX 1

Wiggins on Sortals

Wiggins's treatment of the concept of a sortal, like much else in his book, is extremely obscure. The concept is introduced early, in an extremely misleading footnote where Wiggins says that he is using 'sortal' 'in roughly the manner of the second part of P. F. Strawson's *Individuals*'.[1] What Strawson says is the following: 'A sortal universal supplies a principle for distinguishing and counting individual particulars which it collects. It presupposes no antecedent principle, or method, of individuating the particulars it collects.'[2] But it soon becomes clear that Wiggins is not using the term 'sortal' in anything like this way. It is not unreasonable to take Strawson to be providing necessary and sufficient conditions for sortalhood in this passage, and this is certainly what Wiggins takes him to be doing.[3] That Wiggins does not hold that Strawson's conditions are necessary and sufficient for sortalhood becomes immediately clear in Wiggins's discussion of the thesis, *C*, that: '[T]o specify the something or other under which *a* and *b* coincide is necessarily to specify a concept 𝒜 which qualifies as adequate for this purpose, and hence as a *sortal*, only if it yields a *principle of counting* for 𝒜s.'[4] Wiggins holds that *C* is false. That its falsity conflicts with Strawson's specification of sortalhood is made clear by Wiggins in a footnote: '*C* is commonly supposed to give not only a sufficient but a necessary condition of being a sortal concept. (Cp. Strawson, *Individuals*, loc. cit. See also my '*Individuation*', which is mistaken on this point.)'[5]

This is not the only occasion on which Wiggins explicitly rejects Strawson's account. He says, for example, when dealing with a number of different accounts of what a sortal is that sortals are sometimes described '(not quite correctly, . . .) [as] terms which

---

[1] Wiggins, *Identity and Spatio-Temporal Continuity*, fn. 2 (p. 65). See also Wiggins, 'The Individuation of Things and Places', p. 178.

[2] *Individuals*, p. 168.

[3] Cf. *Identity and Spatio-Temporal Continuity*, fn. 5 (p. 65). [4] Ibid., p. 1.

[5] Ibid., p. 65. The paper to which he refers is his 'Individuation of Things and Places' where he says: 'A term "𝒜" expresses a substance-concept . . . if and only if it is possible to divide up the contents of the world and isolate the 𝒜s in it in one and only one way . . . That is, there must be the possibility of a definite answer to the question "How many 𝒜s are there in region *R* at time *t*?"' (p. 178).

give a principle of counting or enumeration.'[6] And later he explains why this is not correct. It is, he claims, perfectly possible to ask 'whether you at t_1 saw, (e.g.) *the same oily wave* as I saw at t_1, but there is no 'definite way of *counting* the waves or oily waves in the area of sea we are observing'.[7] Thus 'oily wave' is a satisfactory covering concept for an identity statement but does not pass Strawson's countability criterion, nor the one that Wiggins gave in his earlier paper.[8]

Wiggins adds as an after-thought that the Strawson criterion might be all right for 'substancehood in some very strict sense of substance which I leave to those enamoured of it to describe'.[9] For, as he points out, identity statements can be covered by concepts for particulars which 'by certain strict standards, nobody would be entirely happy to call substances'; e.g. 'oily wave', 'volume of argon', and 'area of garden'.[10] These fail the Strawson countability criterion, but can cover identity statements and are therefore, Wiggins implies, sortals.[11] However, the particulars covered by these concepts are not substances in the strict sense; and consequently for this strict sense Strawson's criterion may well provide necessary and sufficient conditions. It is thus quite plain that Wiggins does not accept Strawson's countability criterion. The puzzling thing is why he said, in the first place, that he used the term 'sortal' in 'roughly' the same manner as Strawson.

If the Strawsonian account is not what he wants, Wiggins has to provide an alternative. He considers various ways of picking out sortals, for example, articulating, classifying, drawing boundaries, counting, and division of reference, and says that 'none of these ideas . . . is quite correct enough.'[12] He does not argue for this conclusion, but there is no cause to disagree. He does have a further point against these criteria, namely, that they are not 'quite independent enough of the notion of an *individual* or *object* to bear the weight which has to be borne by an orthodox definition'.[13] In view of his (D)-relative identity theory, I'm not sure why Wiggins thinks the definition of a sortal should be independent of the notion of an individual or an object, nor, indeed, why these accounts of sortalhood are more dependent on the concept of object than some

---

[6] *Identity and Spatio-Temporal Continuity*, p. 28.

[7] Ibid., p. 39.

[8] It will, as Wiggins seems prepared to admit (see fn. 9 below), pass the weaker countability criterion of § 3.3.

[9] Ibid., Appendix 5.2, p. 60. Here Wiggins also goes some way towards distinguishing Strawson's strong countability requirement from weaker ones.

[10] Ibid.

[11] This inference, which is implicit rather than stated, fails both for covering concepts (as we saw in § 3.1) and for (D. II)-completing concepts.

[12] Ibid., pp. 28–9.   [13] Ibid., p. 29.

alternatives, and Wiggins doesn't enlighten us on either point; but his first objection is, I feel, sufficient.

At this stage in the discussion Wiggins seems about to admit defeat in his attempt to define the elusive notion of a sortal. He quotes Frege on the concept of an object: 'I regard a regular definition as impossible, since we have here something too simple [and, Wiggins adds: "too general"] to admit of logical analysis.'[14] But he hopes for clarification in another direction: 'If the general notion of a sortal is a purely formal notion we may at least be able to provide formal criteria for being a sortal.'[15] He begins this task straight away but there is no connected discussion of these formal criteria; the full analysis has to be pieced together bit by bit in the course of his circuitous discussion of (D).[16] However, the first point of his formal analysis is: 'One of the clear facts about sortal concepts is that as a matter of fact they are used to cover identity statements.'[17] And this is the thought which lies behind his Appendix 5.2. Wiggins takes this as his starting-point and makes great use of it. From it, he claims, several things follow.

Perhaps the most important thing which Wiggins thinks follows is this:

[W]e must require of any concept . . . which is a candidate to answer the question 'same what?' that it should give a principle of tracing which can be *relied upon* to preserve the formal properties of identity, sc. symmetry, transitivity, reflexivity, Leibniz' Law. This is of course a criterion of its being a sortal at all. If it cannot do this we shall not have fixed the sense of the identity-statements it covers to be the sense of *identity*-statements.[18]

This is, of course, highly contentious. However, Wiggins holds any statement which fails (DLL) is not an identity statement. If he is right in this, and in the account he gives of the uses of sortals as covering concepts for identity statements, then satisfaction of (DLL) is indeed required.

However, somewhat shady dealings are revealed if we look back to see by what arguments Wiggins establishes the validity of (DLL).

[14] Frege, 'Function and Concept', in Geach and Black (eds.), *Translations from the Philosophical Writings of Gottlob Frege* (Oxford: Blackwell, 1952), p. 32; quoted by Wiggins, *Identity and Spatio-Temporal Continuity*, p. 29.

[15] *Identity and Spatio-Temporal Continuity*, p. 29.

[16] Ibid., pp. 29–40.

[17] Ibid., p. 29.

[18] Ibid., p. 36. We see from this that Wiggins's reference to a concept under which a material particular may be 'counted, individuated and traced through space and time' (ibid., p. 1) was closer to his actual use of 'sortal' than the footnote reference to Strawson's use which was tagged to it. (By 'Leibniz' Law' Wiggins means (DLL).)

The argument for (DLL) takes place in Part I of *Identity and Spatio-Temporal Continuity*; and the bulk of the argumentation is taken up with discrediting examples of (R). But if it is a necessary condition of '$\mathscr{A}$''s being a sortal that '$a =_{\mathscr{A}} b$' satisfies (DLL) it makes little sense to discuss cases of (R), for (R) and (DLL) are (unsurprisingly) incompatible. However, the discussion of the examples of (R) in Part I takes place on the basis of a different account of 'sortal' than the one given in Part II, namely Strawson's account. We can now see what a great, and illicit, service Strawson's account of 'sortal' does Wiggins. In Part I Wiggins uses Strawson's account to reject non-trivially as identity statements statements violating (DLL). Having thus established (DLL) to his own satisfaction, Wiggins goes on to drop Strawson's account of sortals and, in Part II, proposes that the ability to cover an identity statement is a necessary and sufficient condition for being a sortal. Because he thinks that in Part I he has established that satisfaction of (DLL) is a necessary condition for being an identity statement, he then goes on to claim that providing principles of tracing which satisfy (DLL) is also a necessary condition of being a sortal. This enables him to rule out all cases of (R) while giving the appearance of not doing so merely by definitional fiat. The entire argument is based upon an equivocation in the analysis of 'sortal'.

APPENDIX 2

Cartwright on Quantities

We saw in § 4.3 that Helen Cartwright treats 'quantity of $\mathcal{M}$' as a universally applicable sortalization of '$\mathcal{M}$'. She holds, for example, that only 'The gold of which my ring is made is the same quantity of gold as the gold of which Aunt Suzie's ring was made' is equivalent to: 'My ring is made of the same gold as Aunt Suzie's ring used to be.'[1] Moreover, cases in which we cannot replace '$\mathcal{M}$' as covering concept by 'quantity of $\mathcal{M}$' she treats as 'suspicious'.[2] In most, if not all, cases 'quantity of $\mathcal{M}$' can be fitted into the account I proposed in § 4.4. We can always replace 'quantity of $\mathcal{M}$' by 'collection of parts that are $\mathcal{M}$' and when we can replace 'part that is $\mathcal{M}$' by a sortal (as we can replace 'collection of parts that are gold' by 'collection of gold molecules', for example) we can subsume 'quantity of $\mathcal{M}$' under '$Coll(\mathcal{F})$' and define identity criteria as in § 4.4. Moreover, in contexts where we can individuate a and b under a sortal we should be able to give criteria for 'a is the same quantity of $\mathcal{M}$ as b'. However, it is interesting to consider Cartwright's reasons for preferring 'quantity of $\mathcal{M}$' to other sortalizations. I do not want to give reasons for always rejecting 'quantity of $\mathcal{M}$' as a completing concept but merely to argue that Cartwright has given no good reason for always preferring it.

Cartwright rules out, for example, 'piece of gold' and 'cup of coffee' as completing concepts on the grounds that 'they cannot be trusted.'[3] This is because one can diminish the amount of coffee in a cup of coffee by taking a sip, but one cannot diminish the amount of coffee in a quantity of coffee. Similarly, Descartes's wax ceases to be a *piece* of wax on melting, but remains the same quantity of wax.

But, of course, which *sans* you can trust depends on what you want to do. Obviously when mass terms are sortalized in one way the resulting term may very well provide different identity criteria than result when they are sortalized in a different way. (A result which doesn't surprise the relativist.) The point Cartwright makes is that 'Quantities, like sets, cannot grow or shrink.'[4] In other words, in certain respects, 'quantity' will admit of no change at all. (Of

---

[1] 'Quantities', pp. 27–8. [2] 'Heraclitus and the Bath Water', p. 478.
[3] 'Quantities', p. 32. [4] Ibid.

course, in these respects neither will '1·321 grm. of $\mathcal{M}$ precisely'.)
While in other ways (as in the melting of Descartes's wax) it will
admit of very radical changes. On the other hand, 'piece' and 'cup'
will admit changes not admitted by 'quantity', and will not admit
the changes that 'quantity' does. But from this it does not follow
that 'piece' and 'cup' are somehow defective, or, in a vague way,
'not to be trusted'. You pays your money and you takes your
choice. Cartwright must at least show that the modes of change
admitted by 'quantity' ought to be admitted while those admitted
by 'piece' and 'cup' ought not. But she does not do this and I don't
see how she could for, in a general way, the changes we will wish to
admit and those we will wish to exclude will vary from occasion to
occasion.

Moreover, it may be objected that sometimes quantities do
change in ways that Cartwright says they don't. For example, the
volume of my coffee will diminish as it cools (though it remains
the same quantity of coffee as before); Descartes's wax (though the
same quantity of wax) will weigh less on the moon; and the effects
of special relativity may overtake anything. Cartwright considers
this objection and rejects it. She writes:

This objection rests on [a] confusion about measurement. The measure . . .
provided by 'coffee' . . . is neither a method of measurement nor a measure
of amounts of coffee . . . If it is true that two ounces of gold weigh less . . .
on the moon, then it is true of *any* quantity of gold containing the same
amount of gold as one containing two ounces. And the volume of a cubic
inch of ice may or may not be one cubic inch . . . But the *amount* of wax in
a cubic inch of wax does *not* depend on conditions. It cannot be *more wax*,
whatever its volume; two ounces of gold cannot be *less gold*.[5]

This passage seems to me a farrago of confusions which leads to the
absurd conclusion that a cubic inch of wax may be greater or less
than a cubic inch of wax. The trouble seems to be confusion over
the quantity/amount distinction which is made more opaque
because Russell's term 'magnitude' has been dropped. 'Magnitude'
and 'amount' are by no means interchangeable in ordinary language.
We can talk, e.g., of the magnitude of an area, or of a distance and
so on, but we cannot talk of a magnitude of gold—although we do
talk of an amount of gold. Magnitude refers to the measure of a
dimension, 'amount', on the other hand, has substantial connota-
tions which make it easier to confuse with 'quantity'. It seems
altogether better to stick to the Lockean term 'parcel' and the
Russellian term 'magnitude'.

Cartwright seems to believe that a magnitude of gold is something

[5] 'Quantities', p. 34.

over and above a measure of gold (e.g. the weight of a parcel of gold). But it is not. Suppose that a particular parcel cf gold is transferred to the moon, it remains the same parcel of gold even though its magnitude (when measured by weight) diminishes. Thus it seems that a parcel (or quantity) of gold retains its identity through quantitative changes: it is a magnitude (or amount) of gold which does not. Thus if Cartwright is right in ruling out 'piece' and 'cup' on these grounds she should do the same with 'quantity' in favour of 'amount' or 'magnitude'. In fact, I see no reason why she should rule out any of them.

Her claim that cases in which 'quantity of M' fails as a sortalization are 'suspicious', where it is well-founded, indicates no more than the general suspiciousness of mass terms masquerading as completing concepts; and is ill-founded often enough to support my contention that 'quantity' is not a universally applicable *san*. While I see no reason for a total prohibition of 'quantity of M' as completing concept, I equally see no reason for a total prohibition of other sortalizing auxiliary nouns.

Bibliography

[1] ACKERMANN, R., 'Sortal Predicates and Confirmation', *Philosophical Studies*, 20 (1969), 1–4.

[2] ALBRITTON, ROGERS, 'On Wittgenstein's use of the term "Criterion" ', in [100], pp. 231–50.

[3] ANDERSON, A. R., and BELNAP, N. D., *Entailment* (Princeton: Princeton University Press, 1975).

[4] ANSCOMBE, G. E. M., 'Aristotle', in ANSCOMBE, G. E. M., and GEACH, P. T., *Three Philosophers* (Oxford: Blackwell, 1961), pp. 1–64.

[5] —— 'The Principle of Individuation', *Proceedings of the Aristotelian Society*, Supplementary volume 27 (1953), 83–96.

[6] AQUINAS, THOMAS, *Summa Theologica*, edited by T. Gilby and T. C. O'Brien (London: Eyre and Spottiswoode, 1964–   ).

[7] ARISTOTLE, *The Works of Aristotle*, edited by W. D. Ross (Oxford: Oxford University Press, 1929–52).

[8] AYERS, MICHAEL R., 'Individuals Without Sortals', *Canadian Journal of Philosophy*, 4 (1974), 113–48.

[9] BACON, JOHN, 'Do Generic Descriptions Denote?', *Mind*, 82 (1973), 331–47.

[10] —— 'The Semantics of Generic THE', *Journal of Philosophical Logic*, 2 (1973), 323–39.

[11] BARCAN, RUTH, 'The Identity of Individuals in a Strict Functional Calculus of Second Order', *Journal of Symbolic Logic*, 12 (1947), 12–15.

[12] BARCAN MARCUS, RUTH, 'Interpreting Quantification', *Inquiry*, 5 (1962), 252–9.

[13] BENACERRAF, PAUL, 'What Numbers Could Not Be', *Philosophical Review*, 74 (1965), 47–73.

[14] BENNETT, DANIEL, 'Essential Properties', *Journal of Philosophy*, 66 (1969), 487–99.

[15] BOWERS, FRED, 'The Deep Structure of Abstract Nouns', *Foundations of Language*, 5 (1969), 520–33.

[16] BRADLEY, M. C., Critical Notice of Wiggins, *Identity and Spatio-Temporal Continuity*, *Australasian Journal of Philosophy*, 47 (1969), 69–79.

[17] BRODY, BARUCH, 'Locke on the Identity of Persons', *American Philosophical Quarterly*, 9 (1972), 327–34.

[18] BURGE, TYLER, 'Truth and Mass Terms', *Journal of Philosophy*, 69 (1972), 263–82.

[19] BUTCHVAROV, PANAYOT, *Resemblance and Identity* (Bloomington, Ind.: Indiana University Press, 1966).

[20] BUTLER, R. J. (ed.), *Analytical Philosophy* (Oxford: Blackwell, 1965), Second Series.

[21] CALVERT, CARL, 'Relative Identity: An Examination of a Theory by Peter Geach' (University of Washington, unpublished doctoral dissertation, 1973).

[22] CARTWRIGHT, HELEN M., 'Heraclitus and the Bath Water', *Philosophical Review*, 74 (1965), 466–85.

[23] —— 'Quantities', *Philosophical Review*, 79 (1970), 25–42.

[24] CARTWRIGHT, RICHARD, 'Identity and Substitutivity', in [84], pp. 119–33.

[25] CHANDLER, H. S., 'Constitutivity and Identity', *Nous*, 5 (1971), 313–19.

[26] —— 'Wiggins on Identity', *Analysis*, 29 (1968/9), 173–4.

[27] CHAPMAN, TOBIAS, 'Identity and Reference', *Mind*, 82 (1973), 542–56.

[28] CHAPPELL, V. C., 'Sameness and Change', *Philosophical Review*, 69 (1960), 351–62.

[29] —— 'Stuff and Things', *Proceedings of the Aristotelian Society*, 71 (1970/1), 61–76.

[30] CHISHOLM, RODERICK M., 'Problems of Identity', in [84], pp. 3–30.

[31] CHOMSKY, NOAM, *Aspects of the Theory of Syntax* (Cambridge, Mass.: M.I.T. Press, 1965).

[32] CHURCH, ALONZO, *Introduction to Mathematical Logic* (Princeton: Princeton University Press, 1956).

[33] CLARKE, D. S., 'Mass Terms as Subjects', *Philosophical Studies*, 21 (1970), 25–8.

[34] COOK, JOHN W., 'Wittgenstein on Privacy', in [100], pp. 286–323.

[35] COPI, IRVING, *Symbolic Logic* (New York: Macmillan; 2nd edn., 1965).

[36] CROSSLEY, J. N., ASH, C. J., et al., *What is Mathematical Logic?* (Oxford: Oxford University Press, 1972).

[37] DAUER, FRANCIS W., 'How not to Reidentify the Parthenon', *Analysis*, 33 (1972), 63–4.

[38] DAVIDSON, DONALD, 'Truth and Meaning', *Synthese*, 17 (1967), 304–23.

[39] DUMMETT, MICHAEL, 'Frege, Gottlob', in [43], vol. iii, pp. 225–37.

[40] —— *Frege: Philosophy of Language* (London: Duckworth, 1973).

[41] DUNN, J. M., and BELNAP, N. D., 'The Substitution Interpretation of the Quantifiers', *Nous*, 2 (1968), 177–85.

[42] DURRANT, MICHAEL, 'Numerical Identity', *Mind*, 82 (1973), 95–103.

[43] EDWARDS, PAUL (ed.), *The Encyclopedia of Philosophy* (New York: Macmillan, 1967).

222   BIBLIOGRAPHY

[44] ENÇ, BERENT, 'Numerical Identity and Objecthood', *Mind*, 84 (1975), 10–26.

[45] FELDMAN, FRED, 'Geach and Relative Identity', *Review of Metaphysics*, 22 (1968/9), 547–55.

[46] —— 'A Rejoinder', *Review of Metaphysics*, 22 (1968/9), 560–1.

[47] —— 'Sortal Predicates', *Nous*, 7 (1973), 268–82.

[48] FREGE, GOTTLOB, *The Foundations of Arithmetic*, translated by J. L. Austin (Oxford: Blackwell, 1950).

[49] —— *Grundgesetze der Arithmetik* (Jena: Verlag Hermann Pohle, 1883, 1903).

[50] —— 'Function and Concept', in GEACH, P. T., and BLACK, MAX (eds.), *Translations from the Philosophical Writings of Gottlob Frege* (Oxford: Blackwell, 1952), pp. 21–41.

[51] GABBAY, D., and MORAVCSIK, J. M., 'Sameness and Individuation', *Journal of Philosophy*, 70 (1973), 513–26.

[52] GEACH, P. T., 'Good and Evil', *Analysis*, 17 (1956), 33–42.

[53] —— 'Identity', in [54], pp. 238–47.

[54] —— *Logic Matters* (Oxford: Blackwell, 1972).

[55] —— *Mental Acts* (London: Routledge and Kegan Paul, 1957).

[56] —— 'Ontological Relativity and Relative Identity', in [85], pp. 287–302.

[57] —— *Reference and Generality* (Ithaca: Cornell University Press; 2nd edn., 1968).

[58] —— 'A Reply', *Review of Metaphysics*, 22 (1968/9), 556–9. An abridged version is reprinted in [54], pp. 247–9.

[59] GLEASON, H. A., *An Introduction to Descriptive Linguistics* (New York: Holt, 1955).

[60] GODDARD, L., and ROUTLEY, R., *The Logic of Significance and Context* (Edinburgh: Scottish Academic Press, 1973).

[61] GOODMAN, NELSON, *The Structure of Appearance* (New York: Bobbs-Merrill; 2nd edn., 1966).

[62] GRIFFIN, NICHOLAS, 'Ayers on Relative Identity', *Canadian Journal of Philosophy*, 6 (1976).

[63] HAMPSHIRE, STUART, 'Identification and Existence', in LEWIS, H. D. (ed.), *Contemporary British Philosophy* (London: Allen and Unwin, 1956), Third Series, pp. 191–208.

[64] HERBST, PETER, 'Names and Identities and Beginnings and Ends' (unpublished, 1972).

[65] HOBBES, THOMAS, *De Corpore*, in MOLESWORTH, WILLIAM (ed.), *The English Works of Thomas Hobbes* (London: John Bohn, 1839–45), vol. i.

[66] HUGHES, G. E., and CRESSWELL, M. J., *An Introduction to Modal Logic* (London: Methuen; 2nd edn., 1972).

[67] HUME, DAVID, *A Treatise of Human Nature*, edited by E. C. Mossner (Harmondsworth: Penguin, 1969).

[68] JESPERSEN, OTTO, *The Philosophy of Grammar* (London: Allen and Unwin, 1924).

[69] JOSEPH, H. W. B., *An Introduction to Logic* (Oxford: Oxford University Press; 2nd edn., 1916).

[70] KIRWAN, CHRISTOPHER, 'How Strong are the Objections to Essence?', *Proceedings of the Aristotelian Society*, 71 (1970/1), 43–59.

[71] LAYCOCK, HENRY, 'Some Questions of Ontology', *Philosophical Review*, 81 (1972), 3–42.

[72] LEIBNIZ, G. W., *New Essays Concerning the Human Understanding*, edited by A. G. Langley (New York: Macmillan, 1896).

[73] LINSKY, LEONARD, Critical Notice of Geach, *Reference and Generality*, *Mind*, 73 (1964), 575–83.

[74] LOCKE, JOHN, *An Essay Concerning the Human Understanding*, edited by A. C. Fraser (Oxford: Clarendon Press, 1894).

[75] LUSCHEI, EUGENE C., *The Logical Systems of Lesniewski* (Amsterdam: North-Holland, 1962).

[76] LYCAN, W. GREGORY, 'Noninductive Evidence: Recent Work on Wittgenstein's "Criteria"', *American Philosophical Quarterly*, 8 (1971), 109–25.

[77] LYONS, JOHN, *An Introduction to Theoretical Linguistics* (Cambridge: Cambridge University Press, 1968).

[78] MACINTYRE, ALASDAIR, 'Essence and Existence', in [43], vol. iii, pp. 59–61.

[79] MARGOLIS, JOSEPH, 'Dracula the Man: An Essay in the Logic of Individuation', *International Philosophical Quarterly*, 4 (1964), 541–9.

[80] MARTIN, R. L. (ed.), *The Paradox of the Liar* (New Haven: Yale University Press, 1970).

[81] MENDELSON, ELLIOTT, *Introduction to Mathematical Logic* (New York: van Nostrand, 1964).

[82] MOORE, G. E., *Philosophical Studies* (London: Routledge and Kegan Paul, 1922).

[83] MORAVCSIK, J. M. E., 'Subcategorization and Abstract Terms', *Foundations of Language*, 6 (1970), 473–87.

[84] MUNITZ, MILTON K. (ed.), *Identity and Individuation* (New York: New York University Press, 1971).

[85] —— (ed.), *Logic and Ontology* (New York: New York University Press, 1973).

[86] NELSON, JACK, 'On the Alleged Incompleteness of Certain Identity Claims', *Canadian Journal of Philosophy*, 3 (1973), 105–14.

[87] —— 'Prior on Leibniz's Law', *Analysis*, 30 (1969/70), 92–4.

[88] —— 'Relative Identity', *Nous*, 4 (1970), 241–60.

[89] O'CONNOR, D. J., 'On Resemblance', *Proceedings of the Aristotelian Society*, 46 (1945/6), 47–76.

[90] ODEGARD, DOUGLAS, 'Identity Through Time', *American Philosophical Quarterly*, 9 (1972), 29–38.

[91] OWEN, G. E. L., 'Aristotle on the Snares of Ontology', in BAMBROUGH, RENFORD (ed.), *New Essays on Plato and Aristotle* (London: Routledge and Kegan Paul, 1965), pp. 69–96.

[92] PARSONS, TERENCE, 'Analysis of Mass and Amount Terms', *Foundations of Language*, 6 (1970), 362–88.

[93] PEIRCE, C. S., *Collected Papers*, edited by C. Hartshorne, P. Weiss, and A. W. Burks (Cambridge, Mass.: Harvard University Press, 1933).

[94] PELLETIER, F. J., 'On Some Proposals for the Semantics of Mass Nouns', *Journal of Philosophical Logic*, 3 (1974), 87–108.

[95] PENELHUM, TERENCE, 'Hume on Personal Identity', *Philosophical Review*, 64 (1955), 571–89.

[96] PERRY, JOHN R., 'Identity' (Cornell University, unpublished doctoral dissertation, 1968).

[97] —— Review of Wiggins, *Identity and Spatio-Temporal Continuity*, *Journal of Symbolic Logic*, 35 (1970), 447–8.

[98] —— 'The Same *F*', *Philosophical Review*, 79 (1970), 181–200.

[99] PITCHER, GEORGE, 'About the Same', in AMBROSE, ALICE, and LAZEROWITZ, MORRIS (eds.), *Ludwig Wittgenstein: Philosophy and Language* (London: Allen and Unwin, 1972), pp. 120–39.

[100] —— (ed.), *Wittgenstein: The 'Philosophical Investigations'* (London: Macmillan, 1968).

[101] POOLE, ROSS, 'Are There Continuants?' (unpublished, n.d.).

[102] PRIOR, A. N., *Formal Logic* (Oxford: Oxford University Press; 2nd edn., 1962).

[103] —— 'Report on the *Analysis* "Problem" No. 11', *Analysis*, 17 (1957), 122–3.

[104] —— *Time and Modality* (Oxford: Clarendon Press, 1957).

[105] —— 'Time, Existence and Identity', in *Papers on Time and Tense* (Oxford: Clarendon Press, 1968), pp. 78–87.

[106] QUINE, W. V. O., *From a Logical Point of View* (New York: Harper Torchbooks; 2nd edn., 1961).

[107] —— 'Identity, Ostension and Hypostasis', in [106], pp. 65–79.

[108] —— *Mathematical Logic* (Cambridge, Mass.: Harvard University Press, 1955).

[109] —— *Methods of Logic* (New York: Holt; 2nd edn., 1962).

[110] —— 'Reference and Modality', in [106], pp. 139–59.

[111] —— 'Reply to Professor Marcus', in [115], pp. 175–82.

[112] —— Review of Geach, *Reference and Generality*, *Philosophical Review*, 73 (1964), 100–4.

[113] —— 'The Scope and Language of Science', in [115], pp. 215–32.

[114] —— *Set Theory and its Logic* (Cambridge, Mass.: Harvard University Press, 1963).

[115] —— *The Ways of Paradox* (New York: Random House, 1966).

[116] —— *Word and Object* (Cambridge, Mass.: M.I.T. Press, 1960).

[117] QUINTON, A., *The Nature of Things* (London: Routledge and Kegan Paul, 1972).

[118] RESCHER, NICHOLAS, and URQUHART, ALASDAIR, *Temporal Logic* (New York: Springer Verlag, 1971).

[119] ROUTLEY, R., 'Domainless Semantics for Free, Quantification and Significance Logics', *Logique et Analyse*, 14 (1971), 603–26.

[120] —— and ROUTLEY, V., 'Exploring Meinong's Jungle: Items and Descriptions' (unpublished).

[121] —— and GRIFFIN, N., 'Towards a Logic of Relative Identity' (unpublished).

[122] RUNDLE, BEDE, 'Modality and Quantification', in [20], pp. 27–39.

[123] RUSSELL, BERTRAND, and WHITEHEAD, ALFRED, *Principia Mathematica* (Cambridge: Cambridge University Press; 2nd edn., 1925/7).

[124] RUSSELL, BERTRAND, *The Principles of Mathematics* (London: Allen and Unwin; 2nd edn., 1937).

[125] SANFORD, DAVID H., 'Locke, Leibniz and Wiggins on Being in the Same Place at the Same Time', *Philosophical Review*, 79 (1970), 75–82.

[126] SHEEHAN, PETER, '*De Re* Modality' (unpublished, 1972).

[127] —— 'The Relativity of Identity' (unpublished, 1972).

[128] SHOEMAKER, SYDNEY, *Self-Knowledge and Self-Identity* (Ithaca: Cornell University Press, 1963).

[129] —— 'Wiggins on Identity', in [84], pp. 103–18.

[130] SMART, BRIAN, 'How to Reidentify the Ship of Theseus', *Analysis*, 32 (1972), 145–8.

[131] STEVENSON, LESLIE, 'Extensional and Intensional Logic for Sortal-Relative Identity' (unpublished, n.d.).

[132] —— 'A Formal Theory of Sortal Quantification', *Notre Dame Journal of Formal Logic*, 16 (1975), 185–207.

[133] —— 'Relative Identity and Leibniz's Law', *Philosophical Quarterly*, 22 (1972), 155–8.

[134] STRAWSON, P. F., *Individuals* (London: Methuen, 1959).

[135] —— 'Particular and General', *Proceedings of the Aristotelian Society*, 54 (1954), 233–60.

[136] SUPPES, PATRICK, *Axiomatic Set Theory* (Princeton: van Nostrand, 1960).

[137] —— *Introduction to Logic* (Princeton: van Nostrand, 1957).

[138] SWINBURNE, RICHARD, *Space and Time* (New York: St. Martins Press, 1968).

[139] Tarski, Alfred, 'Foundations of the Geometry of Solids', in *Logic, Semantics, and Metamathematics* (Oxford: Oxford University Press, 1956), pp. 24–9.

[140] Taylor, Barry, 'Tense, Energia and Kinesis' (Read at the AAP New Zealand Division Conference, Wellington, 1975).

[141] Thomason, R. H., 'A Semantic Theory of Sortal Incorrectness', *Journal of Philosophical Logic*, 1 (1972), 209–58.

[142] Vendler, Zeno, *Linguistics in Philosophy* (Ithaca: Cornell University Press, 1967).

[143] Vision, Gerald, 'Essentialism and the Senses of Proper Names', *American Philosophical Quarterly*, 7 (1970), 321–30.

[144] Voss, S. H., 'The Indiscernibility of Non-Identicals' (unpublished, n.d.).

[145] Wallace, John R., 'Philosophical Grammar' (Stanford University, unpublished doctoral dissertation, 1964).

[146] —— 'Sortal Predicates and Quantification', *Journal of Philosophy*, 62 (1965), 8–13.

[147] Wiggins, David, 'On Being in the Same Place at the Same Time', *Philosophical Review*, 77 (1968), 90–5.

[148] —— *Identity and Spatio-Temporal Continuity* (Oxford: Blackwell, 1967).

[149] —— 'Identity-Statements', in [20], pp. 40–71.

[150] —— 'The Individuation of Things and Places', *Proceedings of the Aristotelian Society*, Supplementary volume 37 (1963), 177–202.

[151] —— 'Reply to Mr Chandler', *Analysis*, 29 (1968/9), 175–6.

[152] —— 'Sentence-Sense, Word-Sense, and Difference of Word-Sense', in Steinberg, D. D., and Jakobovits, L. A. (eds.), *Semantics: An Interdisciplinary Reader in Philosophy, Linguistics and Psychology* (Cambridge: Cambridge University Press, 1971), pp. 14–34.

[153] Williams, Bernard, *Problems of the Self* (Cambridge: Cambridge University Press, 1973).

[154] Wittgenstein, Ludwig, *The Blue and Brown Books* (Oxford: Blackwell, 1958).

[155] —— *Philosophical Investigations*, translated by G. E. M. Anscombe (Oxford: Blackwell, 1953).

[156] —— *Tractatus Logico-Philosophicus*, translated by D. F. Pears and B. F. McGuinness (London: Routledge & Kegan Paul, 1961).

[157] Woodger, J. H., *The Axiomatic Method in Biology* (Cambridge: Cambridge University Press, 1937).

[158] —— *Biology and Language* (Cambridge: Cambridge University Press, 1952).

[159] Woods, John, ' "None in Particular" ', *Canadian Journal of Philosophy*, 2 (1973), 379–88.

[160] Woods, M. J., 'Identity and Individuation', in [20], pp. 120–30.

[161] —— 'The Individuation of Things and Places', *Proceedings of the Aristotelian Society*, Supplementary volume 37 (1963), 203–16.

[162] Zemach, Eddy M., 'In Defence of Relative Identity', *Philosophical Studies*, 26 (1974), 207–18.

Index